# TV'S GROOVIEST VARIETY SHOWS

# TV's GROOVIEST variety shows

## OF THE '60s AND '70s

## Telly R. Davidson

CUMBERLAND HOUSE
NASHVILLE, TENNESSEE

*This book is dedicated to the memory of my grandparents,
Jack H. Wartenberg and Lauryl M. Wartenberg,
without whom I wouldn't be here to dedicate a book at all.*

TV's Grooviest Variety Shows
Published by Cumberland House Publishing
431 Harding Industrial Drive
Nashville, Tennessee 37211

Cover design: James Duncan Creative
Book design: Mary Sanford

**Photo Credits**
CBS Inc.: 4, 9, 14, 82, 87, 92, 106, 111, 114, 120, 171, 182, 189, 194; Welk Music Group: 26, 29, 34, 39, 42, 45; PhotoFest Inc.: 58, 64, 67, 68, 151, 203, 223; Schlatter/Friendly Productions: 128, 134, 139, 145; SFM Entertainment: 154, 156, 161, 164, 167

**Library of Congress Cataloging-in-Publication Data**
Davidson, Telly R.
  TV's grooviest variety shows of the '60s and '70s / Telly R. Davidson.
     p. cm.
  Includes index.
  ISBN-13: 978-1-58182-550-3 (pbk. : alk. paper)
  ISBN-10: 1-58182-550-1 (pbk. : alk. paper)
  1. Variety shows (Television programs)—United States.  I. Title.

PN1992.8.V3D38 2006
791.45'6—dc22

2006027100

Printed in Canada
1 2 3 4 5 6 7—12 11 10 09 08 07 06

# Contents

ACKNOWLEDGMENTS     VII
INTRODUCTION     IX

## THE ED SULLIVAN SHOW     3
VIDEO VAUDEVILLES: Hollywood
Palace, Kraft Music Hall, NBC Follies     24

## THE LAWRENCE WELK SHOW     27
COUNTRY WHEN COUNTRY WASN'T COOL:
The Johnny Cash Show, The Jim Nabors Hour,
Pop Goes the Country, That Nashville Music,
Barbara Mandrell & the Mandrell Sisters,
Hee-Haw     52

## THE DEAN MARTIN SHOW     61
STAR VEHICLES DERAILED: The Mary Tyler
Moore Hour, Van Dyke and Company,
The Julie Andrews Hour, The New Bill Cosby
Show, Cos, The Don Knotts Hour, Dolly!     74

## THE SMOTHERS BROTHERS COMEDY HOUR     81
THE MOD SQUAD: Operation: Entertainment,
This Is Tom Jones, The Lennon Sisters Hour,
The Music Scene, The Engelbert
Humperdinck Show     98

## THE CAROL BURNETT SHOW     105
TIM CONWAY: A Salute to Variety TV's
Greatest Un-success Story     124

## ROWAN & MARTIN'S LAUGH-IN     129
BLACK AND BLUE: The Leslie Uggams
Show, The Pearl Bailey Show, The
Richard Pryor Show, The Redd Foxx
Comedy Hour     148

## THE FLIP WILSON SHOW     155
MELLOW GOLD: The Tony Orlando &
Dawn Rainbow Hour, The Glenn Campbell
Goodtime Hour, Donny & Marie,
The Captain & Tenille, Make Your
Own Kind of Music, The Golddiggers,
The Bobby Darin Amusement Company,
The Bobby Goldsboro Show, The Bobby
Vinton Show, The Jacksons, Sha Na Na     170

## THE SONNY & CHER COMEDY HOUR     181
DEFINITELY NOT READY FOR PRIME TIME!:
Turn-On, The Beautiful Phyllis Diller Show,
What's It All About, World?, Saturday
Night Live with Howard Cosell, The Brady
Bunch Hour, Pink Lady     198

## WHO TURNED OUT THE LIGHTS?     207
POSTMODERN CLASSICS: That Was
the Week That Was, Shindig, Hullabaloo,
The Jonathan Winters Show, Monty
Python's Flying Circus, Benny Hill Show,
Solid Gold     220

CONCLUSION     228
INDEX     229

# Acknowledgments

There are many too many family members and friends to thank, but all of the below played some special part in the life of the book and/or author. (And if I missed you, feel free to write in your name with my blessing.)

Special thanks to Paul Brownstein and his great assistant Debbie Slavin, without whom this book would never have been possible. Greg Vines at Andrew Solt Productions, SFM Entertainment president Stanley F. Moger (and his friendly, exceptionally able production manager Craig Gilwit) were also among this project's team of Most Valuable Players. Howard Mandelbaum and the gang at Photofest helped, assisted, and generally put up with me far above and beyond the call of duty, as did the ever-patient and reasonable David Lombard at CBS Photo Archives.

Ron Simon at the Museum of TV & Radio has been a friend both to the project and writer, and cleared away much needless baggage from my work. Suzy Vaughan cleared many an obstacle from the book's path, and Keith Cox at TVLand helped open others ahead. Margaret Heron and the folks at The Welk Group gave me so many pictures and ideas, the hardest part was simply picking the best. And besides being one of the sharpest film critics I've ever worked with, Brent Simon was the best editor a writer could have in the glory days of *Entertainment Today,* and one of the best friends anyone could have anytime.

All the "groovy" folks at Cumberland House Publishing—in particular Ron Pitkin, who said "yes"; Mary Sanford, who did a fabulous job editing the book (and putting up with a pushy author); and Michelle Brown, the publicist to thank that you're reading this today. And no writer could ask for a friendlier, more knowledgeable, or connected counsel than Jeffrey Kleinman, Esq., of Folio Literary.

Thanks also to Al Masini, Dana Adam Shapiro, Matthew Florin, Adam Frisch, Sean Hunter and the gang at Nielsen Syndication Service, Gary Snyder, Randy West, Fred Wostbrock, Brent Mann, James Robert Parish, Vincent Terrace, Dave Golden, Chuck Donegan, Steve Herbert, Sandi Byner, Vivien Kooper, Gary and Kathy Young, Tom Heald, Dianne DeLaVega, Brad Schreiber, and the folks at Independent Writers of Southern California (www.iwosc.org).

Special credit to Chris Clark, Larry James Gianakos, the late Peter Tauber, and of course, my mom, for years of friendship, advice, and professional assistance – and to Richard Horgan at FilmStew and Tony Bray at TV-Now for helping to keep me in business. And a final nod to the hardest-working producer in television, Damian Sullivan – who finally unlocked that first closed door.

Note: If this book makes you want to relive some of these shows on your own TV, almost all of the major shows covered here are available on DVD. Check out such Web sites as www.tvclassics.com, www.sfment.com, Rhino Home Video, and Guthy-Renker, as well as PBS, Nick and Nite, and TVLand.

# Introduction

### Or, how we got from there to here . . .

This book covers the greatest, goofiest, and grooviest variety shows of those revolutionary years in the late 1960s and 1970s. For a genre that's all but disappeared from network prime time today, TV variety shows reached their zenith during the flower-power era. Shows like *The Ed Sullivan Show* introduced us to the Beatles and Elvis—and kept stars like Ella Fitzgerald, Gene Kelly, Ethel Merman, Duke Ellington, and Peggy Lee in business into the 1970s. Lawrence Welk kept the big-band era alive, as well as the legacy of Broadway and Hollywood's golden era of song and dance.

Programs like *The Dean Martin Show* and *Rowan & Martin's Laugh-In* defined swinging hipness and cool, while *The Smothers Brothers Comedy Hour* and *Sonny & Cher* brought the youth-movement viewpoint to TV for the first time. *The Flip Wilson Show* helped open the floodgates for minority performers to finally have an equal footing in television, while Carol Burnett made some of the most brilliant and enduring sketch comedy of all time.

But though it was the launch of a new era, it was also the beginning of the end. After these shows faded away, nothing ever really replaced them. These shows were both the pinnacle and the final act of regularly scheduled music, stand-up and sketch comedy, and dance on commercial network television.

There have been numerous books, articles, and documentaries made on those pioneering days of early TV, when the first great variety shows were in their prime—the Berles, Bennys, Gleasons, and Caesars. However, comparatively little has been written about the genre's later years—the ones that Generation X grew up with, the Baby Boomers came of age with, and the Greatest Generation kicked back with, in their middle-aged prime of life. This book sets out to remedy that.

Most importantly, unlike the early TV classics, the shows covered in detail in this book have been in reruns on cable and public television for years and years. They are almost as familiar as a classic sitcom or cop show to younger viewers who weren't even born when they were originally on the air. And now, with the boom in DVD sales, millions of people are rediscovering these classic comedies and magic music moments once again.

However, we can't leave out those pioneering shows in the early days of television, either. Those "Golden Age" classics were the ones that set the standard and laid down the ground rules that even their hottest, hippest, and fastest successors would play by. So here's a look at how we got from those early days of black-and-white postwar kinescopes and video vaudevilles to those fast, frenetic, and fun days in the era of free love, sunshine, and happy-faces.

Television's first three great variety shows made their debuts (along with much of the new medium itself) back in 1948. And their parallel stories would be the first to illuminate the twisting paths that TV variety would travel from its earliest, postwar days to the swinging '60s and the sexy '70s.

First there was Mr. Television himself, Uncle Miltie—the one and only Milton Berle. Already a well-known comedian with several radio shows and a few comedy motion pictures under his belt, Berle was the ultimate vaudevillian, having practically been "born in the trunk" in a traveling showbiz family. (Miltie made his vaudeville debut at the ripe old age of five.) When he began his *Texaco Star Theatre* (later the *Buick-Berle Show*) on NBC in September of 1948, it was the show that launched a million television sets.

Longtime announcer and interviewer Jack Narz (who would go on to his own signature role hosting *Concentration* in nighttime syndication from 1973 to 1978) was just starting his showbiz career in Hollywood when Uncle Miltie first held sway. In a TV interview about those early days, he mentioned offhand that he would sometimes go for a walk down the boulevard near some apartment buildings and town houses, and "you could hear the [Milton Berle] show from the start of the block to the end— uninterrupted! *Everybody* had it on." He wasn't exaggerating. Berle's regular Tuesday-night ratings were as high as an *80 percent share* of viewers! Nightclub, movie theatre, and Broadway attendance plummeted on Tuesday nights—and bars and grilles always kept their sets switched to Berle, where their patrons would crowd around the TV set, laughing themselves silly.

Uncle Miltie's style of comedy was the first to truly utilize the visual aspect of television, rather than just photographing a radio show for TV. The show specialized in broadly played sketches and musical-comedy moments with costumes and wacky sight gags (most especially Berle's signature shtick in a dress and lipstick—it was like watching a Bugs Bunny cartoon come to life!). The showbiz veteran drove both himself and his staff to the max, with seventy-two-hour work-weeks and rehearsals, and as many jokes and gags as could be crammed into each hour.

The first two men that CBS put in the driver's seat were also highly capable, talented, and experienced—but *not* as comedians, actors, or singers. Both were veteran journalists and interviewers instead; one had worked on CBS radio since 1930 and had covered the funeral of Franklin Roosevelt during World War II, as well as hosting countless hours of interviews and talent showcases. Another was the preeminent

Broadway columnist of his time, and one of the most influential Hollywood movie critics and celebrity interviewers in America.

The first of those two was legendary radio star Arthur Godfrey, who moved his *Talent Scouts* radio show to CBS-TV in 1948. He followed it along with the somewhat oxymoronic (given what we now know) *Arthur Godfrey and His Friends* on Wednesday nights. By 1952, Godfrey had also moved his daytime radio show, *Arthur Godfrey Time*, to television as a daily chat show, with a few music and comedy numbers to liven things up. It has often been reported that between his radio and TV shows, Godfrey's success was such that he was responsible for more than one out of every ten dollars that CBS earned in those years.

CBS's other early-TV landmark of variety, of course, was TV's greatest "really big shew"—the one and only *Ed Sullivan Show*. (In those years it was officially titled *Toast of the Town*, "with your host Ed Sullivan"—on the theory that it was the acts that would be introduced, rather than the introducer himself, who were the real "stars" of the program.)

And that was the one difference that would forever determine why one show lasted all the way into the early 1970s while the other—despite being the most successful show on CBS besides *I Love Lucy*—would close up shop before the end of the decade. Ed Sullivan had no illusions about his talents as a performer. (Although with his twenty-year experience writing about the film and stage community, he had an eye for talent that was second to none.) He actively preferred to keep the focus of his show on the guest comedians, actors, and singers that he would bring on. And despite his grim, overbearing image, Ed actually had a pretty darn good sense of humor about himself. He roared with laughter when comedy black belts like John Byner and Will Jordan would take on the boss and do impersonations of him.

Not so with Arthur Godfrey. Godfrey seemed to consider himself a talented entertainer in his own right. Though his performing abilities were pretty much limited to playing the ukulele and singing novelty tunes like the "Too-Fat Polka" and some Hawaiian love songs, Godfrey demanded absolute respect and star treatment from every one of his "friends." The idea of someone satirizing or doing impressions of Godfrey on his show would have been almost unimaginable, and if a performer didn't show the proper degree of respect around His Eminence, Godfrey would have no qualms about firing them on the spot. Those ego issues would cause the ultimate downfall of CBS's earliest variety franchise. After the chart-topping McGuire Sisters left and Pat Boone headed to Hollywood for a movie and solo singing career, by far the most popular performer remaining in Godfrey's mid-1950s stable was the heart-throb crooner Julius LaRosa. But Godfrey was tired of seeing his "friends" leave him in the lurch, to go on to bigger and better things after he had given them their first breaks. Seeing "Julie" getting too big for his britches with the fan magazines, interviews, and screaming bobby-soxers was just too much for Godfrey to take.

He fired a shocked LaRosa, live on the air, right after LaRosa had finished singing a love song—to teach the young singer a hard and fast lesson in humility. But it was Arthur Godfrey who ended up humiliated instead. His ratings took one of the sharpest dives on record, and the show started to get more negative publicity than any TV program until the quiz-show scandals of 1958.

Godfrey's reputation recovered, but that was hardly good news given how it happened: In 1958, he was diagnosed with lung cancer, and the prognosis wasn't good. (This wasn't the indefatigable Godfrey's first bout with a life-threatening situation. In 1931, Godfrey was in a severe auto accident that damaged some nerve endings in his lower back and required several later surgeries. Some people believe that his fiery offscreen personality and bad temper were due in part to the excruciating flare-ups he suffered from time to time.) While he would still maintain a fairly active presence in radio, Godfrey retired all of his TV shows from the air by the spring of 1959.

Less than eighteen months after Milton Berle's show premiered came two more early-TV variety showcases that were built for the ages. During the early '50s, there was no better reason to stay home on Saturday night than the two hours from 9 to 11 o'clock on NBC. For a way to unwind at home on the weekend, only CBS's legendary mid-'70s Saturday lineup could compare to the ninety minutes accurately titled *Your Show of Shows*. Sid Caesar and Imogene Coca were in front of the cameras, and Mel Brooks, Neil Simon, and Carl Reiner were behind them.

*Your Show of Shows* was notable as television's first truly hip and sophisticated variety hour. Sure, there was plenty of pie-in-the-face comedy and mugging for the camera (Imogene Coca's funny faces were second to none) but *Your Show of Shows* was distinctly made by and for a literate, urban, in-the-know audience. As did that other pioneer of early-TV comedy, Ernie Kovacs, the show satirized such targets as pretentious literary-fiction authors, space cadet jazz musicians, politicians, and popular motion pictures. (Twenty years before Carol Burnett, *Your Show of Shows* had the funniest movie spoofs in town—their sendup of *From Here to Eternity*'s beachfront love scene, with the two lovers repeatedly splashed by a bucket of water, ranks alongside Carol's "Went With the Wind" as an all-time comedy classic.)

*Your Show of Shows* had a perfect follow-up in the TV version of the radio favorite *Your Hit Parade*, with big-band vocalists like Dorothy Collins, Helen O'Connell, Gisele MacKenzie, and Snooky Lanson recapping the week's top songs in one staging and setting after another. *Your Hit Parade* had almost as impressive a behind-the-scenes cast as *Your Show of Shows* did, too, including the likes of Bob Fosse, Tony Charmoli, and Dwight Hemion.

After nearly five years of punishingly hard work and enough funny faces and eye tricks to qualify for an Olympic gold medal, Imogene Coca left *Your Show of Shows* on a full-time basis. The show was then retitled *Caesar's Hour* and downsized appropriately to a one-hour slot on Monday nights. There, Caesar's throne was ably supported by movie-musical comedienne Nanette Fabray and a twenty-one-year-old writer named Woody Allen. *Caesar's Hour* stayed a big hit until NBC got greedy and rescheduled the show back to Saturday nights—which were by then the province of another early-variety veteran, *The Lawrence Welk Show.*

The year 1950 also brought the debut of legendary radio, vaudeville, and movie comedian Jack Benny's show to TV. Benny brought all of the best supporting players from his long-running radio show, including wisecracking black valet Eddie "Rochester" Anderson, voice-over and cartoon legend Mel Blanc, singer Dennis Day, full-size announcer Don Wilson, and of course Benny's wife, Mary Livingstone. The program pioneered the "show within a show" format that later programs like *The Dick Van Dyke Show* would bring to perfection. It was part variety show and part sit-com about the life of a famous movie and TV star *making* a weekly show, and his other showbiz adventures. It ran for nearly fifteen years, and even after that, the seventy-one-year old Benny kept going in Las Vegas and Hollywood and made memorable appearances on *Laugh-In* and *Lawrence Welk* in the early 1970s. After claiming to be thirty-nine years old for about forty years, Jack Benny died the day after Christmas 1974.

By 1953, Jackie Gleason and Red Skelton had both joined the CBS stable of stars. Skelton had started in vaudeville before he was even in double-digits, and as a grownup he starred alongside the Queen of Laughter herself, Lucille Ball, in several MGM comedy movies. Red was universally acknowledged as America's clown prince (the "king" being his mentor, the legendary Emmett Kelly)—even Jerry Lewis said he considered Red "the clown master." Red's slapstick comedy and repertoire of characters like boxer Cauliflower McPugg, Sheriff Deadeye, Willie Lump Lump, and the Mean Widdle Kid became a fixture on Tuesday nights.

As for "The Great One," Jackie Gleason—what can we say? His "Honeymooners" sketches, usually in the second half-hour of his variety show, were enough on their own to ensure his place in American culture forever. Gleason's show was top-quality from start to finish. It boasted an incomparable cast of real-life characters like Art Carney, Audrey Meadows, and Joyce Randolph, plus comic Frank Fontaine (often seen as "Crazy Guggenheim"), the June Taylor Dancers, and legendary announcer Johnny Olson (who would "come on down" to iconic status in his own right as Bob Barker's sidekick on *The Price Is Right* in the '70s.)

Like Milton Berle, Jackie Gleason had been knockin' em dead since he was a kid, and had played minor roles in movies, appeared on Broadway, and preceded William Bendix in the early TV sitcom *The Life of Reilly.* Jackie had developed a one-man repertory company of master-crafted characters in his vaudeville and cabaret days, and they all became regular "guests" of his show. They included wealthy snob Reginald Van Gleason, Charlie the Loudmouth, (the vastly politically incorrect) Pedro the Mexican, nebbishy Fenwick Babbit, and his lovably pathetic Poor Soul.

He also had a running skit as Joe the Bartender, who'd greet the camera as it bellied up to the bar (from our POV) as his favorite patron, "Hiya, Mr. Dunahy!" But his signature character would, of course, be ill-tempered "honeymooner" Ralph Kramden, who achieved immortality alongside Lucy Ricardo and Archie Bunker as one of the two or three most notable characters in all TV history.

The mid-1950s brought more stars into the mix. Veteran big-band leader Lawrence Welk came off a trial summer-replacement run in 1955 on ABC so successful that the network didn't even wait until midseason to bring the show back. They wanted it to continue uninterrupted, and it did—for decades! Big-band singing 1940s superstars Perry Como and Dinah Shore were next in line to capitalize on the new trend towards singers and music. Como had started his TV career with a fifteen-minute, twice-a-week show leading in to the news back in 1948, and Dinah Shore joined the fun with her own fifteen-minute show by the end of 1951.

Como and Shore were each upgraded to hour-long variety shows on NBC by mid-decade. The *Dinah Shore Chevy Show* was the first hour-long variety showcase to be successfully hosted by a woman—it wasn't for nothing that Hollywood's epitome of Southern charm and good humor was referred to as "The Hostess with the Mostess." Having starred in several movie musicals of the '40s, Dinah was as at ease with comedy skits and characters as she was with singing and dancing, and her show attracted everyone from Benny Goodman and Frank Sinatra to top film and TV series stars.

Dinah also showed remarkable courage for a white Southern woman of the time in insisting that the show be integrated, with guests like gospel great Mahalia Jackson and jazz legends Louis Armstrong, Ella Fitzgerald, and Nat King Cole all making regular guest shots. And each week she would smooch her audience goodbye, as she belted out variety TV's most famous anthem of all, "See the USA—In Your Chevrolet!"

Perry Como's signature easy-listening show would also run for several years, until 1963. The avuncular Como was so easygoing and relaxed he made Dean Martin look like he had Attention Deficit Disorder. Comedians would turn Como's style into a punchline—even twenty years later, *SCTV*'s Eugene Levy would play Perry Como in skits where he'd be falling asleep in mid-song, drooling on himself, and so on. After Como's show ended, he went on to make regular holiday specials and guest-hosted *The Hollywood Palace* more times than just about anyone besides Bing Crosby himself.

Iconic entertainer Steve Allen would be NBC's final find of the '50s variety slate. Like many of the others, Allen's parents were vaudevillians, and he had started his own highly successful grown-up career with a Hollywood radio interview show just after returning from service in World War II. The witty and extremely intelligent Allen attracted top movie names, comedians, and his favorites—jazz and big-band swing musicians—to his radio show. The bespectacled Allen caught the eye of the new visual medium of television just as it was getting started.

As we all know, Allen "invented late night," as a recent book on his show titled itself, hosting the first incarnation of *The Tonight Show* when it started in 1954. He stayed with it until turning the reins over to Jack Paar in 1957 so that he could concentrate on his new Sunday-night variety hour, which had already been battling with the formidable Ed Sullivan for a year.

Both of Steve Allen's shows were like a Who's Who of Comedy, with Don Knotts, Louis Nye, Pat Harrington, Tom Poston, Al "Jazzbeaux" Collins, and future *Match Game* master Gene Rayburn among the regular performers. The show kicked itself off with the A-list roster of Kim Novak, Vincent Price, and Sammy Davis Jr. It would fight Ed Sullivan until 1959 and then move to a Monday-night time slot for the show's final season.

By then Allen and his glamorous wife, movie musical and Broadway star Jayne Meadows, had moved back to Hollywood, and "Steverino" would keep a near constant presence in TV for the next two decades. There would be *I've Got a Secret* from 1964–67 (and again 1972–73 in syndication), and his own syndicated talk shows from 1962–64 and 1968–71. He also wrote dozens of books, both fiction and nonfiction, and hosted the unique PBS series *Meeting of the Minds*, which ran from 1977 to late 1981 and won a Peabody Award. Steve Allen died an icon of both Hollywood and the intellectual world alike in October of 2000, just shy of his seventy-ninth birthday.

CBS's last big variety hit of the '50s was with Garry Moore, who had already hosted a highly successful CBS daytime radio talk show for years. The genial, easygoing Moore had been a top radio comedian since the early 1940s (he was the young "straight man" second banana on Jimmy Durante's radio show), and starred in the popular *Club Matinee*. Garry Moore launched his prime-time variety hour on CBS in the fall of 1958, bringing along his longtime best friend and sidekick Durward Kirby—and most fatefully, a twenty-five-year-old Broadway comedienne and aspiring movie star with a face of rubber and a heart of gold. Her name was Carol Burnett.

Moore's show ran until 1964 in prime time on CBS (he also hosted the long-running panel show *I've Got a Secret* from its 1952 debut until Steve Allen took it over in 1964). By 1966, Garry was back, but not for long—he was crushed by *Bonanza* and replaced by the considerably more youthful and cutting-edge Smothers Brothers. However, Garry reclaimed his crown in 1969 with the syndicated era of *To Tell the Truth* (complete with a psychedelic, *Laugh-In*–style set). The congenial Moore retired one year before *Truth* told its last in 1978 (Joe Garagiola did the final year), and died at seventy-eight in 1993.

And while country music and comedy wouldn't really break through to the mainstream until 1970s shows like *Hee-Haw* and *The Dukes of Hazzard*, down-home comedian George Gobel and baritone country crooner Tennessee Ernie Ford both had relatively popular shows during the late 1950s and early 1960s.

By the early 1960s, though, this first wave of TV variety was coming to an end. As television spread out into the heartland of the South and midwest, the Borscht Belt comics, greasy-haired singers, and bow-tied radio interviewers who were TV's first superstars were giving way to suburban, upper-middle-class sitcoms like *Leave It to Beaver* and *The Donna Reed Show*. Soon they would be joined by the other preeminent trend of comedy: the country-com, from the gently homespun *Andy Griffith Show* to the hillbilly hee-haws of *The Beverly Hillbillies, Mister Ed,* and *Green Acres*.

The Hollywood movie studios that had once been TV's sworn enemy (at least on the surface) now became television's best friend—selling off their libraries of feature films to the networks, and switching their "B" movie production arms over to filming weekly cop shows and medical dramas. The quintessential TV genres of westerns, doctor shows, lawyer shows, and crime shows started coming into their own during this era.

But that didn't mean that variety shows were instantly obsolete, or out of the picture just yet. Five variety veterans held on all through the 1960s with their carry-over shows, two of which we'll cover in detail (*The Ed Sullivan Show* and *The Lawrence Welk Show*). A sixth, starring that classic movie clown Danny Kaye, would also hold forth with a CBS variety hour on Wednesday nights from 1963 to '67. It was everything that a fan of Kaye's style of physical comedy and voice impersonations would like, and it probably could have run even longer had CBS not foolishly scheduled the show at 10:00 p.m.—an early-evening time slot would have been far more appropriate, in light of Kaye's tremendous popularity with young children.

Veteran singing star Andy Williams launched a successful variety hour in 1962 on NBC, coming off the million-selling hit record of his signature song, Henry Mancini's "Moon River." Williams's show essentially replaced Dinah Shore's, which had left the airwaves earlier that year. The dynamic host and his wholesome series ran until 1967 on the network, and launched the careers of an unusually talented Mormon family of entertainers named the Osmonds.

As for Jackie Gleason, his original "Honeymooners"-era show closed up shop in 1957. But "The Great One" returned to CBS in 1961 with "that bomb!"—a disastrous celebrity game show called *You're in the Picture*, which was deservedly axed after just one airing. Gleason turned the format into a talk/interview half-hour until its thirteen weeks ran out later that spring. A year later in 1962, he was back with an extension of the idea he'd had during that time—*Jackie Gleason's American Scene Magazine*. That show would be music, variety sketches, and light interviews tied to a different human-nature topic or issue each week. The show owned its Saturday 7:30 time slot for four years.

In 1966, Jackie and CBS both decided that the "magazine" format to his Top 25 show was played out, and they formally retitled the show what everyone always called it anyway, *The Jackie Gleason Show*. (While Jackie did want to keep the show somewhat relevant, he had no interest in doing "magazine" spots on race riots, flag-burning hippies, and bra-burning feminists, or the other issues of the week that were dominating society by the late 1960s.) For the first time in a decade, new *Honeymooners* sketches were resumed, with Sheila MacRae playing Alice and Jane Kean as Trixie. (Jackie pleaded with Audrey Meadows to rejoin the fold, but she politely declined. She had married a business executive who was the love of her life and wanted to keep her appearances confined to TV guest shots and movie cameos. Jackie understood, and the two "honeymooners" wished one another the best.) Despite having a successful career on Broadway, Art Carney just couldn't say no when his best friend invited him back, and he rejoined the cast on a full-time basis.

By now the already laid-back Jackie started taking his cue from Dean Martin, doing fewer and fewer actual onstage rehearsals and meetings. He also demanded that CBS relocate the series to where he had his winter palace vacation home, "The Sun and Fun Capital of the World," Miami Beach. With Jackie still pulling in first-place ratings in his weekend time slot, CBS agreed, and they upgraded the studio facilities of their Miami/Ft. Lauderdale flagship with top-quality equipment.

With his usual loyalty, Jackie did what he could to prevent the relcoation from causing an undue disruption to his colleagues' lives. He simply wouldn't hear of anyone but lifelong friends like Art Carney and Johnny Olson continuing on with him, and saw to it that they were pampered in the grand style. First-class airfare was provided for them to commute to and from Miami to New York, and top hotel accommodations awaited them to use at their will.

But by the spring of 1970, the clock was running out for *The Jackie Gleason Show.* After giving Jackie a free pass with little competition for most of the decade, NBC and ABC both had the show in their sights. ABC countered with two red-hot game shows, the nighttime versions of *Let's Make a Deal* and *The Newlywed Game*, while NBC installed a revamped *Andy Williams Show* directly opposite.

Following a two-year absence, Andy was brought back to NBC in the fall of 1969 for two more years. NBC wanted what they hoped would be a more dynamic and contemporary variety show—but still one with a proven "name" performer—to force a showdown with Gleason on Saturdays. To that end, they hired Saul Ilson and Ernie Chambers, fresh from CBS's just-cancelled Smothers Brothers show, to produce the Williams redux. The writers were told to speed the show up with quickies and *Laugh-In*–style skits, and to be sure and book contemporary folk and rock acts as guests, including Mama Cass Elliott, Judy Collins, and a new British singer named Elton John.

Really young viewers were also to be taken care of, with mime and puppeteer Janos Prohaska hired to play "Cookie Bear," a bear who shared a culinary appetite with a certain blue monster on another 1969 show called *Sesame Street.* For continuity, and to further ensure the presence of families where the kids controlled what the families would watch, the Osmond family was also invited back.

Jackie Gleason still finished the season ahead of the others in general ratings, but the audience demographics told a different story. While an obsession with younger viewers wouldn't really hit the networks for another twenty years, CBS was getting panicky about their image as the country-and-western, old-fashioned network. They realized what a royal screw-up they had made by smothering the Smothers Brothers, and they were about to launch new fare like the Norman Lear sitcoms and *Sonny & Cher* to try to get some of those urban sophisticates and young viewers back. After close to twenty years working with CBS, Jackie was notified that the honeymoon was over.

The same thing happened that year to Red Skelton. By 1969, the fiftysomething veteran had been hearing the rumors that CBS wanted to start going youthful, and Red started booking rock acts like Sweetwater and Chicago in a last-ditch attempt to make young adults give his venerable show a second look. Meanwhile, his far-out regular guests like Tiny Tim, Big Bird, and Soupy Sales kept young children tuning in by the millions. But Red's movie-star salary, and his agent's demands for a firm three-year contract, broke the deal.

Since Red's seventeen-year-old show still managed to finish in the Top Ten, NBC scooped up Red as soon as CBS let him go. Some older NBC execs still hadn't forgiven CBS for pirating Red when he was a top comedy movie star doing NBC radio and TV specials back in the early 1950s. They gave Red a primo half-hour slot leading into *Laugh-In* on Monday nights and promised the industry trades a new, contemporary approach.

While Red's show was still hilarious to his main fans, most reviewers were unimpressed. One said that the "new and improved" *Red Skelton Show* was just the same old "low comedy verging on the vulgar, broadly played sketches, and painfully unsophisticated jokes" that it had always been. It wouldn't have mattered anyway; Red's new NBC show was clobbered by *Gunsmoke* and *Let's Make a Deal*. He saw the inevitable cancellation coming and thanked NBC for giving him his second chance, signing off the show with his usual "God bless." Afterward, Red decided that he'd earned a rest, and he semi-retired to enjoy the rest of his life after having worked nonstop in films, radio, television, and the stage since childhood. He died in 1997.

Jackie Gleason, as always, had the last laugh. He gleefully started taking advantage of the many movie and casino offers that he had earlier turned down out of loyalty to the show. By 1977, Jackie took on his greatest comic role besides Ralph Kramden, as the corrupt country Sheriff Buford T. Justice, who was Burt Reynolds's nemesis in his blockbuster hit *Smokey and the Bandit*. Not only did Jackie play the part in the sequel, the role served to inspire other car-screeching comic characters on the small screen, like *The Dukes of Hazzard*'s Boss Hogg, and Claude Akins's 1979–80 semi-embarrasment *The Misadventures of Sheriff Lobo*. The Great One died in 1987 at age seventy-one, shortly after making his final film alongside Tom Hanks, the bittersweet comedy-drama *Nothing in Common*.

Jackie's sidekick, Art Carney, surpassed even his boss in big screen work during the '70s. He played in the original Broadway production of *The Odd Couple* and walked away with a Best Actor Oscar for his 1974 signature role in *Harry & Tonto*. Art then starred alongside Lily Tomlin in *The Late Show*, and with legends George Burns and Lee Strasberg in the 1979 classic *Going in Style*.

Arthur Godfrey helped relaunch *Candid Camera* on CBS in 1960, but left to concentrate on his radio show and on emceeing stage and charity revues for the rest of the decade. He later joined Dennis James and Rich Little at the helm of *Your All-American College Show* from 1968 to 1970. In 1972, Godfrey (not altogether willingly) retired from CBS radio, making occasional talk- and game-show appearances, until his cancer returned in the early '80s. After cheating death more than once, Arthur Godfrey signed off the air for good in March of 1983, just shy of his eightieth birthday.

Danny Kaye also busied himself with appearing on other variety shows, awards ceremonies, talk shows, and *Hollywood Squares* until his passing at age seventy-four in 1987. Milton Berle continued on as the showbiz trouper he was, making feature film appearances in movies like the classic *It's a Mad Mad Mad Mad World*, guest shots on other series from dramas to comedies, writing books, and appearing onstage, until his death at eighty-five in the spring of 2002.

Andy Williams hosted the Grammy Awards for years in the 1970s and was one of the pioneers of the new middle-American entertainment capital of Branson, Missouri, where he opened his "Moon River" Theatre in the 1980s. Ironically, the quintessentially wholesome and friendly singer found himself at the center of a strange controversy in 1976 when his estranged wife, singer Claudine Longet, "accidentally" shot and killed her lover, ski champion Spider Sabich. Longet was eventually acquitted, and though Andy stood by her during her murder trial, the two officially went their separate ways afterward.

Sid Caesar made some lesser comedy movies, as well as having a great supporting role as the Coach in 1978's John Travolta/Olivia Newton-John blockbuster *Grease*. He appeared regularly in Vegas and nightclubs in the '60s and '70s. (I think we all know what happened to Mel Brooks, Neil Simon, Carl Reiner, and Woody Allen.)

And while Dinah Shore probably tied with Perry Como as the most low-key of the bunch, in her unpretentious and friendly way, it would be she who would have the longest-running television career. She "kissed" her classic *Dinah Shore Chevy Show* goodbye in the spring of 1962 (she was then undergoing a painful divorce from her longtime husband, Western star George Montgomery), but the woman who had been the top big band "girl singer" of the '40s just couldn't stay away from the microphone for long.

After making several TV specials and doing club gigs, by 1970 she was back with a half-hour talk show called *Dinah's Place*. After four years on NBC, the show moved into hour-long daytime syndication and carried on until 1980. Dinah also raised money for March of Dimes, had a headline-grabbing four-year romance with (a considerably younger) Burt Reynolds, and cemented her status as one of the first ladies of game shows with appearances on *Password*, *Hollywood Squares*, and *Cross-Wits*.

Most importantly, she founded a golf tournament in 1972 that did more to "put women's sports on the map" than anybody this side of Martina Navratilova and Billie Jean King. ("The Dinah" also became the ultimate party destination for the lesbian community, with a weeklong celebration of parties and disco dancing that continues to this day.) Even after her 1980 retirement, the always vibrant Dinah continued with her signature golf and tennis tournaments, made several specials for the Nashville Network, and guest-starred on *The Love Boat* and *Murder, She Wrote*. She passed away at the age of seventy-seven, in early 1994.

In the revolutionary 1960s, TV variety shows shook their 1950s styles and conventions and burst open into being some of the most revitalized, energetic, and fun shows on television. Of course, not every variety show that aired between 1965 and 1980 receives in-depth coverage here—there were simply too many. Well over fifty shows are described in this book, and when you add in the summer replacements, the specials, the six-week limited series, and so on, the tally for prime-time variety in the '70s reaches well over one hundred!

Yes, this ultimate retro-vision format was at one time the most popular type of prime-time programming. In the 1970–71 season alone, there were no less than fifteen variety hours on the air each and every week—and that was back when there were just three networks! What we have endeavored to do is cover the best-remembered, most notable, and most uniquely of-their-time variety shows in pop culture history.

So for now, pretend it's 8:00 on a Saturday, Sunday, or Monday night. As Gary Owens used to say, "Get ready, America"—for a night of familiar fun and exciting thrills, and a true "variety" of personalities, artists, styles, and fashions. We're about to turn back the clock to the 1960s and '70s, so enjoy the groovy trip and relive the world of classic TV's "really big shews"—starting with the biggest one of 'em all . . .

# TV'S GROOVIEST VARIETY SHOWS

# The Ed Sullivan Show

**STARRING**
Ed Sullivan

**ON THE AIR**
June 20, 1948–June 6, 1971

**NETWORK**
CBS

**MUSIC**
The Ray Bloch Orchestra

**ANNOUNCERS**
Lee Vines, Ralph Paul

**ORIGINATION**
The Ed Sullivan Theatre, New York, NY

"We've got a reeeeeel big shew tonight!"

*Clockwise from left:* Louis Armstrong, Bob Hope, and Joan Rivers.

FOR TWO FULL decades, from the post–World War II settling-down of the '40s and '50s to the tumult of the Woodstock era of the late '60s, there was a show on CBS every Sunday night that was the premiere showcase for top talent of all kinds. *The Ed Sullivan Show* was a North American institution, the "Big Shew" that had something for everyone—from stuntmen to Streisand, from Bach to the Beatles, from George Burns to George Carlin.

But it was much more than just that. Ed's show was a testament to "the power of TV in its infancy," said singer and frequent guest Carol Lawrence. Joan Rivers said, "when Ed put his arm around you and said, 'You know, she's a really funny little lady,' *America* said, 'You know—she's a really funny little lady!'" For twenty years, as Joan correctly called it, "Ed Sullivan . . . was *America's taste.*"

Ed Sullivan was born on September 28, 1901, in New York City. The tough Irish kid from the apartments of New York at first wanted to become a boxer, enthralled by the fights at Madison Square Garden and in the city's YMCAs and gyms. But Ed found his first love and calling in the field of journalism. In the 1920s, after finishing school, the young aspiring writer worked a succession of jobs at various New York papers, finally securing a column in that quintessential New York sensation, *The Daily News.*

In 1930, Ed married his longtime sweetheart, Sylvia Weinstein, and a few years later the young couple would welcome a baby daughter into their family, Elizabeth. The 1930s would also mark the beginning of Ed's forty-year love affair with broadcasting.

In the early '30s, Ed secured an interview show in New York City on the then new and growing medium of radio. The burgeoning success of his column on Broadway life provided the perfect nexus to the radio show, as popular stage stars, vaudevillians, and bandleaders would make themselves available to the new program. Jack Benny was one of Ed's earliest guests, and he recalled that show as one of his first—if not his very first—major radio appearances. However, the strains of starting a family, managing his column, and seeing to his and Sylvia's active New York social life was quite a load on the thirty-year-old writer. Ed elected to give up the radio show after a relatively short run on the air.

He quickly regretted the decision, as radio only grew and grew in stature and popularity during the decade. By the 1940s, it had soundly eclipsed the print media as the nation's foremost force in communication. Ed later recalled, shortly after the debut of his television show, "I got in at the ground floor of radio and dropped out of it—like a dope. Now," Ed continued, "I'm in on the ground floor of television—and I'm not giving up my lease until the landlord evicts me!"

Still, Ed Sullivan stayed quite visible and successful in the 1930s. During the Depression, the entertainment industry was one of the few stable industries out there, as families who were unable to spend money on expensive travel escaped their worries with mental "vacations" in front of the Golden Age of Hollywood's movies and Broadway's plays and musical revues. Ed stayed on top of it all, wining and dining with stage stars and visiting movie figures in Manhattan on an almost nightly basis. His column was so successful by the early 1940s that only the likes of Hedda Hopper, Louella Parsons, and Walter Winchell held more sway or importance for film and stage stars' exposure.

During the war years, Ed expanded his publicity and influence by hosting and putting on several servicemen's balls and stage canteens. By 1945, Ed had finally returned to the radio medium that he'd walked out on "like a big dope" almost fifteen years before. Now, he was tapped to host New York's annual Harvest Moon Ball, which was being broadcast by CBS Radio.

Ed claimed that he was unaware that the film footage of the 1947 Harvest Moon Ball was televised on CBS that year. Whether or not that was more (false) modesty than truth, it proved to be a turning point in his life. At the time, the growing radio network of CBS was actively branching out into television and wanted to establish itself firmly as a leader in that new medium.

But NBC had almost all the biggest stars—Bob Hope, Jack Benny, Bing Crosby, Red Skelton, Milton Berle; and CBS chairman William S. Paley was a firm believer in the Metro-Goldwyn-Mayer–style "star system" of bringing the absolute best in marquee names to your company and then building shows around them to showcase their talents. CBS's program committee needed a new show that would be an avenue for exposing the best and widest range of possible talents to the viewing audience: The new show should be "bait" for stars who had commitments to rival networks to come by and visit CBS—and equally importantly, it should be a place where young talent on the rise could get their breaks, so that if the audience's response was especially positive, CBS might be able to develop them further, and perhaps build new shows around them.

Providentially, as CBS started looking for a master of ceremonies for their new showcase show, an executive brought up that shy yet commanding man who'd hosted the Harvest Moon Ball . . . what was his name . . . oh yeah—that guy who writes that column for *The Daily News*. Ed Sullivan would be able to handle running the new show firmly and fairly, but he wasn't so much of a performer himself that he would detract attention from the all-important guest stars. Plus, as a respected (and somewhat feared) entertainment columnist, he would be able to secure top-name Broadway and nightclub acts and Hollywood movie stars—who otherwise might be "allergic" to TV—for the very asking.

On June 20, 1948, the first of what would become *A Thousand Sundays*, as a book on the Sullivan show appropriately titled itself, premiered on CBS: *Toast of the Town*, hosted by Broadway columnist Ed Sullivan. The show's title was appropriate; it was a celebration of the people who were the "toast" of the entertainment world, especially

New York's. The show had a pathetic—even by 1940s standards—talent budget of roughly $500 total for the first episode. But Ed's clout and the chance of exposure on the hottest new show in TV was enough to lure the red-hot comedy team of Dean Martin and Jerry Lewis onto the show, plus the Broadway composing team of Rodgers and Hammerstein.

The new show exuded a certain kind of sophistication and was unlike any other show on the air. While other variety shows were silly, Ed's was serious—although not without a big dollop of humor and comedy. It gave you the impression that, with all due respect to the Ringling Brothers and Barnum & Bailey, you really were seeing "The Greatest Show on Earth."

Still, some CBS officials (and viewers) were a little uncomfortable with the awkward, ill at ease, and not conventionally handsome Sullivan. Already some of Ed's competitors in the entertainment press had dubbed him "Old Stone Face" and "that Zombie." It was reported that for the first six months of the show's run, CBS put Ed on trial, asking sponsors if they had anything against his handling of the show, or if they would rather CBS send out a casting call for a new emcee for the new program. Fortunately for the history of television, none of the sponsors reacted so negatively to Sullivan that they made an issue of it. Ed Sullivan finally had a secure "lease" in the new high-rise of television.

The late '40s and '50s would establish Ed Sullivan, and *The Ed Sullivan Show*, as television's premiere variety showcase. While all the variety shows on the air had comedy skits and musical moments, Ed would invite acrobats, Broadway stars, prima ballerinas, and animal acts onto the show. Music acts would range from '40s big-band era stars like Patti Page, Jo Stafford, Peggy Lee, Benny Goodman, Rosemary Clooney, and Teresa Brewer in the show's early years, to Steppenwolf, Vanilla Fudge, Janis Joplin, and Jimi Hendrix before the show's run was over.

And of course, through it all there was primordial puppeteer Señor Wences. He had a simple yet sweetly funny act in which he would hold his hand, which he painted to suggest a face, over a small rubber "body," creating a "boy" he named Jimmy (or "Chimm-ey," as he pronounced it in his thick accent). He would converse with "Jimmy," and then hold up a box with a plastic head in it, talking with the mumbling head-in-the-box for a bit and then finally asking, "Okay?" and opening the box, which responded, "Saw-right!" Simple stuff, but such was the stuff of early TV's heyday.

Most importantly, the show succeeded beyond anyone's hopes in luring proven talent into the CBS stable of stars. Veteran journalist Ed (and CBS) could barely contain their glee that they had "scooped" NBC's flagship himself, Bob Hope, giving Bob his East Coast television debut in September of 1948. Legendary composer Irving Berlin made his first TV appearance on the Sullivan stage, as would Walt Disney, Victor Borge, Harry Belafonte, Richard Pryor, and Fred Astaire in the years ahead.

By 1950, CBS had nabbed Jack Benny, George Burns and Gracie Allen, and Frank Sinatra to star in their own CBS television shows. Red Skelton and Jackie Gleason would soon follow, and before the 1950s were over, a young comedienne named Carol Burnett would receive one of her biggest breaks on the program. *The Ed Sullivan Show* was drawing talent into CBS's family like a magnet, as well as viewers to CBS itself. *Toast of the Town* was second only to Uncle Miltie himself as the highest-rated television show of the 1949–50 season.

Already famous for his Hollywood and Broadway journalism and radio interviews, Ed Sullivan now became a superstar across the United States and Canada. Comedians had a field day with Ed's robotic mannerisms and pretentious delivery. "Ed Sullivan will be around as long as someone else has talent," joked early-TV and radio icon Fred Allen, adding that, "a dog could do that, so long as you rubbed meat on the performers." John Byner, Rich Little, Frank Fontaine, and Frank Gorshin would be among the many impressionists who would "do" sidesplitting imitations of Ed (often right alongside the real thing). Everyone agreed, however, that Will Jordan, who made his first appearance in the mid-'50s, was the definitive one. His jut-toothed, ill-tailored Ed was so funny that even "Old Stone Face" himself would crack up watching.

What was perhaps the show's most obvious weakness—Ed's ill-at-ease presence on camera and lack of interest in lengthy interviews—was also its greatest strength. "Let me just introduce the acts and get off," Ed once said. The greatest singers, actors, and comedians—who would have otherwise not even thought about doing television—were eager to appear on the Sullivan show, because they knew that they would be the "stars" of their segments, without any fear of being upstaged or lampooned.

All this meant, of course, that whenever Ed *did* appear in a comedy skit or alongside one of the comics or musicians it was all the more memorable and funny! One early episode even featured a hilarious *I Love Lucy* sketch where Lucy and Desi are preparing to go on *The Ed Sullivan Show*, and are panicked waiting for Ed's impending visit. Another episode in the '60s, making note of Ed's Sunday-night neighbor *Bonanza*, had a mustache-clad, badge-wearing, pistol-packin' Ed a-headin' into a saloon, to clean up them dadgum varmints out in the old West!

1956 would be a huge turning point for *The Ed Sullivan Show*. At the start of the 1955–56 season, CBS finally dropped the by-then-irrelevant title of *Toast of the Town* and formally retitled the program *The Ed Sullivan Show*. But less than a year after this high-water mark, Ed would experience two of the lowest points of his career.

In the summer of 1956, NBC decided to return the compliment of CBS's earlier cannibalizing of their talent roster. NBC installed Steve Allen, then at the height of his popularity (hosting the first incarnation of *The Tonight Show* and starring as Benny Goodman in a major motion picture) in an hour-long variety show smack opposite Ed's on Sunday night.

*Clockwise from above:* Barbra Streisand, George Burns, and Judy Garland on-stage at the Ed Sullivan Theatre.

Using the same strategy that they were hoping would knock off an ill-at-ease veteran big band leader named Lawrence Welk (in their disastrous attempt to counter-program that show with Sid Caesar), NBC painted Ed as old-fashioned, aging, and square.

As if that wasn't enough to make the temperamental Ed irate, Allen's show gave Ed the ultimate humiliation, by "scooping" him with hot young rocker Elvis Presley's TV debut. Watching Allen's show wipe the walls with his in the ratings, Ed became consumed with fury. He announced the very next day he was booking Presley for three appearances for the then astronomical sum of $50,000 (at that time, fifty grand could pay for a house in Beverly Hills or Brentwood).

Unfortunately, that was just the beginning of the bad news that 1956 held in store. In the late summer of 1956, while traveling to his vacation home on Long Island, Ed was involved in a severe car accident and spent several weeks in a hospital bed recovering, with guest hosts taking over the show until he was better. (Ed would, from then on, often sign his show off with good wishes and an exhortation to "drive safely.")

Back on the show, Ed wasted no time in using the power of his columnist's pen to let America know what he thought of NBC and the upstart Allen show. Venting his considerable pain and frustration (both physical and emotional), Ed was especially blunt and to the point. Calling Allen's rival show a "Johnny-come-lately to Sunday nights," in *TV Guide*, he said that he wasn't worried about future incidents of "guest-stealing" because, "[since] our show can claim to have originated most of the techniques" of the variety-show format, it didn't need to "steal" anything from the Allen program. "From now on, I just wouldn't trust Allen—it's as simple as that."

Later, when asked what he thought of Steve's (very polite and deferential) response to his missive, and of Allen's producer and manager Jules Green, he said, "I have no comment on either of those two punks!" (Fortunately, like so many other show-business "feuds" this one eventually blew over, not long after Allen's NBC show ended in 1960.)

Ed could take some comfort in the fact that his "debut" of Elvis Presley in 1956 attracted the highest audience in television history to that point, as well as an around-the-block line of screaming fans. Despite his first instincts, Ed had shown Elvis in all his glory on the first two appearances, but by the third and final one, Ed gave in to letter-writing viewers and station managers, who didn't much care for Elvis or his sexy, swivel-hip pelvis. Ed insisted that Elvis be photographed from the waist up, although it was clearly discernible that his lower quarters were giving their all to the live studio audience.

It would be Elvis's last appearance on the Sullivan stage, but Ed graciously provided the twenty-two-year-old phenom a wonderful sendoff. "I just want to say to you," Ed addressed the camera, "that this is one decent, fine boy. And Elvis, wherever you go on your travels, I want you to know we've never had a more enjoyable time with a big-name star that we've had with you. You're thoroughly all right—so let's have a big hand for a very nice person!"

As stodgy as Ed Sullivan looked, and may have been in actual fact, as Michelle Phillips recalled in a salute to the Sullivan show, "he was [ultimately] in charge of who got booked for that show." Rock acts might not have been to his own taste as much as show tunes, swing, and opera. But Ed's nose for entertainment "news," and his instinct to objectively report the facts as they were, led him to book the greatest rock acts of all time.

And that's not all. In the horrifyingly racist world of the late '40s, '50s, and early '60s TV, *The Ed Sullivan Show* was in some cases the *only* major venue for top-name black talent. Sammy Davis Jr., Louis Armstrong, Ella Fitzgerald, Lena Horne, Harry Belafonte, and Pearl Bailey were regular guests from start to finish. In later years, Ed would give the biggest breaks to Richard Pryor and Flip Wilson, as well as Diana Ross and the Supremes, the Jackson Five, and all the other great Motown bands of the '60s. And since Ed's show was by then such an institution, it was inconceivable for even the most segregationist Southern TV stations to use their shopworn threats of boycotts or blackouts against the show. *The Ed Sullivan Show* was above it all, in every way.

Ed scored an altogether different (and perhaps literal) kind of "coup" in 1960, and it had nothing to do with singers or dancers. In 1960, Ed was one of the only North American journalists allowed to interview Fidel Castro, who had just taken over Cuba's government. (A year earlier, Sullivan had made history and headlines when he shot an episode of his show on location in the Soviet Union.) Sullivan asked the communist dictator no-holds-barred questions, to which the Cuban chairman could only stammer halfhearted responses.

By the early '60s, Ed's show was one of the only remnants of the first wave of TV variety left on the air. Milton Berle, Arthur Godfrey, Steve Allen, and Sid Caesar had already seen their initial shows go off the air (although they would all remain active and visible in TV for years to come). Also by then, Ed's beloved daughter Betty had grown up and was starting a long and fulfilling married life with young *Sullivan* show producer Bob Precht. In the "Camelot" days of the Kennedy era, the Sullivan show was *the* show to watch at 8 o'clock on Sundays. But as we all know, those days—and all the innocence of the late '40s and '50s—were numbered. On November 22, 1963, that era ended with an assassin's gunshot in Dallas.

The nation was panicked and stunned and went into a dazed period of mourning as 1963 turned into 1964. It has often been said that the nation was looking for something new, something entertaining, to take their minds off the national tragedy—especially America's youth, now that the rock-and-roll, doo-wop, drive-ins, and sock-hops of the '50s had firmly established a teenage culture in the United States. On February 9, 1964, *The Ed Sullivan Show* delivered it.

Throughout 1962 and '63, a fabulous foursome of a rock group called the Beatles were making headlines across England. Influenced by Elvis, Buddy Holly, and several of the black R&B acts of the '50s, the four lads from Liverpool were fast becoming Europe's most popular rock-and-roll band. Ed had traveled to London in the fall of 1963 and had found himself swimming through a mob of young people waiting for the Beatles' plane to arrive at Heathrow Airport. Before Ed's London holiday ended, he had signed the band for the top-dollar price tag of $25,000 to make two appearances on his show.

Once again, the show broke all the records for TV ratings. Virtually all of the United States and Canada watched as the Fab Four made their *Sullivan* premiere, singing "She Loves You (Yeah Yeah Yeah)"—only to be almost drowned out by the roaring, screaming fans and weeping teenage girls in the packed-to-the-rafters audience. A new era in music—in all of society and culture—was born, and Ed Sullivan was the doctor-in-attendance.

For the next six years, *The Ed Sullivan Show* was not only the ultimate destination for acts like the Beatles, the Rolling Stones, the Supremes, Four Tops, the Fifth Dimension, the Temptations, James Brown, Aretha Franklin, and Barbra Streisand, it would set the standard for the presentation of musical acts on television. And as for comedy: how about Joan Rivers, Richard Pryor, Flip Wilson, Henny Youngman, George Burns, Jack Benny, and George Carlin—to name a few?

In contrast to the inviting, closeup style that Dean Martin and *Laugh-In* used and that Lawrence Welk insisted on for members of his "musical family," *The Ed Sullivan Show* would photograph musicians and comedians in long, floor-to-ceiling shots. It had huge background sets, and emphasized the fact that it was being broadcast from a prominent stage theatre CBS had taken over for television production. Even the casual viewer couldn't be mistaken about the Sullivan show's viewpoint. It was like a museum, something awesome, something bigger than big. *The Ed Sullivan Show* was the Supreme Court of live entertainment.

Especially after up-and-coming TV directors Tim Kiley and John Moffitt took over the show's direction in the late '60s, the twenty-year-old show proved it could still lead the league in innovative TV techniques. Rock bands would often have a psychedelic, electronic effects–generated background, or re-looped footage of them performing in rehearsal, projected in back of them via Chroma-Key (or superimposed on the screen while they were singing). "We used mirrors, computers—everything!" recalled a justifiably proud Moffitt in interviews years later.

By then, NBC had found an increasingly successful opponent to Ed on Sunday nights, the equally influential *Disney's Wonderful World*, which drew off families with children by the millions. Ed's show responded by booking Jim Henson's and Sid and Marty Krofft's puppet acts. He frosted the cake by introducing a funny, New York

Italian "mouse" puppet named Topo Gigio, with whom Ed would often stop by and "visit" with at the end of the show. The effect was to attract kids and soften Ed's grim, "Stone Face" image.

"Eddie," a pajama-clad Topo would intone, with a Jerry Mouse–like smirk on his face (at nearly 9:00 p.m., it was probably past his bedtime), "Kiss-a me-a good night!" "Eddie" always did as he was told, and Ed probably smiled and laughed more with Topo Gigio than all the top-name comedy acts he had put together. (Little Topo was probably the only performer on the show who could ever get away with calling Mister Sullivan "Eddie," too!)

Even in 1970 after more than twenty years on the air, Ed's show still proved it had what it took. On March 1, 1970, the Sullivan show presented a sentimental, campily over-the-top salute to the Fab Four (who were just about to announce their breakup), called "The Beatles Songbook." It boasted an incomparable lineup of Peggy Lee, Peter Gennaro, the Muppets, Duke Ellington, Steve Lawrence & Eydie Gorme, and Dionne Warwick recapping the Beatles' best-loved hits, with a filmed performance of the Beatles' last recording session at Twickenham Studios signing off the show with "Let It Be."

The episode would be the Beatles' last-ever television appearance together, which was certainly appropriate, since the Sullivan show had been their first live U.S. appearance just six years earlier. A few weeks later, when Paul McCartney debuted his solo album, he gratefully saw to it that Ed could "scoop" everyone else again—with an avant-garde video John Moffitt made of Linda McCartney's photography, zoomed and fast-edited to "Maybe I'm Amazed."

Alas, those shows didn't just signify the end of the Beatles' era in music—they also marked the beginning of the end of the Ed Sullivan era in television, too. Ed finished 1969–70 in a more than respectable twenty-seventh place, and CBS knew that they had no other show that could even hope to draw that kind of viewership against the crushing competition of Disney, *The Bill Cosby Show,* and *The FBI.* But as the 1970–71 season got under way, the once-unbeatable program would find itself placing an embarrassing third in its Sunday-night time slot.

Ed pulled out all the stops for the show's September 1970 premiere, with "groovy" pop-art advertisements featuring colorful text design and a hilarious mirror image print photograph of him laughing and applauding. He also proved that his show was still the prestige destination for top-name talent, booking otherwise ungettable, to-die-for guests Barbra Streisand, Flip Wilson, Lucille Ball, Bob Hope, and Blood Sweat & Tears for the premiere.

Over the next few months, it was old home week at the Sullivan show, with Joan Rivers, Gladys Knight & the Pips, the Fifth Dimension, Wayne & Shuster, Alan King, Jackie Mason, and the rest of the Sullivan gang (and of course Topo Gigio and Señor Wences—can't forget them). As 1971 opened the show gave the first big break

The Fab Four *(top)*, the King *(bottom)*, and the Doors *(left)* lit *The Ed Sullivan Show*'s fire.

to young stand-up comedian Albert Brooks and brought back George Carlin and Richard Pryor for some of their riskiest (and funniest) material yet.

But CBS had other plans for 1971, and unfortunately Ed Sullivan just wasn't a part of them. After a decade of relying on country comedies, vintage sitcoms, and variety shows, new CBS chief Robert Wood was refocusing the network on an updated slate that would carry the network through the new decade. CBS was finally building a successful stable of newer shows, from Archie Bunker and Mary Richards to *Hawaii Five-0* and *Mannix*. And with a drastic cutback in available network time for the fall of 1971 due to new FCC regulations, it was clear that *The Ed Sullivan Show* was on its last legs at the network it had helped build.

On Sunday, June 6, 1971, *The Ed Sullivan Show* finally closed the book on its unforgettable twenty-three-year run. At the time, it was the longest continuously running television show in history besides the news and public affairs. The last show was actually a rerun of a February episode (the last first-run episode aired March 28, with select shows filling out the rest of the season).

Even though he was pushing seventy, Ed was determined not to be forced into an unwanted retirement. He continued writing columns for New York newspapers and national magazines, traveled to Las Vegas regularly, and even booked several appearances on talk shows and *What's My Line*. He also made uproarious guest appearances on his longtime guest Flip Wilson's new top-rated variety hour, as well as on ABC's short-lived *ABC Comedy Hour* program (where he played a dirty-old-man newscaster!) and on the Friar's Club roasts.

Less than two years later, however, everything changed. Ed's beloved wife of more than forty-two years, Sylvia, died suddenly in March 1973. Ed was devastated by the loss and made far fewer appearances in public as he began making the adjustment to life alone. However, it turned out Ed didn't have much time left either. On October 13, 1974, Ed Sullivan passed away in New York City, just two weeks after his seventy-third birthday.

Just a few months later in January of 1975, Dick Cavett hosted a salute to TV's ultimate variety show, with the most memorable clips from the program. A few local stations here and there would occasionally rerun the show, and the Elvis and Beatles episodes were in perpetual demand by media professors, collectors, and Hollywood pros for TV specials and clip shows. But over the next sixteen years, the once-ubiquitous Ed Sullivan presence in TV would slowly fade from memory.

In the fall of 1990, CBS decided to mount a salute to their most popular and influential programs of the past forty-five years. The network already had specials planned for the spring of 1991 celebrating the twentieth anniversary of groundbreakers like *The Mary Tyler Moore Show* and *All in the Family* (as well as the "nineteenth" anniversary of the first Bob Newhart show). CBS felt it was time to look back at what had been, along with Sid Caesar and Milton Berle, the most influential and important variety program in early-TV history. The network commissioned veteran researcher and producer Andrew Solt to organize and edit a two-hour, prime-time special featuring the best of *The Ed Sullivan Show*'s limitless archive of memorable moments.

In February 1991, *The Very Best of The Ed Sullivan Show* aired appropriately on Sunday night, following CBS's top-rated Sunday duo of *60 Minutes* and *Murder, She Wrote*. The two-hour retrospective was hosted by CBS's other variety-show standard-bearer, Carol Burnett. Wraparound segments for the show were taped on the stage of the Ed Sullivan Theatre in Manhattan (which would become ground zero for David Letterman's *Late Show* just two years later, after he jumped ship from NBC to CBS in 1993).

The show also featured spot interviews with a veritable panoply of surviving *Sullivan* guests, from Ella Fitzgerald, Michelle Phillips, Ray Manzarek, and Carol Lawrence to Joan Rivers, Alan King, Jackie Mason, and even Steve Allen and ninety-something Señor Wences himself. The show's dozens of clips were jam-packed with showstopper performances.

From Elvis and the Beatles and the premiere rock bands of the '60s to jazzy jaw-droppers like Louis, Ella, Bobby Darin, and Sammy Davis Jr.; from what-was-*that?* novelty and circus acts, to a Who's Who of stand-up comedy, impressionists, and magicians; even the original-cast performances from Broadway shows like *Man of La Mancha* and *Camelot* were there—ending with Ethel Merman's appropriate 1968 belting-out of "There's No Business Like Show Business."

*The Very Best of the Ed Sullivan Show* was the single highest-rated TV special of the 1990–91 television season. No sooner were the overnight ratings in than CBS ordered another special, this time hosted by Burt Reynolds, for the fall of 1991. In light of this (and their 1987 success with reruns of *The Lawrence Welk Show*), PBS stations began inundating Andrew Solt's production company for repackaged episodes of *The Ed Sullivan Show* to re-air on stations across the country.

*The Ed Sullivan Show* was more than just another TV variety show. It was an honest-to-God time capsule of the absolute best the entertainment industry had to offer in the Golden Age of Hollywood and Broadway. The program launched innumerable careers and kept going hundreds more. Alongside an invite for Johnny Carson's *Tonight Show*, nothing in the mid-twentieth century said that you had "made it" in show business more than the perfumed note to appear on Ed Sullivan's stage.

In 1993, *TV Guide* understandably chose *The Ed Sullivan Show* as the most important variety show in TV history. "Today, Sullivan's all-encompassing mandate is spread across the dial," careening all the way from late-night talk shows to MTV to PBS. "*The Ed Sullivan Show* wasn't just 'a real big shew,'" they noted. "It was *the biggest*."

## FUN FACTS

Alan King recalled in a 1990 interview that "Ed Sullivan was a great, great friend— and a terrible, terrible enemy. But if he liked you," King added, "nobody in the world could be kinder to you." The following bits of information would seem to bear this out.

- Ed Sullivan actually had a twin brother when he was born! Sadly, he died of complications during the delivery.

- Ed's daughter Betty's best friend in high school was child actress Peggy Ann Garner. Garner was living the unfortunately typical life of a '30s and '40s child performer, with an abusive "stage mother" who took most of Peggy Ann's earnings and worked her like a dog. After Peggy broke down in tears and told Betty what her home life was really like, Ed and Sylvia marched straight to Mrs. Garner's house. While Sylvia cleared out all of Peggy Ann's things, Ed told the shocked Mrs. Garner that they were taking Peggy to live with them, and added that if she didn't cooperate, they'd fight her in open court for custody, with all the gossip columnists watching! Peggy Ann enjoyed the rest of her teenage years, and remained best friends with Betty Precht until Peggy's untimely death at age 50 in 1984.

- In perhaps the unseemliest moment of both men's careers, Ed and Walter Winchell once got into a fight in a men's bathroom—with Ed reportedly dunking Winchell's head in a urinal! Fortunately, later on the two rival columnists made up, with Ed calling Winchell "The best we have" in a book.

- In the truest sense of the phrase "adding insult to injury," Ed Sullivan was absent from the first show that Elvis Presley performed on—he was still recuperating from his car accident. British actor Charles Laughton, the guest host, introduced Elvis (or as he pronounced it, "Elvin") Presley to the Sullivan show viewership.

- Influential New York columnist Harriet Van Horne was an apprentice writer in her twenties during World War II. She was put off by reading columns where, as her boyfriends and family members went off to fight, Ed (at age forty and way past draft eligibility) seemed to make himself out to be a "war hero," promoting bond rallies and servicemen's benefits starring himself. She took her frustrations out some years later when the Sullivan show was in its prime, giving it a particularly nasty review in the newspaper in which she had by then secured a column. Ed responded by wiring her a heartfelt note: "Dear Miss Van Horne: You bitch. Sincerely, Ed Sullivan."

- When legendary vaudevillian and black movie star Bill "Bojangles" Robinson died in 1949, alcoholism and medical expenses had taken their toll on the performer, and he had next to nothing left in his estate. Ed personally picked up the tab for, and arranged, a state funeral for Robinson, with his rose-bedecked casket paraded by limousine down the main boulevards in Harlem. Thousands of his fans lined up to say goodbye, with television and newsreel footage taken of the funeral, giving Mr. Bojangles the send-off he richly deserved. And it was because of Ed that they were able to do so.

## MEMORABLE MOMENTS

Where does one even *begin* to account for the memorable moments on *The Ed Sullivan Show*? Every episode of the roughly one thousand produced was almost guaranteed to have at least one show-stopper, be it an incredible daredevil "stunt" or acrobatic act, a dazzling dance routine, a breathtaking operatic or ballet recital, a surefire Borscht Belt comedy crack-up, or one of the greatest music acts in history. Nonetheless, here is just a sampling of Sullivan show delights:

### memorable music moments

- Well, of course, February 9, 1964, was perhaps the single most important date in pop music history. "Ladies and Gentlemen—the Beatles!! Here they are!!!"
- And the close runner-up for most important date was September 9, 1956, when Elvis (and his pelvis!) made his Sullivan show premiere. The episode was the single-highest-rated regular episode of a television program in TV history up to that time, with an audience of over 60 million people! (Remember, this was in 1956, when TVs were just beginning to become commonplace household items.) Even now, only things on the level of "Who Shot JR?" and the finales of *Friends* and M*A*S*H can boast higher numbers.
- And of course, the end of the era: March 1, 1970, the last time all four Beatles played together on a U.S. or Canadian television program.
- As if that wasn't enough, the "father" of jazz himself, Louis Armstrong, considered Sullivan's show his favorite to appear on, and did so regularly. Who can ever forget "Pops'" versions of "Bill Bailey, Won't You Please Come Home," "I Found My Thrill on Blueberry Hill," "Sleepytime Down South," or "Hello, Dolly" (for which he was paid the then top-dollar fee of $5,000 for the one song alone; it goes without saying he was worth that and ten times more.)
- Just after New Year's in 1970, the "Ike & Tina Turner Revue" gave an astounding soul-music tour de force. They kicked off the show with Tina's incomparable "Big wheels keep on turnin'!" screamin' version of "Proud Mary"—with her lightning-fast backup singers dancing and "diving underwater" at nuclear pace! Then, before the show was out, Tina fairly radiated the black woman's anthem of liberation, "Bold Soul Sister."
- Two of the greatest entertainers in history joined forces in a stunner of a 1964 episode, when Sammy Davis Jr. and Ella Fitzgerald scatted their way through an impromptu duet that was arranged on the spot by Sullivan on that night's show.
- Then there was the Fifth Dimension's amazing appearance in state-of-the-art 1970 computer technology. They started by riding an orange-carpeted "flying saucer" through a painted set of space stars, which was enlarged via Chroma Key to look as though they were really in outer space, singing "Aquarius"—at one

point with a blue crystal image of the Aquarius sign superimposed on the screen. Then, for the big finish, they "flew" straight to the sun itself, finishing off with an impossible-not-to-sing-along-with rendition of "Let the Sunshine In."

- Janis Joplin's incendiary appearance a year earlier, with Big Brother and the Holding Company, was a lacerating tour de force, with Joplin belting out her anthems "Try Just a Little Bit Harder" and "Raise Your Hand." As always, Joplin wrung every drop out of each note, with Big Brother providing relentless support in the background.

- The Beach Boys' 1966 rendition of "Good Vibrations" and "Wouldn't It Be Nice" was a psychedelic panorama, with split-screen video, as "America's Beatles" reclaimed their crown with their "Pet Sounds" premiere on *The Ed Sullivan Show*.

- More interesting than psychedelic rock band Vanilla Fudge's January 1968 appearance were the mutton-chop sideburns on sixty-five-year-old Ed Sullivan. He looked like a cross between a Muppet and the "Tall Man" from the Phantasm horror movies!

- James Brown's 1966 appearance was to R&B fans almost what the Beatles' was to rock-and-rollers two years earlier. Showing that he wasn't named "the hardest-working man in show business" by accident, his performance of "I Feel Good" and "Papa's Got a Brand New Bag" was so emotional and red hot, a sweat-soaked Brown literally collapsed at the edge of the elevated stage by the time the number was over.

- Ed admitted that he felt "a little busted up" when he heard that The Mamas & The Papas were breaking up in 1968, but Ed had the satisfaction of scoring some of their last TV appearances together. On an earlier show in '66, they gave the definitive TV renditions of "Dedicated to the One I Love" and "California Dreamin'."

- The Rolling Stones made several *Sullivan* appearances early in their career, but none as controversial as the one in 1967, when they planned to sing their free love–era hit, "Let's Spend the Night Together." Ed and son-in-law/producer Bob Precht strongly "suggested" that they change the lyric to the tamer, "Let's Spend Some Time Together"—much to Mick Jagger's disdain. (It would be one of the Stones' last appearances.)

- Then there was the most important act that never was on *The Ed Sullivan Show*. Folk singer Bob Dylan was scheduled to appear in the early '60s, but the controversy over his booking prompted Dylan to pull out rather than tame his lyrics, or cause Ed's show unnecessary grief.

- But no act ever gave as good as they got from *The Ed Sullivan Show* as Jim Morrison of the Doors. The Doors were booked in '67 to sing their hit "Light My Fire," a fairly straightforward rock love song—if it weren't for Morrison's stunningly handsome looks, animal sexuality, and head-to-toe leather outfit! CBS drew the line at the lyric, "Baby, we couldn't get much higher" (as in "high" on drugs), and insisted that Morrison trim the line. Morrison promised he'd be a good little boy—and then promptly sang the line as pointedly and erotically as he could, live, on the air! A furious CBS censor stormed into the band's dressing room afterward carrying a pile of legal contracts. "You see these?" the censor cried. "We were gonna book you for *six* more Sullivan shows!" he exclaimed (reportedly at a price of over $25,000), while tearing the contracts to shreds. "But now—you've blown it! You'll never do *The Ed Sullivan Show again*!!" To which a relaxed Jim Morrison just grinned and replied, "Hey man—we just *did The Ed Sullivan Show*!!"

## comedy classics

- In the early '60s, a ventriloquist was on the show whose dummy had the unusual occupation of teaching other people the art of ventriloquy. Ed expressed interest when the dummy told him that "Any dummy can learn to do this!" "Really?" Ed smiled—then took a double take and laughed, "Oh—very funny . . ."

  Ed got the dummy back a moment later. "The first thing you have to do," said the dummy-teacher, "is put a great big smile on your face." The dummy then did an up-and-down survey of Ed's as-always-grim countenance, and wailed, "I see now that I'm working against impossible odds!"

- Albert Brooks did a routine a decade later that earned him the title of the "worst" ventriloquist ever to appear on the Sullivan stage. Brooks's mouth (and everything else, it seemed) moved right along with his dummy's (the point of the routine being how *bad* a ventriloquist he was).

- "I'm a big believer in diet and exercise," rotund comedienne Totie Fields announced. "I mean, that's how I stay firm!" she laughed, shaking her fleshy arms. Then she showed off a favorite facial-firming tip of hers (massaging her double chin with the back of her hand). "See how pretty my fingers are!"

- Joan Rivers once said she'd put on so much weight while trying to squeeze into skimpy bathing suits, she had to walk around Long Island like a zombie. People came up to her, she said, and pointed at her, saying, "Look—it's Ed Sullivan!"

  Ed came up to Joan waggling his finger in the middle of her act after that one. "Oh no, Ed, I didn't mean it," Joan apologized. "You'd have looked thinner!"

- A debonair, cigarette-smoking Alan King lamented the fact that his house had just burned down—and what's more, his insurance company was refusing to pick up the tab. "What kind of policy do you have, sir?" the clerk had asked. "Fire and theft," King replied. "Oh—there's your mistake," the insurance analyst grinned. "You should have had Fire OR Theft! Under your policy, the only way you can get paid is if the house is robbed while it's burning down!"

- Phyllis Diller gave an assessment of married life that in 1969 you'd only have gotten on *The Newlywed Game*. "When I first married Fang, I thought that our week-ends would be a loaf of bread, a jug of wine, and va-va-va-voom!" she exulted. "Turned out, it's a bag of popcorn, a can of beer, and The Green Bay Packers!" She added that Fang drank so much, "he could kill a six-pack during an Instant Replay!"

- Henny Youngman asked us to "take my wife—please!" after reciting her new sensuous-woman attempts to be worthy of his affections. He said that she put so much cold cream, mudpacks, Oil of Olay, and eye makeup on her face, when she came into the room to say "Good night," he said, "Take me to your leader!"

- Kiddie-show legend and future *What's My Line* regular Soupy Sales was seen wearing a Clark Gable mustache and tuxedo, massaging the hand of his sexy "date" at a romantic restaurant. Then the bouffant-haired "date" turned around to face the camera. It was Ed Sullivan—wearing diamond earrings and a blond flip!

- The comedy team of Charlie Brill and Mitzi McCall appeared on the show that was also the Beatles' premiere. They found the audience so unruly and excited to see the Fab Four, they could hardly get through their routine!

- Ed's most notorious moment with a comedian came in 1964: the show was running overtime and Borscht Belt legend Jackie Mason was the guest. Ed and the show's director kept giving Mason offstage "cues," with their fingers, of how much time he had left, while Mason was performing his forcibly shortened routine. This rattled Mason and understandably insulted him a bit. At the end of his act, he made fun of the cues, saying, "Here's a finger to you—and a finger to you—and a finger to you!"—allegedly using his middle finger when pointing in Ed's direction!

  Ed was shocked—his "Stone Face" flared like something out of a Walt Disney cartoon, as he stamped his foot with barely contained fury! Jackie Mason was off the Sullivan show from that moment on. However, after both sides had gotten their fair share of tabloid headlines and embarrassing gossip stories in the Hollywood trades, the two men finally mended their fences when they ran into each other at the Las Vegas Airport. Ed welcomed Jackie back onto his stage in 1966, and both men said they wanted to "clear up any misunderstanding." Jackie remained a regular and popular guest of the show for the rest of its run.

- Not only was the Canadian comedy team of Johnny Wayne & Frank Shuster one of the most popular acts on the Sullivan show—Frank Shuster was also the father of a young lady named Rosie Shuster, who would become Lorne Michaels's first wife and his colleague on the original *Saturday Night Live*.

## AND AN ENDOWMENT FOR THE ARTS...

- Legendary dance star Gene Kelly showed that he still had what it took, in 1962 at age fifty, when he lifted Ed up and did a sort of Jack LaLanne–like "reverse push-up" with Ed after dancing a marathon lindy-hop from one end of the stage to the other!

- Jacques D'Amboise "handed off" his dancing partner, ballerina Karel Shimoff, to a stunned Ed in 1970!
- Respected stage and screen actor Richard Kiley gave a bravura rendition of "The Impossible Dream" from the Broadway show *Man of La Mancha,* which was incomparably dramatic, with Orson Wellsian "looking down" crane shots and a full costume and stage show set.
- Richard Burton and Julie Andrews defined the Kennedy era with their full stage showing of *Camelot* at the Sullivan theatre.
- Julie Andrews, Barbra Streisand, Beverly Sills, Joan Sutherland, Maria Callas, Ella Fitzgerald, Judy Garland, and Aretha Franklin—all made showstopper appearances on *The Ed Sullivan Show.*

## AMAZING ACTS AND FANTASTIC FEATS

During the twenty-three-year run of *The Ed Sullivan Show,* there was a plethora of plate-spinners, a jubilee of jugglers, an abundance of animal acts, and more. Among the more notable:

- The young French ladies who could "sit" on their backs on orthopedic lounge chairs and spin full-size dinner tables in the air with their feet.
- A trio where two men supported a girl in the middle who held onto a wire held in the mens' mouths, while the men simlutaneously spun themselves from a trapeze ladder's platforms.
- An Asian man who could balance a razor-sharp spinning wheel with a tiny pivot point on the edge of a paper folding fan.
- And a lady who was strong enough for a man—she could tear telephone books and dictionaries in half with her bare hands—who, when she was pre-empted due to news conferences and break-ins, tried to tear Ed in half. (Fortunately, an army of burly New York security guards stopped that before it started!)

## BLOOPERS, BREAKUPS, AND QUOTABLE QUOTES

Were you watching when . . .

- Despite his mastery of the English language when writing his columns, Ed could be . . . well . . . a wee bit undiplomatic in his way of putting things—even with friends. If Gladys Knight & the Pips were expecting a gushing introduction for their fall 1970 hit "If I Was Your Woman," they didn't get it! "Gladys Knight & the Pips have been on our show I don't know how many times, and each time they seem to have a new hit. Well—damned if they didn't do it again!"
- "Dusty," Ed intoned to Irish soul singer Dusty Springfield. "Come on over here, and tell us your real name!" Dusty responded by rattling off a long Mary-Margaret-Catherine style litany of Irish-Catholic names and middle names until getting to

the "Springfield," as Ed beamed with pride. "So, you're an Irishman like me, eh?" Ed preened, smoothing out his tie. "No," Dusty winked. "I'm an Irish *girl!*" "WELL!" Ed coughed.

- "And now, here's rock singer Jose Feliciano. He's blind, and he's Puerto Rican!"

- Then there was the notorious time that Ed had a bit of trouble with operatic singer Sergio Franchi's name on a mid-'60s Easter telecast. "And now, here's Sergio Frankie-Finky-Funky-Phooey. . . . uhh . . . umm . . . er . . . Oh heck—let's hear it for The Lord's Prayer!!"

- In rehearsal, Jack Jones came over to Ed to be "interviewed" after finishing his song for the night, and Ed said, "Say, your father was Allan Jones, right?" to which Jack replied, "He still is!" The crew completely broke up laughing, and Ed said, "Well, I'll ask you that again, on the air!" Cut to the live show—Jack finishes his number, goes over to Ed, and Ed says, "Your father *is* Allan Jones, right?" Then Ed waited and waited for the "laugh" that was supposed to come. It took several explanations of why the first way of putting it "worked" and the other didn't before Ed "got it."

# Video Vaudevilles

While none of these shows had the panache or influence of their spiritual forefather Ed Sullivan, they nonetheless made a definite impact on their own.

## The Hollywood Palace

*Network: ABC; On the air: January 4, 1964–February 7, 1970*

ABC's answer to *The Ed Sullivan Show*, *The Hollywood Palace* started production at the end of 1963 to replace the disastrous *Jerry Lewis Show*, on which ABC had pegged all their hopes for the fall 1963 season. The new show was taped at Hollywood's famous El Capitan Theatre, which had been the home of many of TV's earliest hits to be taped on the West Coast (most notably the 1952–61 run of Ralph Edwards' classic *This Is Your Life*.)

*The Hollywood Palace* even managed to exceed Ed Sullivan in pomp and circumstance, with a bigger-than-big theatrical feel, although that was likely a case of overcompensation on its part. It did beat Ed (and ABC's own Lawrence Welk) in being one of the first variety shows shot in color, in early 1964. Rather than finding a regular host of the program, the show inaugurated the format later used to perfection on *Saturday Night Live* of having a top-name weekly "guest host" to run each week's show. After their monologue and introduction, they would introduce and converse with the usual cavalcade of popular music, opera/ballet, stand-up comedy, and novelty acts that paraded by.

In its earlier episodes, the show also featured a sexy young go-go girl who served as the "card holder" and model for the show, as each major act was introduced with a campy vaudeville-style card and easel announcing their name. The "card girl" later became as big or bigger a name than any of the acts she would help introduce—her name was Raquel Welch!

*The Hollywood Palace* was and is remembered to this day as being essentially "The Bing Crosby Show," and no wonder: Crosby hosted the show more often than any other performer, and was by far the most closely associated with it as well as the most popular. Fittingly, the legendary enter-tainer and singer hosted both the first and the last telecasts. Crosby's star power and warm charm made the show a success in the beginning, and made *The Hollywood Palace* the perfect "lead-out" for *The Lawrence Welk Show* on ABC's Saturday night lineup. (Crosby was such a big fan of Welk's show, he reportedly wrote fan letters to the program himself; and Welk for his part "saluted" Crosby and his best friend Bob Hope so many times one loses count.)

Several memorable moments occurred on the show, too. Marx Brothers diva Margaret Dumont made her last TV appearance on the show before her death in 1965, and the Rolling Stones made their American TV debut on the show a year earlier, on an episode hosted by Dean

Martin. (His introduction was classic Dino: "Let me tell ya—I've gotten rolled when I was stoned, too!") And Diana Ross helped "discover" the Jackson Five on this show when she hosted it in 1969. Following Andrew Solt's spectacular success with the *Ed Sullivan Show* specials of 1991, ABC ordered two retospectives on *The Hollywood Palace* for the 1992–93 season.

## The Kraft Music Hall

*Network: NBC; On the air: September 13, 1967–September 1, 1971*
Judy Carne, Don Ho, Alan King, Johnny Cash (until he got his own variety show, which played opposite the *Music Hall* on ABC), and Des O'Connor were the most frequent and the most popular guest hosts of this show, similar in format to *Hollywood Palace*. The show would be hosted by a different performer (or group of performers) each week. The major difference was that many if not most "Music Halls" would be structured similarly to a musical-comedy theatre production, or a "salute" to such-and-such a theme ("Tonight, So-and-So salutes the wacky world of modern marriage," and so on).

The show held down its time slot from '67 to '70, but by late 1970 both ABC's *Johnny Cash* and CBS's *Medical Center* were closing in. Des O'Connor was appointed the permanent host of the show in the spring of 1971 to strengthen its identity as a stand-alone variety series, but by the fall of 1971, *The Kraft Music Hall* had expired.

## NBC Follies

*Network: NBC; On the air: September 13, 1973–December 27, 1973*
Despite being hosted by Sammy Davis Jr. and Mickey Rooney, this freewheeling hour of video vaudeville came when the time of old-fashioned big-name-act shows like *The Ed Sullivan Show* and *The Hollywood Palace* had already passed. *NBC Follies* was probably doomed from the minute it was assigned the 10:00 spot on Thursday nights. Virtually all the fans of NBC's Thursday 9:00 lead-in, *Ironside,* switched over to the perfectly compatible *Streets of San Francisco* over on ABC at 10:00. *NBC Follies* was replaced by *Music Country,* an hour focused on country and western performers as incompatible with *Ironside*'s city-folk audience as pork rinds were with veal Prince Orloff and chocolate mousse. Both series were given the death penalty by the spring of 1974.

# The Lawrence Welk Show

## Vital Stats

**STARRING**
Lawrence Welk and the Champagne Music Makers

**ON THE AIR**
May 2, 1951 (Los Angeles); July 2, 1955 (ABC)

**OFF THE AIR**
Summer 1982

**NETWORKS**
ABC (1955–71), Syndicated first-run (1971–82),
KTLA (local Los Angeles, 1951–55)

**MUSICAL DIRECTORS**
George Cates, Myron Floren, Bob Ballard

**ANNOUNCER**
Bob Warren

**ORIGINATION**
Aragon Ballroom, Santa Monica (1951–55),
ABC Prospect/Talmadge Studios (1955–76, 1979–82),
CBS Television City (1976–79)

"Wunnerful, ah-wunnerful!"

TELEVISION'S LONGEST-RUNNING variety show was, like its longtime contemporary *Ed Sullivan*, as much a product of the 1950s and early TV as it was of the groovy, shagadelic '60s or the disco decade after. Nonetheless, no Baby Boomer or Gen Xer can forget the garish '70s costumes, yellow and orange bandstands, or Broadway comedy–style musical numbers that kicked off every weekend in the '60s and '70s.

More than that, the story of the "wunnerful" alternate universe of *The Lawrence Welk Show* is the story of television itself in its growing-up and adolescent phase—a bridge that runs from Truman and Eisenhower through Ford and Carter, and from Uncle Miltie's day to MTV's.

Lawrence Welk was born on March 11, 1903, in the rural hamlet of Strasburg, North Dakota. His parents, Ludwig and Christina Schwann Welk, were turn-of-the-century immigrants who had escaped the political turmoil and upheavals of Germany and Alsace-Lorraine in the late 1800s, and settled in to homestead their own farm in the New Country. Welk was among several brothers and sisters born during the late 1800s and early 1900s on the Welks' North Dakota farm.

In the grim turn-of-the-century conditions of life in the freezing country, the social life of the town revolved around the fun barn dances and "jam sessions" where the young men of the town would get together to play and sing. Young Lawrence was enchanted by seeing the world of enjoyment that these things brought from everyday life, and from listening to his father play his accordion for the family at the end of the day. By the dawn of the 1920s, the teenage Welk had no doubt in his mind that he wanted to make his life one of music.

Welk's parents took rather a dim view of their son's obsession with being an entertainer, although much to their credit they didn't put any permanent roadblocks in his way. Still, even soft-spoken mother Christina sometimes referred to young Lawrence as *dummer-Esel* ("dumb-ass"!) for his "frivolous" attentions to showbiz, instead of buckling down to the serious struggle for existence on the freezing-temperature farmland.

Already Welk had had to leave his own education behind after elementary school, in order to help his father run the farm. And after several more years of what a deploring yet amazed *New York Times* book reviewer called "indentured slavery" to his father, Ludwig Welk returned the favor by paying the then-outrageous price of $400 for a professional-quality accordion for his son. By now Welk was twenty-one years old, and it was clear to his parents that, despite his ox-like work ethic and respect for his elders, their *dummer-Esel* was much more at home on the bandstand than in the barnyard. Ludwig and Christina Welk bade their son goodbye, as the young Germanic musician set out into the new country he loved so much to find his fortune.

Needless to say, it wasn't easy. The sheltered, devoutly Catholic Welk could barely speak English, and had precious little knowledge of the cutthroat, cosmopoli-

All in the musical family: *(clockwise from right)* Bob Lido and the Lennon Sisters, Guy and Ralna, Norma and Jimmy, and Joe Feeney and Myron Floren with Lawrence Welk.

tan ways of roaring '20s nightlife. At first all he could gather were desultory one-nighters in barn dances and regional pickup bands.

But in the late 1920s, Welk received his biggest break as vaudeville legend George T. Kelly hired Welk as one of his stable of performers dubbed "The Peerless Entertainers." While the versatile vaudevillian became Welk's mentor onstage, Kelly's warm and generous wife became Lawrence's "second mother," brushing up the eager-to-learn young man on English at night, and encouraging him to broaden his horizons reading literature and philosophy.

In 1931, the twenty-eight-year-old musician married his sweetheart Fern Renner, a highly capable young nurse who was using her career as a stepping stone for the then unheard-of (for a woman) role of doctor, studying at medical school at night and earning top grades. The twenty-seven-year-old had silky long black hair and "bedroom eyes" on a warmly smiling, cameo face, and was as at ease in the kitchen as she was in the operating room, well known among friends and family for her gourmet cooking.

The newlywed bandleader struck out on his own in a rickety collection of short-lived combos (like the "Honolulu Fruit Gum Orchestra"), and his perseverance finally started to pay off. By the late '30s, Welk had established himself as one of *the* premier minor-league big bands, and was finally starting to secure posh bookings in prominent hotels, restaurants, and ballrooms. After several managers and apprecia-tive fans told Welk that his "light and bubbly" sound reminded them of a refreshing glass of champagne, a trademark was born. By 1938, Lawrence Welk and his "Cham-pagne Music Makers" were fully in business, and Welk inaugurated his signature of hiring talented "girl singers" to hold the coveted position of "Champagne Lady."

During the war years, Welk solidified his hold on success, establishing himself in the midwest's capital of culture, Chicago, as one of the pre-eminent dance bands going. While he hadn't attained the coast-to-coast recognizability of Tommy Dorsey, Benny Goodman, or Duke Ellington, his opulent perch at the sumptuous, world-renowned Aragon and Trianon ballrooms in Chicago firmly ensconced the band in the big leagues. By then he also had a growing family of three children—young daughters Donna and Shirley, joined by son Larry Welk Jr., in March 1940.

Toward the end of the decade Welk added a highly successful radio show spon-sored by Miller High Life—"The Champagne of Bottled Beer." And in 1950, he brought a genial red-haired, thirty-year-old accordion prodigy named Myron Floren to the band. Floren would achieve stardom in his own right as one of the greatest accordionists of the twentieth century, and he had a likeable, slyly good-natured per-sonality—which is exactly what Welk's managers feared! "Would Dorsey hire another trombonist to do solos, or Goodman another star clarinetist or saxophonist? I mean, this guy's better than you!" To which Lawrence Welk responded proudly, "That's the only kind of musician I hire!"

By 1951, the Lawrence Welk Orchestra was getting ready to play a late-spring and summer engagement at the Aragon Ballroom's satellite showplace in Santa Monica. At the time, new local TV station KTLA-5 was telecasting most of the reputable big bands that came to play at the Aragon. And with some prodding by Welk's manager Sam Lutz, KTLA chief Klaus Landsberg agreed to a trial run of a "Lawrence Welk Show" during the time.

With its debut bolstered by the TV premiere of the then-recent Bogart and Bacall blockbuster *To Have and Have Not,* the new *Lawrence Welk Show* soon became KTLA's most popular TV attraction. An elated Welk sent word to his family that they had "made it" in Hollywood, and could move out to the land of beaches and movie stars, "where the sun shines every day." With the income from the new show and his ballroom gigs, Welk could afford a down payment on an elegant mansion in the hills of Brentwood, with full-size pool and a lush, ocean-view backyard. Welk's teenage children jumped at the chance to trade windy Chicago for the beaches and surf of southern California. Fern Welk smilingly gave in, and the family made the move before 1952 was out.

During the early 1950s, Welk also started gathering the "Musical Family" that fans would come to know and love throughout his show's run. Tall, elegant male lead vocalist Jimmy Roberts, Irish tenor Joe Feeney, jazzy singer and violinist Bob Lido, and "Champagne Ladies" Roberta Linn and Alice Lon came on board during Welk's KTLA era.

By early 1955, the local *Lawrence Welk Show* was a Southern California TV institution, regularly creaming its nationally promoted network competition everywhere from San Diego to San Luis Obispo. That fact did not go unnoticed by an ambitious television producer who'd already had two humongous successes launching popular local shows nationally.

Don Fedderson was a young producer who had built a track record of successful series. He had helped get Los Angeles station KCOP-13 off the ground and was known for his diplomacy in cementing alliances with movie studios fearful of the new medium of TV. He had already made stars out of Betty White and Liberace, both of whom had started their television careers on local L.A. shows, and he knocked it out of the park with the 1954–60 anthology series *The Millionaire*. Fedderson felt that a national big-budget version of the local Welk show would have the potential to bring in the same fan letters and ratings points. If the down-to-earth, unpretentious program could do this well in sophisticated Hollywood, he knew it could *own* its time slot in the southern and midwestern heartland.

In 1955, he learned that the Dodge Division of Chrysler Motors was shopping for a new variety show that they could sponsor for the upcoming 1955–56 television season. Don Fedderson knew just the man to put in the driver's seat. (In 1959, Welk and Dodge would part company as friends—though Welk, whose own tastes ran to

BMWs and Cadillacs, bought Dodges for his wife for the rest of his years. Welk's new sponsor would be the JB Williams Pharmaceutical Company, the makers of Sominex, Aqua-Velva—and especially "GERITOL," as the huge lighted sign over the Welk bandstand would proclaim.)

After a four-year run on local TV, the tension was mounting to an all-time high as the countdown neared to the July 2, 1955, national premiere of the new *Lawrence Welk Show* on ABC.

At first the ratings were dismal—a 7 rating, and a less-than 20 percent share of audience—outright failure in those three-network days. However, as befit the folksy, homespun show, word of mouth and favorable publicity quickly spread in Welk's favor. To the amazement of ABC executives, each week the summer show's popularity grew almost exponentially. By the end of the eight-week trial run, the show was winning its time slot, and had more than tripled its rating from its initial telecast!

Shortly after the show went national in 1955, fifteen-year-old Larry Welk brought home as his date the daughter of a prominent Santa Monica Chamber of Commerce president and country-club executive. Her name was Dianne "Dee Dee" Lennon, and she happened to have three equally talented and appealing sisters who sang and danced, named Kathy, Janet, and Peggy. Soon, four new stars were born. *Da luffly* Lennon Sisters would instantly become the show's starring attraction, becoming a "sister act" outdone only by the likes of the Andrews and McGuire siblings, with their Connie Francis–like sound and effortless harmonies.

By the start of the 1960s, the final parts of the Welk firmament were installed. Talented eighteen-year-old dancer (and ex-Mouseketeer) Bobby Burgess, and his first partner, the winningly smiling Barbara Boylan, were added as the show's dynamic dance team. And two ladies would break down the all-male barriers of the Champagne Music Makers: the elegant cellist Charlotte Harris, who at little over thirty had already had prestige spots with several symphonies and movie studio orchestras; and the ultra-talented piano-playing whirlwind Jo Ann Castle.

Jo Ann's vivacious personality, flair for comedy, and ever-more-outrageously campy costumes made the beautiful twentysomething performer one of the most popular on variety TV throughout the 1960s. (Jo's outfits were matched by the what-are-they-going-to-think-of-THIS-week repaintings of her upright piano. It went from pink-and-white vaudeville style to go-go era flashing neon to rhinestone-and-mirror appliques that made the piano look like it had mugged one of the Supremes!)

Also in 1959, lovely operatic-voiced vocalist Norma Zimmer succeeded the vivacious Alice Lon as "Champagne Lady," and would remain as the most famous one in the role until the show went off the air more than twenty years later. Alice left the show in 1959 because—according to Welk—she wanted to take advantage of new opportunities. Gossip columnists instead suggested that it was because Welk disapproved of her so-called "cheesecake" image and clothes! Whatever the case, Alice

Lon went on to use her fame and money to open up a nightclub near Malibu Beach, which soon became *the* trendiest and hippest spot on the Pacific Coast Highway. Whatever differences there may or may not have been between Alice and Mister Welk were obviously soon resolved, as her club was also a proving ground for new Welk show talent, giving tap-dance trouper Arthur Duncan and Jo Ann Castle regular engagements, among many other performers. Later on, when Alice was diagnosed with terminal cancer, Lawrence kept in constant contact with her, until the day she passed away at age fifty-five in the spring of 1981.

Jazz legend Pete Fountain also left the show around this time, after a brief stint getting his first big break with the Welk show band. According to the columns, the twenty-nine-year-old, beatnik-bearded clarinetist and saxophonist left the straitlaced *Welk* show after two years because Welk disapproved of him "jazzing up" a Christmas carol (even though Welk often said Dixieland music was a personal favorite of his).

And speaking of Arthur Duncan, the versatile African American song-and-dance man who tapped his way to stardom on the *Welk* stage, his hiring caused an especially unseemly controversy. While racist stations in the Deep South and Midwest were uncomfortable, certainly, none made too much of an issue of it, as Welk's show was already second only to Ed Sullivan as a cultural institution. But Welk received little credit for the then-gutsy move in the new civil-rights era. And worse, some black journalists and spokesmen were actually upset at Arthur (at least at first) for joining the "white-bread" *Welk* program.

At the time, as historian Ken Burns noted in his landmark PBS documentary *Jazz*, some of the most talented black performers who ever lived—Sammy Davis Jr., Nat King Cole, and Louis Armstrong among them—were being tarred by younger blacks as being "Ooftah" (minstrel-like, pandering). The community was understandably tired of having to do insulting Jim Crow routines or pretend that they had the exact same culture as white America in order to make it, and at the woefully limited exposure African Americans had in movies and television. Now, there was a backlash against black performers deemed too acceptable or friendly to white audiences.

The fact remains that Duncan was one of the most talented dancers of his era. He would later be cited as an inspiration and influence by stage stars of the caliber of Gregory Hines and Ben Vereen, and would consult and choreograph for them and numerous other productions in Black Theatre. Welk treated Arthur the same as he did the white regulars, and Duncan immediately became one of the most popular members of the Musical Family.

The year 1965 marked two major moments for *The Lawrence Welk Show*. It was the show's tenth anniversary on coast-to-coast ABC, and it was also the show's first season in living color (or at least as close to living color as 1965 technology allowed). The color process took some getting used to—the sets and bandstand were notably

Accordion master Myron Floren (*above*) in his prime, and the lovely Anacani (*left*), looking *muy caliente*.

drab that year, compared to the more lavish and outrageous sets and costumes to come in the later episodes. Also new in 1965 was Philadelphia-born singer and entertainer Natalie Nevins. Natalie had already had her own local TV shows in Los Angeles and Philadelphia and was a close friend of comedy legend Stan Freberg. Her Irish charm, high soprano, and pixie-like appearance would brighten the show for four years.

By 1967, the set was finally "colorized" with the bandstand boasting wood-carved "LWs" and painted light blue, with huge swags of chiffon curtains and crystal chandeliers hanging above (along, of course, with the ever-present "GERITOL" sign). And the band's uniforms went color (and would only get more outrageously so as the years progressed, as any fan of the show can tell you).

Two talented young singers joined the show that year, Andra Willis and soon-to-be country superstar Lynn Anderson; their tenure on the show would be relatively short before leaving to pursue other options. Bobby Burgess also found his most famous (and best) dancing partner in the energetic and dynamic person of Cissy King. The tall and toothsome Bobby and the shag-haired, sweetly sexy Cissy would be the definitive young dance couple for the next decade.

Unfortunately, the show wasn't just *adding* members to the cast. That was made all too clear at the end of 1967 when, after twelve years, the Lennon Sisters announced that they were leaving *The Lawrence Welk Show*. They were now all grown up and besieged by Hollywood talent agents and promoters to strike out on their own while the iron was still hot. Welk had always (he said) encouraged the Lennons to take other occasional performances on other shows, like *Ed Sullivan* and *Perry Como*. Now the ladies asked Lawrence if they could do the show part-time, so that they could keep up their in-demand schedule of Vegas and Tahoe headlines, stage and resort shows, and TV guest appearances.

Welk felt that that would be an unfair indulgence, and that it would violate his favored-nations policy toward his "Musical Family." He also didn't feel all that comfortable with *the girls-ah* recording the more modern Beatles, Stevie Wonder, and Lesley Gore songs that were their personal favorites, still insisting on old-fashioned standards for the four. Most significantly, even aside from the law of diminishing returns, the four "girls" were now grown women with careers, dating, marriage, and establishing their own lives on their minds. In the changing world of 1968, the time had come for the fab foursome to make it on their own.

After the Lennons left the show, Lawrence Welk seemed to reevaluate things. He decided—correctly—that, as one reference book put it, "something approaching a modern beat" with "modern young singers," wasn't necessarily such a bad thing after all. During 1968, Welk added twenty-year-old pop singer Tanya Falan, whose sultry Italian looks and mod jazzy style soon caught the eye of Welk's twenty-eight-year-old son Larry. They were married within a year. And while he didn't exactly go psychedelic, Welk did start becoming a lot friendlier to Burt Bacharach, Nancy Sinatra, and even several of the Beatles' hits, with relatively modern arrangements.

Welk also brought on the quintessentially dynamic duo of Sandi & Salli that year, who beat out literally *hundreds* of acts vying for the spot left open by the Lennons. Sandi Jensen (later Griffiths, after her 1969 marriage to college sweetheart Brent) and Salli Flynn were students at Brigham Young University in Utah and had formed a singing act together that had toured Vietnam-era Army bases and was one of the college's most popular attractions.

Effervescent redhead Sandi and raven-haired Salli drove the audience absolutely "mod" with their groovy rhythm harmonies of the day, like "Do You Know the Way to San Jose" and "Raindrops Keep Fallin' On My Head." (Their pink lipstick, up-to-date hairdos, and leggy miniskirts and go-go boots didn't hurt either!) Salli also bore a distinct resemblance to the actress Susan Saint James, and in 1971 when Saint James was cast in *McMillan & Wife* alongside Rock Hudson, her fancy-free character was named Sally. Coincidence? You be the judge. . . .

In early 1969, young singer Ralna English made her debut on the show, with a soft-rock repertoire of songs like Glen Campbell's "By the Time I Get to Phoenix" and the Woody Guthrie anthem "This Land Is Your Land." The beautiful twentysomething Ralna had already starred alongside other up-and-comers like Steve Martin and Mason Williams at the fabled Horn nightclub and several other top L.A. nightspots. Ralna started her career before she even started high school, singing with rock and doo-wop bands from the age of thirteen in her home state of Texas. (She even beat a then-unknown Buddy Holly in a "Battle of the Bands" back then!)

Ralna would bring her husband, Mississippi native Guy Hovis, onto the show by December. Guy's curly black hair and tenor-voiced Elvis style paired with Ralna helped to make them one of the preeminent soft country duos of the 1970s. (In the mid-'70s, Guy and Ralna would enjoy several gold records in their own right.)

Before the new season started, Welk would also add Glen Campbell–style country vocalist Clay Hart to the show, who kept it all in the family when he married Salli Flynn after she left the show in 1972. (Clay stayed until 1975). Also brought aboard was Ken Delo, a thirtyish song and dance man from Detroit who had found a measure of fame working in television Down Under, where he hosted a talk show and the Australian version of *Name That Tune*.

Pianist and singer Gail Farrell was hired fresh out of college in Oklahoma, where she had majored in classical piano performance and graduated near the top of her class. Along with Gail came her longtime friend and singing partner Mary Lou Metzger, who danced, sang, and acted. Mary Lou was also just finishing up college when she auditioned for the Welk show's 1970 casting call on the recommendation of her grandmother, an ardent Welk fan. Mary Lou initially doubted that she would be so lucky as to get a plum variety show gig at twenty-one. But showing the pluck and spunk that would be her signature, she tried out for it anyway—and got it! (Mary Lou also "kept it in the family" in 1973, when she married young bassist and brass player Richard Maloof.)

It wasn't all champagne and music, though. In 1969, Natalie Nevins was let go from the show in one of the program's low points. Details of the dismissal were unclear, but it apparently stemmed from Natalie having been absent from a premiere night opening of a Welk "Musical Family" event on stage. Natalie claimed she had been sick, but according to Welk's representatives she failed to obtain a doctor's note to that effect. Natalie later tried to make a peace offering by baking Welk some homemade pastries and apologizing, but it was clear that the damage was done, and it was an uncomfortable situation for both.

Leaving the show on much happier terms would be piano-playing dynamo Jo Ann Castle, who exited the show at the end of 1969. Jo Ann had told Welk months in advance that she wanted to see what she could do on her own, and that she felt the timing was now right to capitalize on her fame to build a solo career. Now with some financial security, Jo Ann wanted a free hand in making her busy work schedule, since she was expecting a child. Welk accepted the decision gracefully, and gave Jo Ann a beautiful full-show send-off.

As *The Lawrence Welk Show* headed into its sixteenth season on ABC (and its twentieth on the air), Welk presented what he considered his most important and meaningful show ever: the Thanksgiving 1970 episode titled "Thank You America." Some critics groaned that it was embarrassing, right wing, and reactionary—which it may well have been, considering the era. But looking back, "Thank You America" seems no more conservative or flag-waving than a typical Fourth of July salute today. For his part, Welk also was careful not to "take sides" on the divisive Vietnam issue— indeed, he even started the show off with a Thanksgiving-table rendition of "A Prayer for Peace."

Welk's core audience, many of whom had sons or grandsons serving in Vietnam, and lived in terror each day that they would get "the call," thought of the show as nothing less than a lifeline. The episode drew more fan letters and near-tearful words of gratitude than any other *Welk* show in history. (And for unintentional comedy, whatever your outlook, it was hard to beat Bobby and Cissy's stars-and-stripes dance uniforms, Welk's white polyester suit with red shirt and blue tie, or Norma's fashionable French roll and eye makeup while "playing" a homespun Pilgrim mama!)

The show also started booking more and more top-flight guest stars; the 1970–71 season alone would feature formidable names like Kate Smith, Irving Berlin, and Jack Benny among several others. But, as Welk noted in his autobiography, despite the success there were some unsettling "straws in the wind." The FCC's Prime-Time Access Rule was phased into effect in 1971 and 1972, disallowing all network-fed programming besides news and sports events from the 7:00–8:00 p.m. Eastern/Pacific time period from Monday through Saturday, turning the hour over to syndicated programming.

ABC had been trying to establish a show on Saturdays that would successfully follow Welk's show, but nothing worked. After his longtime Bing Crosby companion *The Hollywood Palace* ran its course at the beginning of 1970, ABC tried *The Lennon Sisters Hour* and *Engelbert Humperdinck* at 9:30 p.m., both to lackluster results. The network's latest effort, *The Most Deadly Game*, was an outright failure. Meanwhile, CBS was throwing their hat in the air at 9:30 on Saturdays with the *wunnerful* new *Mary Tyler Moore Show*.

By the end of 1970, it was clear that the overwhelming majority of Welk fans were off to Mary and Rhoda's apartment the minute Welk signed off at 9:30, and there they stayed for CBS's hit detective drama *Mannix* at 10:00. Early in 1971, ABC would write the rest of Saturday night off entirely, installing a ninety-minute movie at 9:30 p.m. for the rest of the season. And finally, like his longtime CBS companion *Ed Sullivan*, Welk's show and audience were beginning to show their age. The show was facing stiff competition in its once-unbeatable time period—particularly for what little was left of the young professionals and sophisticated households most prized by advertisers.

By the time the final episode of the season was about to be taped in spring 1971, tension was running at an all-time high. Welk's managers Sam Lutz and Don Fedderson felt like throwing water on themselves to see if it was all real—if the show that had been *the* linchpin of ABC's schedule for most of its run, the network's most reliable moneymaker, would be back or not for the fall. Making things even more nerve-wracking, ABC executives placed a strict gag order on their programming department until all the decisions were set in concrete.

Shortly after (trying to) celebrate his sixty-eighth birthday, Welk was taking part in a charity golf tournament held at his country club just south of upscale Orange County, and fighting a miserable head cold. He tried to keep a game face despite it all, but he knew that ABC would be announcing their new fall schedule in only a matter of days. This would be the week that would make or break the fate of his show, and of his "Musical Family."

While nearing the eighteenth hole, Welk was called off the golf course for an emergency phone call. The caller was longtime UPI television and movie columnist Rick DuBrow. He had an urgent message for Welk, and would be calling back in five minutes. After being sped back to the clubhouse in a golf cart, Welk waited nervously for the phone to ring.

Just a few minutes later, it did.

With almost unthinkable disrespect, ABC had decided to leak the news of the show's cancellation to the press, without even so much as warning Welk or his producers beforehand. DuBrow informed Welk that his show had indeed been formally cancelled by ABC and asked the shocked maestro for a quote.

Lawrence (*above*) shows a different side of himself than usual—and how! Cissy King, Arthur Duncan, and Jo Ann Castle (*right*) celebrate Easter 1969.

Lawrence showed uncommon grace in his response. "Naturally, I am very, very sad," he stammered, fighting to keep his composure. "No, as for me, it's not so bad. I have all the money I'll ever need. But as for my Musical Family . . . I hope I can think of something for them."

He didn't have to. Within the month, station after station—including many in the NBC and many more in the CBS "family"—all hungry for a new hour-long syndicated show to fill their Saturday-night 7:00 "access" slot—sent in requests, begging the Champagne Music Makers to pop the cork on a syndicated run. Matthew Rosenhaus, CEO of longtime sponsor J. B. Williams Pharmaceuticals, met with Don Fedderson to create a deal commonly known in the business as "barter."

J. B. Williams would essentially underwrite the full cost of the program (and provide a sumptuous retainer to Fedderson's production company for producing the show) in exchange for five or six minutes per hour of commercials built into each episode. The show would then be offered free to the station offering the best time period for it in each market. The remaining five to six commercial minutes per hour were left open in the tape for each local station to sell their own ads in—and keep all the profits to themselves.

And what profits they were! The Welk show's 30, 40, and 50 shares in weekend access and the program's proven familiarity to national ad agencies buying "spot time" on local stations made a fortune for almost every station that carried it. Since Welk would only produce roughly thirty new shows per year, with twenty to twenty-two of those episodes rerun in the summer (meaning no extra production costs)—the millions for both Welk and Fedderson flowed like a river of French champagne.

On September 11, 1971, one week after the last of the ABC episodes aired, *The Lawrence Welk Show* entered first-run syndication. By agreement, it was required to be shown between 5:00 p.m. and 10:00 p.m. on Friday, Saturday, or Sunday evenings. This ensured audience continuity, and the two-hundred-plus stations that placed their orders happily agreed.

Welk later laughed in a 1974 *Los Angeles Times* interview that in some ways "being cancelled by ABC was the best thing that could have happened to us! If we'd been retained, we would have had to go up against *All in the Family*." Instead, Welk "led in" to that show, and the rest of the Saturday night lineups of the 1970s, in the 7:00 access hour in most cities. Not only was Welk the number one syndicated TV show from 1971 to 1976—in some cities it was *the* number-one show, period. In cities like Philadelphia and Boston during 1973–74, it boasted a phenomenal 60 percent share of the viewing audience.

Flush with success, Welk expanded his Musical Family in 1972, with clarinet and saxophone great Henry Cuesta joining the band, and the appealing young singers Tom Netherton and Anacani. Anacani's discreetly sexy outfits and effervescent personality drew young and Hispanic viewers to the show in never-before-dreamed-of numbers, and she went on to enjoy several huge hit Spanish-language records during the decade.

By the mid-'70s, talented country singer Ava Barber joined and immediately became another "Welkome" part of the cast. Salli Flynn left the show in late 1972 to work in voice-overs and commercials, but Sandi Griffiths remained until 1980, forming a trio with fellow "Welk girls" Mary Lou Metzger and Gail Farrell.

The show's sets grew even more elaborate, and costumes and production values even more upscale. Following the lead of his Saturday-night neighbor Carol Burnett, Welk mounted lush full-show tributes to Hollywood's Golden Age of movies and musicals. There were big production numbers and comedy skits, top-dollar sets, and dignified musical director George Cates providing Boston Pops–like arrangements. The show culminated with several all-out specials during the 1975–76 season to celebrate the Bicentennial.

In 1976, following the retirement of longtime Welk drummer Johnny Klein, Welk recruited top African American studio drummer Paul Humphreys to the band, and fresh-from-college vocalist Kathie Sullivan. Continuing to keep an eye out for young talent to try to keep the show fresh, a year later Welk added young singers Sherri and Sheila Aldridge and Roger and David Otwell to the show, and country-and-western singer Jim Turner in early 1979.

Two departures changed the face of the Welk show in the fall of 1978. After over sixteen years with the band, cello queen Charlotte Harris decided to concentrate on her first loves of classical music and movie soundtracks, and on teaching her highly prestigious and sought-after clinics and classes. Charlotte knew that Welk probably would not want to continue his show too much longer at his age. She also knew all too well that variety TV was beginning to fade from the horizon. Their parting was a fond one, with only happy feelings.

Cissy King's departure was initially not quite as fond, but it thankfully did nothing in the long run to affect her status as an immortal part of Welk's Musical Family. As with Natalie Nevins a decade before, the official reason for her contract not being renewed was tardiness to several live shows and taping sessions. Cissy was fired by a Welk associate at first, but an embarrassed Welk soon offered Cissy her job back.

However, Cissy politely refused the offer, not wanting to prolong an unpleasant situation further. She also recalled in a 1985 book on the Welk show that Lawrence seemed confused and troubled about the whole affair, and that he reportedly commented after the first incident, "I just fired Cissy King, and I don't know why." By the time the show was off the air, though, Welk and Cissy had completely mended fences, and Lawrence would refer to Cissy's work with nothing but praise in the years ahead.

Cissy was replaced by Dorothy Hamill–hairdo'd dynamo Elaine Niverson (later Elaine Balden, when she married ABC cameraman Jim Balden in late 1980), and

Welk ended all of his shows by taking a turn around the dance floor with all
"da luffly" ladies.

Charlotte's replacement was symphony cellist Ernie Ehrhardt. A year later in 1979, when sax man Dave Edwards left for Hollywood and Nashville studio work, Welk convinced seventy-year-old saxophone and clarinet legend Skeets Herfurt to postpone his upcoming retirement. (In an irony both men laughed heartily about, Skeets had led a jazz combo that was one of Welk's main competitors during Skeets's college days in the late '20s. In the intervening years, Skeets had performed with a Who's Who of jazz—including Doc Severinsen, Frank DeVol, and several big bands, and had also played the title theme on *My Three Sons*.)

By the end of the decade, the program still remained a hugely profitable weekend draw for over 180 stations. But as the 1970s came to an end, so did the support from Welk's staunchest ally—Matthew Rosenhaus died of a massive heart attack in the summer of 1980. And Don Fedderson, who had as many as five or six top-rated shows on the air when Welk left ABC in 1971, now had only Welk's program left.

And Lawrence himself was now over seventy-five, world famous, and a millionaire several times over. His family (including his wife, Fern) began urging the workaholic midwesterner to semi-retire and just enjoy the rest of his life. While he still loved making music, Lawrence Welk finally came to the liberating realization that he didn't have to "prove" anything anymore.

Nighttime soap operas, sexy sitcoms, and gritty crime shows like *Hill Street Blues* and *Cagney & Lacey* were ruling the ratings by the early 1980s. A full decade had passed since ABC had discarded the show for having outlived its usefulness back in 1971. Longtime Welk singer and saxophonist Dick Dale even remembered some younger station managers saying things like, "I don't give a damn if it's Number One—the show is *not* [getting renewed] on my station!"

In February of 1982, *The Lawrence Welk Show* taped its final episode, after thirty years straight on the air. (It aired the weekend of April 16–18, with reruns into the summer.) At the time of its demise, the show was the longest running program besides news and public affairs in TV history. The taping was an emotional event, and the audience was packed with former regulars like Jo Ann Castle and the Lennon Sisters, who came to wish the series a fond farewell.

After a summer farewell tour in several top-line concert venues, Lawrence Welk finally slowed down. Still, the nearly eighty-year-old performer taped a series of "intros," "outros," and updates, complete with humorous behind-the-scenes anecdotes, for a select series of reruns that were made available to local stations. In 1987, the show moved to PBS under the aegis of Oklahoma public-TV executive Robert Allen, where it remains to this writing.

Lawrence Welk also busied himself sitting on the board of his music-publishing empire, traveling the world, taking it easy golfing and swimming, all with the love of his life, Fern—and of course, being a doting grandpa to his bevy of grandchildren and great-grandchildren. He also made a handful of personal appearances and talk-show interviews during the 1980s, and gave lectures and commencement speeches on issues close to his heart.

But in the early 1990s, the always-active Welk's health finally took a turn for the worse. In May of 1992, with his wife of sixty years and his family by his side, Lawrence Welk died of old age in Santa Monica. He was less than a year away from his ninetieth birthday. (Fern Welk would join Lawrence almost ten years later, in February 2002 at the age of ninety-eight.) It was perhaps appropriate that Lawrence Welk passed away the very same week that fellow entertainment legend Johnny Carson retired from his thirty-year career at the helm of *The Tonight Show,* as the voices of two of the twentieth century's biggest cultural icons fell simultaneously silent.

Longtime Los Angeles anchorwoman Ann Martin spoke for everyone when she smiled at the end of that night's news broadcast and said, "Somehow, I never thought that the bubble machine would really go off." *Newsweek*'s full-page obituary dubbed him "Lawrence of America," citing his transformation from near-illiterate immigrant farm boy to well-read, successful businessman and entertainer. Even President and Barbara Bush sent their personal condolences.

Even all these years later, despite the diverse paths their lives and careers took, the bond evident in the Welk "Musical Family" is still as strong as ever. Stars from the show routinely reunite for shows and revues in Branson and on public television. And books, records, tapes—even Internet sites (all the sweeter for a show accused in its later years of appealing only to geriatric viewers)—help keep the series' many memories alive and well.

One gets the feeling that that's just the way Lawrence Welk would have wanted it. Successful in solo careers—yet with a bond that's as strong as a family reunion. Even those who thought that the midwestern bandleader with the thick accent, straitlaced ways, and campy old show was a joke had to acknowledge that Mister Welk had the last laugh in the end—becoming an icon of unintentional comedy and easy listening whose status outlasted his own life. As such, our look back at the *Wunnerful* world of *The Lawrence Welk Show* is best completed by the longtime sign-off of the Maestro himself: "Now keep a song in your heart, and may all your memories be happy!"

## WHERE ARE THEY NOW?

Welk's many stars went on to a varied list of accomplishments in the two decades after the show ceased production. Jo Ann Castle, Lynn Anderson, Ralna English, Anacani, and the Lennon Sisters in particular had successful solo careers, as Vegas and nightclub headliners, and on other television shows.

- Following the demise of their own variety show in 1970, the Lennon Sisters became favorite guests of Mike Douglas's popular talk show, and near-regulars on

Welk and Norma celebrate the show's silver anniversary in 1980.

the original *Hollywood Squares*, appearing alongside Joan Rivers and Harvey Korman on the show's last episode in 1981. In recent years, they released a memoir of their career, *Same Song, Separate Voices*.

- Jo Ann Castle's fabulous personality and comedy timing made her a natural for similar TV guest appearances, and she kept up a packed touring schedule in the 1970s. She soon became one of PBS's most popular and often-seen entertainers, hosting innumerable music specials and making talk show appearances throughout the 1970s, '80s, and '90s. On a much sadder note, Jo had to cope with the tragic death of one of her daughters from complications of cerebral palsy in 1978. Jo thankfully survived to move on to a fulfilling life partnership with her longtime boyfriend, jazz trumpeter Lin Biviano. Jo is still one of the top draws in Branson and on the festival and fair circuit.

- "Our Country Gal" Ava Barber became a near-regular on Ralph Emery's 1983–93 talk/variety show *Nashville Now,* on cable's The Nashville Network, and she performed her 1978 hit "Bucket to the South" at the Grand Ole Opry. Around the time *Nashville Now* ended, Ava and Welk-saxophonist/singer Dick Dale opened up a successful musical theatre in Pigeon Forge, Tennessee, along with Ava's husband and manager, drummer Roger Sullivan.

- Lynn Anderson also became a household name in the country and western field, and had a very successful career on her own, most notably with 1970's pop hit "I Never Promised You a Rose Garden."

- Ralna English and Guy Hovis amicably divorced in 1984, but remained friends and shared custody of their daughter. Ralna maintained a successful solo career in both secular and gospel music, and headlined several live shows with her close friend Peter Marshall during the 1980s and early '90s. Ralna kept busy with appearances on major talk shows and most of the remaining Goodson-Todman celebrity game shows throughout the '80s, and was also the on-camera spokeswoman for RB Furniture Stores. ("RB" was rumored to humorously stand for "Rich Bitch"—but of course, only the "R" applied to Ralna.) Meanwhile, Guy pursued a political career, and was a part of Republican power broker Trent Lott's inner circle.

- Joe Feeney semi-retired, but continues to make appearances in *Welk* show reunions and revues.

- Ken Delo pursued a business and speaking career after the show, and hosted several PBS "updating" segments on Welk show reruns.

- Natalie Nevins retired from show business and moved back to Philadelphia. The always-refined Natalie cherished her privacy but remained active with the Catholic church and in charity work through her brother, a prominent Philadelphia area priest and clergyman.

- Bass-voiced pianist and singer Larry Hooper battled arterial sclerosis in the late '60s and took an extended leave of absence from the show. (Welk kept him on salary and paid for his health insurance.) The avuncular Larry temporarily beat his illness and returned part-time in the '70s, his good cheer and knowing smiles intact. In June of 1983, Larry passed away at sixty-six. He is still fondly remembered by everyone associated with the show.

- Bob Lido, the jazz violin virtuoso who had a big hit singing "Winchester Cathedral" and led the Hotsy Totsy Boys combo, passed away at age eighty-five in 2000, and is remembered with equal fondness for his dynamite personality and top-notch comedy timing.

- Andra Willis wrote songs for John Denver and worked with Tennessee Ernie Ford, as well as pursuing a nightclub career and working with the rock band Chicago on the soundtrack for the 1973 counterculture classic *Electra Glide in Blue*.

- Myron Floren, far from settling into retirement, made as many as two hundred appearances a year throughout the '80s and early '90s, until age and health problems slowed him down. By the time of his passing in 2005, the genial showbiz trouper had secured his status as the undisputed Master of the Accordion.

- Cissy King moved into Hollywood talent and public relations, while keeping up a career as an in-demand choreographer for top theatre, stage shows, and operas.

- Anacani became one of the queens of Spanish-language TV and married top attorney Rudy Echeverria in 1978, giving birth to a daughter, Priscila, in 1984. Gorgeous Ana continued to star in Spanish-language variety specials and made guest shots as sophisticated women on sexy Latin soap operas and "telenovelas." She was also spokeswoman for Crisco and Alpha-Beta on Univision all through the '80s and early '90s.

- Tom Netherton opened a fashionable travel agency, and continued to work in live musical theatre.

- Bobby Burgess taught choreography and dance in sought-after Hollywood classes.

- Gail Farrell made guest appearances on shows like *Match Game* and *Super Password* and did numerous radio voice-overs and commercials. She bought property in Hendersonville, Tennessee, with husband Ron Anderson in the late '80s, and she continues to do live singing and theatrical performances across the South and midwest.

- Mary Lou Metzger and Richard Maloof continued their careers as well as their longtime marriage, Mary Lou in musical theatre and singing in doo-wop revival groups, and Richard as a Hollywood studio musician.

- Arthur Duncan became a mentor and colleague to the likes of Gregory Hines and Savion Glover, and made appearances on Broadway and in TV shows like *Diagnosis Murder*.

- Kathie Sullivan made a memorable appearance on ABC's *Fridays* (more on that later), continued a career in the gospel field, and wrote children's books.

- Tanya Falan and Larry Welk amicably divorced around the time Tanya left the show in 1977. Their son Larry Welk III grew up to become the top news-helicopter pilot and aerial television/radio reporter for the CBS news stations in Los Angeles.
- Lovely Champagne Lady Norma Zimmer moved to Park City, Utah, and enjoyed an appropriately regal retirement with her real-estate developer husband Randy in a posh, rose-bedecked mansion above her beloved ski slopes. Norma also continued her longtime avocation of oil painting, and her artwork has been exhibited in galleries.
- Her longtime singing partner, Jimmy Roberts, retired to a deluxe beach estate in Tampa Bay, where he enjoyed life with his new wife, Vi. Easy-listening fans around the world mourned when he passed away at age seventy-four in the spring of 1999.
- Fern Welk stayed active well into her nineties and kept her mind razor-sharp, making sure that her three doctor grandchildren and her son-in-law (Shirley Welk's husband, also a prominent physician) kept her up to the minute with the latest advances in medical technology and science.
- And musicians like Johnny Zell, Bob Havens, Bob Ralston, and Paul Humphreys went on to successful recording-studio careers, in both jazz and classical arenas.

## QUOTABLE QUOTES

Some of the many memorable lines spoken by Lawrence Welk include:

- "Wunnerful, ah-wunnerful!"
- "A-one and a-two and ah . . ."
- "And now, here's a medley of songs from World War Eye!" (on the wisdom of poorly-written cue cards)
- "Settle down-ah—you guys sound like that 'Fred Zepperling!'" (staying in touch with the rock generation)
- "There are good days, and there are bad days, and I'm having one of them!"
- "Now, here comes beautiful Tanya Falan—so boys, let's give her a nice sound, and a good feel!"

## FUN FACTS AND MEMORABLE MOMENTS

- Comedian Paul Lynde was such a huge fan of the Lennon ladies, he insisted they sit two-to-a-square on either side of him when they appeared on *The Hollywood Squares.* When Lynde died of a heart attack early in 1982, the Lennon Sisters sang an acapella rendition of "The Lord's Prayer" at his funeral.
- Norma Zimmer was approached by Tyndale to write her autobiography in the mid-seventies, detailing her life working with Walt Disney, Bing Crosby, Welk,

and Billy Graham. Her 1976 memoir, *Norma*, was a bestseller at Christian bookstores from coast to coast.

- Bing Crosby was such a fan of Norma, he actually wrote fan letters to her on a regular basis. When Crosby died in 1977, Norma was reportedly one of the guests at his private Hollywood funeral.

- Kathie Sullivan was rehearsing for the show in 1981 when comedian Andy Kaufman was taping an episode of ABC's early '80s late night show *Fridays*. Kaufman spotted her in the hallway and asked Kathie if she'd like to "get married" right then and there! The stunned young singer was game and went on the *Fridays* show with her "new husband."

- During the Halloween episode in 1975, Ken Delo had to "bandage" his rear end with stage curtains when, dressed as Frankenstein, he split his slacks on the air. (Luckily for him, he was facing the camera.)

- Welk decided to shoot his first-ever color show, the fall 1965 premiere, on location at his country club village in San Diego County. The lovely Lennon girls, who by then were all grown up, sang a number at the poolside—wearing modest but modern one-piece bathing suits. Some of Welk's most elderly and conservative viewers actually sent shocked letters in response, wondering how he could show "that sex stuff" on the air!

  From then on, modern bathing attire was a thing of the past on Welk's show. Even in 1980, when the show's fall premiere was set aboard the *Love Boat*, Anacani, Elaine, and the Aldridge girls wore business suits and slacks—even while lounging on-deck at "poolside!"

  Well, there was *one* exception. In September 1972, Welk celebrated the success of his first syndicated year by filming the first show of the new season beachside at the Sheraton Towers in Honolulu. The show had set pieces, songs, and skits in the sky-view elevators, on the roof of the hotel with the city lights below, on a canoe in the ocean—and yes, on the beachfront and at the pools and spas. It ended with a Hawaiian-shirt-and-lei wearing Welk, surrounded by Sandi, Salli, Cissy, Tanya, and Charlotte, wishing his audience "Aloha" as the program faded away.

- Lawrence Welk might not have been quite the prude some thought he was. His girls revealed that he would sometimes whisper gently off-color jokes in their ears when he would dance a turn with each of the ladies during the end credits, to mischievously see if he could break any of them up!

- Accordion maven Myron Floren was given a draft deferment during World War II, due to a heart murmur brought on by his childhood bout with rheumatic fever. "Go home and enjoy what little of life you've got left," the Army doctor commanded. (Myron showed him—he didn't even have a heart attack until 1975, and lived thirty more years until the age of eighty-five.) Not wanting to "shirk" (his word) his duty, Myron saw his own doctor and did medical research to see if there was anything he could do to improve his health and be able to serve in the war effort. He embarked on a strict physical-fitness and diet regimen, and finally convinced the service to give him noncombatant status with the USO. Floren almost choked up as he recalled riding in an entertainment caravan following the liberation of France, as the passersby cheered at him, "Vive Le France! Vive Les Americains!"

- Welk showed his playful side in the fall 1975 premiere, when he had a "beauty pageant" of his bevy of beautiful and talented ladies, reintroducing each one and reading off a list of their interests and accomplishments as they paraded by in designer evening gowns. At the end, Lawrence winked, "As you can see, even at age seventy-two, there's nothing wrong with my eyesight!"

- Martin Scorsese played Welk's longtime sponsor, Matthew Rosenhaus, the controversial chairman of the J.B. Williams pharmaceutical empire, in the 1994 movie *Quiz Show*. Rosenhaus was widely believed to have been the man who ordered the infamous rigging of the prime-time game show *Twenty-One*, which Geritol also sponsored. (As with today's "reality TV" shows, back then a big-money quiz-show contestant could achieve true celebrity-of-the-moment fame. Rosenhaus allegedly wanted *Twenty-One* fixed so that only the most telegenic and personable contestants would return week after week to be associated with his product.)

- What camp aficionado can forget the 1971 "Salute to the Academy Awards"? Where to begin? Middle-aged Norma and Jimmy popped out from behind the camera wearing lettermen's turtlenecks, singing the chorus to "Hey There, Georgy Girl!" Sandi and Salli gave the least "butch" impersonation of Butch & Sundance on record—riding a pink Western carriage in saddle clothes and dungarees singing "Raindrops Keep Fallin' on My Head." Joe Feeney sang a bravura rendition of "Born Free," and Norma played the "fairy godmother" in the salute to Walt Disney.

  Later that same episode, Jack Benny made one of his last TV appearances, and actually played his violin—playing his own theme song, the vaudeville chestnut "Love in Bloom." "Well, let's look at this violin a minute," he said in mid-song when he hit a wrong note. "You know—this is a real Stradivarius violin! See, it says right here, 'Antonio Stradivari, area code 213. . . .'"

- Once, the show had an actual water-filled pond constructed onstage, with trees and grass in the background and a canoe for Norma and Jimmy to row while singing a love song. Everyone was awed by the elaborate set—except Norma and Jimmy, whose canoe tipped over in mid-song and dunked the two not-so-young "lovers" in the water!

- In a 1969 show, Lawrence Welk hilariously poked fun at his "square" image by opening the show with a rocking version of "Aquarius" and "Let the Sunshine

In." At the very end, Lawrence himself came out—wearing a long black Cher wig and John Lennon granny-glasses, complete with headband, fur vest, and peace sign! The audience for the show was laughing so hard they could barely finish the rest of the program!

# country when country wasn't cool

Hard to imagine in today's era of Faith, Reba, Kenny, Dolly, Toby, Garth, and Shania that it wasn't so long ago when country music was considered total white trash and completely out of the mainstream. A halfhearted exception was made for Patsy Cline, Dottie West, Loretta Lynn, Tennessee Ernie Ford, Tammy Wynette, Johnny Cash, and Hank Williams—and sometimes even that was pushing it. Network executives openly discriminated against country and western performers as much as they did against black and Hispanic artists, on the fear that they would give shows a downscale "hillbilly" look and feel.

Here are some of the shows that knocked down those barriers—and as such, changed the futures of both TV and country and western music forever.

## The Johnny Cash Show

*Network: ABC; On the air: June 7, 1969–May 5, 1971*

ABC's most innovative, and in some ways, most important variety show of the late '60s started as a summer replacement for *The Hollywood Palace*. The show was the brainchild of the late TV producer Bill Carruthers, who would later hit the motherlode with the 1983–86 cult classic game show *Press Your Luck*. At the time he was working as a consultant to the Screen Gems television arm of Columbia Pictures Studios. Carruthers had worked with Cash on some specials, and he thought Cash would bring the name value and cutting-edge style that ABC so desperately needed in their prime-time variety schedule. Carruthers also knew that Canada's CTV had recently broadcast a highly popular and well-received Johnny Cash special, which had topped that country's "Enjoyment Index," according to the ratings services in Canada. ABC approved the idea.

Carruthers appproached Cash about the idea of doing the summer replacement show, which, if it took off, would be a firm go for the mid-season 1969–70 schedule. Cash was interested. He wanted to reach a wider audience and have the chance to give some of his country colleagues and outlaw singers a national platform.

He did have some firm ground rules for the new series, though. For one, the new show would absolutely, positively, under no circumstances originate from some glitzy studio in Hollywood or some coldhearted theatre in Manhattan. It would be produced on location in country capital Nashville—or it wouldn't be produced at all. Not only that, but Cash wanted the show to be shot in the Mother Church of Country Music itself, the Ryman Auditorium, then the home of the fabled Grand Ole Opry.

*Variety*'s Les Brown noted in his book *Televi$ion* that "the interests of Cash and those of his producers" were "at somewhat of a variance." Johnny Cash, like the Smotherses before him and *Satur-*

*day Night Live* after, simply wanted *The Johnny Cash Show* to be a Johnny Cash show, and that meant a distinct outlaw-country and folk-music flavor. He assumed that if ABC wanted him for a series, it was because they wanted *him,* and the talents and attitudes he represented. What arrogance, thought ABC executives! Don't tell me he really believed all that high-falutin' business about artistic freedom . . . I mean, this is showbiz!

True to TV, the only producers and directors and writers that had enough of a track record or connections where ABC would approve them were all straight from Los Angeles and Toronto—not Nashville. As Les Brown recognized, they would all "be going back to Hollywood for their next job" after the Cash show inevitably ran its course. And if they wanted to use this show to advertise their own talents as producers, it would be only by "producing the sort of the slick and elaborate variety hour the Hollywood circle could appreciate," not necessarily by tailoring the show all that specifically to Johnny Cash.

The trendy, power-lunching New York and Hollywood ABC executives who set foot into the Grand Ole Opry (no doubt for the first time in their lives) were shocked at what they saw. Despite having been home to local-local-local Southern TV telecasts and radio broadcasts all across the South and Midwest, the Opry was then in no condition for even the cheapest-looking nationally televised show.

In order to make the country palace cool, the network ended up spending tens of thousands of dollars for lighting equipment, computers, and switchboards that were shipped in from Hollywood. The show also had to pay first-class transportation to the show's technical consultant, Jim Kilgore, who refused to leave Beverly Hills for the hillbillies on a full-time basis. A doctor of physics who played a part in the creation of sonar frequency was paid top-dollar retainers to fix the sound reverberation problems, too. Cash had also evidently refused to pre-record his numbers in a recording studio only to lip-sync them on stage. This was standard operating procedure on most musical variety shows, on account of the difficulty of "singing" live with set pieces clunking in the background and so on. But again, the Man in Black's show was not "most" variety shows!

And as if that wasn't enough of a challenge, all of the high-tech equipment and whatnot had to be removed from the Opry on Friday morning, as soon as the Thursday-night tapings were finished, so that the Opry would have full seating capacity. Then it had to be trucked into storage, only to be built back up again and installed on Monday morning.

But because of his talent and insistence on doing it his way or the highway, *The Johnny Cash Show* was top quality all the way. It had the opening that would become his signature from then on—with a darkened set and the Man in Black intoning in tight closeup, "Hello—I'm Johnny Cash" as the lights came up (and the crowd went wild.) Each episode had a segment that was close to Cash's heart, called "Ride This Train"—a sort of tramp's-eye view of a trek cross-country, with location footage, that combined the feel of a PBS travelogue with that of an MTV music video.

And there were some true showstoppers in the music itself, on a par with even the best of *Ed Sullivan*. Not far into the summer 1969 run, none other than Bob Dylan himself appeared on the show. It was one of the only—if not *the* only—major variety shows he ever would appear on. He delivered a performance with Cash that was so stunning, it made VH1's 100 Coolest Music Moments of All Time list.

When the show returned at mid-season in January of 1970, Johnny's first guests were hippie iconoclast Arlo Guthrie and folk diva Bobbie Gentry. Like the Smothers Brothers before him, Johnny Cash showed no fear whatsoever in booking music acts that network "suits" thought were on the fringe. And the hippest acts in rock, folk, and jazz (Paul Simon and Judy Collins to name a few) never turned down his invitation. And each of his shows ended with a "Musical Family" jam session, with his country legend wife June Carter Cash and her mother Maybelle (and often the rest of the Carter Family), that was like money from home to the country fans who tuned in. The show won its time period and placed a healthy seventeenth place in the 1969–70 ratings race.

Unfortunately, the 1970–71 season brought less encouraging news. ABC was growing more and more lukewarm to variety shows and was beginning to think of them as relics of TV's past. CBS's *Medical Center*, in third place in the time period for 1969–70, continued to grow as the popularity of the similar and superior *Marcus Welby* grew as well. What with the frustration and expense of commuting staffers and ABC watchdogs from Hollywood and the neverending cycle of installing the equipment and sets and then taking it all down again, ABC just gave up. Two years after it had began, ABC put the "whammy" on Bill Carruthers and *The Johnny Cash Show*.

Perhaps it was all for the best. As much as both he and ABC may have tried, the Man in Black simply was not meant to be a "Guy Smiley" TV-show host week after week. However, the fact that the show was ultimately canceled after only two years actually worked in its favor. *The Johnny Cash Show* was pure in its goals; thanks to Cash's star power and determination, it rarely strayed from being the unique, singular program that it was. It didn't compromise itself into another bland, run-of-the-mill TV show, and it didn't run on and on and on until there was nothing left worth watching. *The Johnny Cash Show* was a country comet that flared across the skies of 1969 and 1970 and died young in a blaze of glory, like the outlaw rebel it was.

## The Jim Nabors Hour

*Network: CBS; On the air: September 25, 1969–May 20, 1971*
After five years, the classic sitcom *Gomer Pyle* finally ran its course in the spring of 1969. The show was the second most popular TV show in the 1968–69 ratings race, second only to *Laugh-In*. But by then, its slapstick jokes set in the supposedly "contemporary" Marine Corps of 1969—even as

the Vietnam war raged in real life—made *Hogan's Heroes'* nutty-Nazi hijinx seem positively tasteful in comparison.

But CBS didn't want to lose Jim Nabors—especially knowing that he had a reasonable singing voice and a flair for sketch comedy. Nabors was also Carol Burnett's "lucky charm," and he would appear to help her kick off the season-premiere episodes of her variety show from first year to last.

*The Jim Nabors Show* picked up where *Gomer Pyle* left off in more ways than one, with many of *Pyle's* cast carried over as regulars or frequent guest stars. Since the show's lead-in was the classic kids' sitcom *Family Affair*, and its competition the grim and serious *Ironside*, the Nabors show aimed squarely at children and family viewers, bringing on singer Karen Morrow to direct "The Jim Nabors Kids."

Despite finishing in the Top Thirty in 1970–71, *The Jim Nabors Show* fell victim to the same bout of de-ruralizing of the CBS schedule that ensured the cancellation of all of their major country comedy shows. Nabors continued to make occasional TV appearances and did a hilarious job with his role as Burt Reynolds's deputy sheriff in 1982's *The Best Little Whorehouse in Texas*. Beyond that, Nabors spent most of his time on his Hawaiian estate enjoying his success. From Mayberry to Mauna Loa—well, "gaw-all-ee" indeed!

## Pop Goes the Country/That Nashville Music

*Syndicated first-run: 1974–1983*
Ralph Emery, the legendary Nashville radio personality dubbed the "Dick Clark of country music," hosted *Pop Goes the Country* from 1974 to 1980 (Tom T. Hall succeeded him for the final three seasons). *That (Good Ole) Nashville Music* was another "regional" success—a sort of weekly concert series of country performers tied together under the same banner. Of only marginal popularity in the major cities, the shows were must-see TV in lucrative 7:30 "prime access" in the South and midwest. They also boasted remarkably pricey production values and high-quality videotape and camerawork for late-'70s syndie half-hours. (Especially ones that didn't attain anywhere near the financing or fame of a *Sha Na Na, Name That Tune, Gong Show, Muppet Show,* or *SCTV.*)

Of course, Ralph went on to his greatest fame hosting the Carson-style talk/variety show *Nashville Now* on cable's The Nashville Network from 1983 to 1993, followed by several interview specials on that network thereafter, until it was folded into CMT in the year 2000.

## Barbara Mandrell & the Mandrell Sisters

*Network: NBC; On the air: November 18, 1980–June 26, 1982*
Country music's best light variety show proved to be one of the few successes of the Fred Silver-

man era at NBC. The show had great main stars—Barbara Mandrell had been performing since the age of twelve, and she had risked her life while barely into her twenties performing in Vietnam, singing and entertaining the troops (her husband was among them). By 1980, the barely thirty-year-old performer had won Country Music Entertainer of the Year Awards and made guest appearances on everything from *The Lawrence Welk Show* to *Hollywood Squares* to *Merv Griffin.*

Campy comedy specialists Sid and Marty Krofft's production team ensured that the new show would also be replete with the funniest over-the-top outrageousness and showbiz shtick, having just come off their success with ABC's *Donny & Marie.* Appropriately, the show was assigned the same stage at the Sunset/Gower Studios in Hollywood where Chuck Barris and Sandy Frank had just finished taping Rip Taylor's 1978–80 camp classic, *The $1.98 Beauty Show,* the previous winter.

There was no price tag adequate for the beauty and talent on the Mandrell show's stage. Barbara Mandrell and the Mandrell Sisters had the biggest "babe factor" of any program then in prime time besides *Charlie's Angels.* The three drop-dead-gorgeous young women were the hostesses with the mostesses in their designer jeans, sprayed-on New Wave slacks, and evening gowns and dresses.

The trio also proved they were as bountiful in the talent department as they were in their natural gifts. Raven-haired beauty Louise Mandrell could play red-hot Dixieland jazz and country fiddle; Barbara could do guitar, steel guitar, bass, and saxophone; and youngest sister Irlene ruled on the drums. And each show started off and wrapped up *Sonny & Cher*–style, with a driving musical number and a jokey "conversation" between the three ladies, with the fun only having just begun.

*Barbara Mandrell and the Mandrell Sisters* was probably the best example of a somewhat sophisticated prime-time country-music show since Johnny Cash's program a decade earlier. It had a humorous but affectionate weekly musical salute to "American Things"—"Horseshoes—hot dogs—the way that Willie [Nelson] sings! These are just a few genuine American Things!" It also had a regular feature of Southern gospel favorites toward each episode's end, with Barbara and her guests performing renditions of sacred songs.

Barbara Mandrell did more than *be* country when country wasn't cool—she and her show helped *make* country music cool. The show was sexy and sophisticated without apologizing for it, and yet as down-home, comfortable, and genuine-article as a fried chicken dinner, carried by people with undeniable talent and versatility. It embraced guest stars straight from the heart of country like Roy Acuff and Minnie Pearl, as well as current country stars like Loretta Lynn, Mel Tillis, Marie Osmond, Conway Twitty, Tammy Wynette, and Glen Campbell. And it also welcomed rock acts and old-favorite variety veterans like Joan Rivers and Phyllis Diller, making the show a truly master blend of variety and entertainment.

And it was reflected in the show's ratings. The show easily defeated *WKRP in Cincinnati,* its competition, forcing CBS to move that show back to its old Monday-night time slot. But despite the clear success of the show, bad news was on the way. Barbara was reluctant to distance herself too much from live concerts and performances, which was seemingly invitable given the pressures of doing twenty-five to thirty episodes a year of a prime-time musical-comedy show. She also worried about becoming just another TV personality with nowhere left to go once the show ran its course.

By early 1982, the pressures of carrying a successful weekly variety hour—the *only* weekly variety hour still left in prime time besides the syndicated *Solid Gold* and *Hee-Haw*—plus raising a family, touring, and doing club dates was getting to be just too much for Mandrell. In June of 1982, Barbara made the sudden and totally unexpected announcement that the show would go on indefinite hiatus as she backed away to catch her breath and regroup.

As it turned out, even if the show had gone on, it could only have lasted another year or two. In 1984, Barbara was in a severe car accident with her children—one that would have certainly been fatal for all of them if they hadn't been wearing seat belts or if she'd been in a smaller car than her top-of-the-line Jaguar. As it was, Barbara had to endure painful physical and maxillofacial therapy and was bedridden for months with depression following her surgery to remove scars and tissue damage.

Fortunately for her and her fans, Barbara Mandrell proved that not even a near-fatal car crash could slow her down for long. (Thankfully, her children also survived with no permanent injuries.) She spent the rest of the 1980s and '90s doing the live performances and tours she knew and loved best, with her band the Do-Rites. And she managed to keep up a very active presence in television, making acting appearances in shows like *The Commish, Touched by an Angel,* and *Diagnosis Murder,* as well as several TV movies, and serving as matriarch of NBC's late-'90s afternoon soap, *Sunset Beach.* Barbara's sisters also did her proud. Louise regularly appeared on Ralph Emery's *Nashville Now* throughout the '80s and early '90s, and Irlene went on to star on *Hee-Haw* for the rest of that show's run.

Barbara's show also marked the very last prime-time network variety hour to be successful on the network television until the arrival of *The Tracey Ullman Show* and *In Living Color* on the upstart Fox network at the end of the '80s. All in all, with the top talent and Southern hospitality of the Mandrell Sisters, the genre couldn't have gone out on a nicer note.

## Hee-Haw

*Network: CBS; On the air: June 15, 1969–July 13, 1971; Syndicated first-run: 1971–1993*
No other show of the 1970s—not the Chuck Barris game shows, not the sleaziest sitcoms and soaps—got as unrelentingly negative a reaction from movie and television critics as this one. And

Roy Clark shares a musical moment with the Hee-Haw Honeys. Yep, that there's Kathie Lee Gifford on the right.

yet, in many communities and among its millions of fans, this show was TV's best-loved variety show.

It should be noted that the men responsible for creating and developing television's most country-hick series were not country-and-western performers or even Southerners. *Hee-Haw* was developed by two city-slicker Canadians, Frank Peppiatt and John Aylesworth, and a New York talent agent named Bernie Brillstein—whose biggest hit would be *Hee-Haw*'s absolute antithesis, *Saturday Night Live*. And it wasn't over a nice plate of PoFolks' fried chicken and mashed potatoes, either, but in the ultra-chic, exclusive dining room of the Beverly Hills Polo Lounge.

Like *The Johnny Cash Show*, *Hee-Haw* started in the summer of 1969 as a summer-replacement series on CBS, and would score well enough to be brought back in December as a mid-season replacement, also on Wednesday nights. And like Cash, the show was shot in Nashville (at the studios of CBS affiliate WLAC.) But while Johnny Cash had insisted on Nashville-or-nothing for his show to ensure its authenticity, *Hee-Haw* was shot in Music City USA mainly because it depended on a huge cast of regulars, almost all of whom were based in the South. It would have been just as expensive to do the show in L.A. or New York and provide first-class airfare and hotel accommodations to the giant rotating cast as it was to bite the bullet and upgrade WLAC's facilities to national-grade.

The show itself was just as Brillstein, Peppiatt, and Aylesworth had presented it when they pitched the idea to CBS. "A cross between *Laugh-In* and *The Beverly Hillbillies*," with a heapin' helpin' of the Grand Ole Opry thrown in. The show would be hosted by the likeable country and western stars Roy Clark and Buck Owens. And it would borrow *Laugh-In*'s format of quickie jokes, wacky sight gags, rapid-fire one-liners, and a farmland equivalent of a "joke wall" (a cornfield complete with scarecrow and wood fence)—but the similarity would end there.

Instead of risky political shafts and risque liberated jokes, the show's level of humor was epitomized by the buck-toothed grinning donkey that started and ended the show, braying (what else), "Hee Haw! Hee Haw!" There was also the regular feature, "Pickin' and a-Grinnin,'" where Roy Clark (who even the most die-hard *Hee-Haw* haters acknowledge is a master of the acoustic guitar) would join with some other musicians for a good old-fashioned country hoedown, with dueling banjos and guitars or a nice down-home fiddle.

One definite accomplishment of *Hee-Haw* was to introduce country personalities that were legendary within the country and western world—but relatively little known elsewhere—to mainstream, across the board fame. "Cousin" Minnie Pearl, with her flower dresses and price-tag hat; Grandpa Jones, country music's answer to "Charley Weaver" of *Hollywood Squares* fame; and country-music founding father Roy Acuff were among the more notable. Jeannine Riley, David "Stringbean" Akeman (who was murdered along with his wife during a 1973 home invasion), Junior Samples, and full-figured Earth mama Lulu Roman would be the most prominent of the regulars. And perhaps *Hee-Haw*'s biggest find was singer and actress (and Hugh Hefner honey) Barbi Benton, who parlayed her fame into appearances in several movies and TV shows, and a career as a relatively respected pianist.

*Rowan & Martin's Laugh-In* struck back at the obvious plagiarization of their format. One *Laugh-In* skit showed a slow fade on the closed-door of "CBS Program Development." "Mike, we've got a great idea for a new variety show," one voice intoned from behind the door. "Let's call it *Laugh-In*!" "No, Perry," the other voice said, "that's already taken." After a pause, the first voice suggested, "All right then—how about *Hee-Haw*!" "GREAT IDEA!" exclaimed the other voice.

The fact is however, that *Laugh-In* lasted only six years, whereas *Hee-Haw* lasted four times that.

It was cancelled in 1971 by CBS despite Top Ten ratings due to what some critics called CBS's "de-bumpkinizing" of their comedy schedule, only to become an immediate hit in first-run syndication. Even the staunchest *Hee-Haw* fan would have to concede that *Laugh-In* was the more influential and better respected of the two. But *Hee-Haw* was some good old-fashioned country comfort food for its core audience of fans.

Despite the fast-paced psychedelic trappings of quickies and blackouts, the show was as relaxing and satisfying as chicken-fried steak with cream gravy and some homebaked pecan pie for the millions who looked forward to it. In its favor, it was also the only variety show appropriate for young children after the *Muppet Show* went off the air, as opposed to the sex-sational likes of *Solid Gold, In Living Color,* or *Saturday Night Live.*

By the end of the '70s, *Hee-Haw* was still in the syndicated Top Ten, with only the likes of *The Muppet Show, PM Magazine,* and *Family Feud* ahead of it. This was a truly amazing accomplishment. In most of the nation's largest cities, the Saturday 7:00 to 8:00 p.m. "prime access" hour was firmly filled by Lawrence Welk's rival show, or weekend editions of popular game shows. *Hee-Haw* had to draw what little audience it could in the major cities during undesirable little-watched afternoon slots or against prime-time shows on independent stations. But the series made up the difference in the huge, overwhelmingly Number One ratings it had in major Southern cities and Midwestern markets. It was as popular as any prime-time hit in most of those areas—if not even more.

In 1978, *Hee-Haw* mounted a notoriously bad and painfully sexist spin-off called *Hee-Haw Honeys,* starring Lulu Roman and Kenny Price, along with Gailard Sartain, Misty Rowe, and Kathie Lee Johnson (who would later go on to become Kathie Lee Gifford). The show was dropped after only twenty-six weeks of production. The original program however, remained popular for several more years. *Hee-Haw* kept a-pickin' and a-grinnin' all through the '80s, finally wrapping production at the end of 1992. By then the show's ratings had slipped even in the Southern cities most dear to it, and it had long since been banished to Saturday-morning time periods or other unlikely hours in the big cities that bothered to carry it at all.

That probably said as much about the changing dynamics of the South as it did about TV itself. By 1993, *Designing Women,* Molly Ivins, Ted Turner, and a newly elected couple named Bill and Hillary Clinton were as much representative of the new South as the hillbilly world of *Hee-Haw*—and much more so when it came to younger Southern folk. MTV and a newfangled contraption called the Internet had already started globalizing and merchandising national culture from coast to coast.

So depending on your outlook, you either harrumphed a "good riddance" to *Hee-Haw* or said a fond goodbye to a show that, for better or worse, epitomized a kinder, gentler era in television. An era that was now gone with the wind.

# The Dean Martin Show

## VITAL STATS

**STARRING**
Dean Martin

**ON THE AIR**
September 16, 1965–May 24, 1974

**MOST VALUABLE PLAYERS**
Nipsey Russell, Charles Nelson Reilly, Dom DeLuise,
Kay Medford, Lou Jacobi, Marian Mercer, Ken Lane—
and, of course, The Golddiggers

**NETWORK**
NBC

**MUSIC**
Les Brown and His Band of Renown

**ORIGINATION**
KNBC Studios, in Beautiful
Downtown Burbank

"Everybody loves somebody sometime...."

The most sophisticated variety show of the 1960s was appropriately run by the performer who epitomized laid-back cool in postwar America. Dean Martin brought a level of star stature to the variety format that it hadn't had since the earliest days of the medium. In his typical, up-for-anything casual style, Dean came to NBC as almost a "joke" on the network, who badly wanted him to host a weekly show after seeing his ultra-popular specials and his appearances guest-hosting *The Hollywood Palace*. Movie star Dean laughed. "Sure," he'd do TV for NBC—provided they guaranteed him almost a million dollars, a schedule that allowed him to come in only on taping days with almost no rehearsal beyond the final dress, and absolute creative control.

Dean was sure they'd laugh him right out of the boardroom—but to his shock, NBC agreed to everything! He kept his word, and for nearly nine years, *The Dean Martin Show* defined the swinging '60s, and launched an entire era of Vegas-style comedy, talk, and game shows across the dial. The series broke down barriers by the dozen with its integrated cast, venturesome sexuality and jokes, and its upscale, casual elegance. And for many of Dean's fans, it was the very pinnacle of his career.

Dino Crocetti was born to Italian immigrant parents in June of 1917, in the working-class steel town of Steubenville, Ohio. In the late 1930s and early '40s, while trying to get a career together as a big-band singer, Dean supported himself by staging "prize fights" with his roommate, and cobbling together enough nightclub gigs and pickup work to get by. Dean married his first wife Betty McDonald around this time, and they started a family.

Deferred from the draft of World War II due to a double hernia, Dean found some success as one of the few handsome male singers in their early- to mid-twenties available to work the circuit. But in 1946, Dino struck career gold when he teamed up with a twenty-one-year-old up-and-coming Borscht Belter named Jerry Lewis.

The combination was a match made in comedy heaven: Dean, the debonair, Italian stallion, crossed with the vulgar vaudeville comedy of Jerry "Hey Laaayyyy-deeee!" Lewis. The two solidifed their fame in New York by appearing at all the top clubs, and alongside guests like Rodgers and Hammerstein on the first episode of *The Ed Sullivan Show* in June of 1948.

A year later, in 1949, the thirty-two year old Dean divorced Betty and married the beautiful twentyish blond singer and actress Jeanne Martin, setting up housekeeping in Beverly Hills soon after. The two had more children, including Dean's son Dean-Paul, who would grow up to become a tennis pro of note (and, more fatefully, a flying enthusiast). As the 1940s ended and the '50s began, Dean Martin seemed to have it all: a happy home life, blank-check offers from nightclubs, and movie deals for the Martin & Lewis act. The duo also cut their variety-show teeth as the most frequent and popular of the rotating hosts of the *Colgate Comedy Hour*.

Sadly, it wouldn't last long. By 1956, the ego battles and personality clashes that have been the basis for a dozen books and countless articles took their toll. Martin and Lewis shocked the industry when they announced that they were going to go their separate ways. The two would not "reunite" on stage for another twenty years, until Martin's surprise appearance on one of Lewis' annual Muscular Dystrophy Telethons in the mid '70s. Show business tabloids and papers predicted great things for Jerry Lewis.

They were less optimistic about Dean Martin. The thinking was that he simply didn't have the range, gravitas, or interest to hold people's attention like the maniacally funny Jerry. But with the redoubtable personality that had defined his life, Dino Crocetti wasn't going to let go of his well-earned fame without a fight. Dean also pursued the movie connections that he had made with Martin & Lewis, and found roles in considerably more dramatic and challenging Westerns and dramas. Dean proved that he was as natural an actor as he was a singer and comedian, and by the early 1960s, his star shone as brightly as ever.

Also by then, Dean and his close friends Sammy Davis Jr., Peter Lawford, and the Chairman of the Board, Frank Sinatra, had formed the legendary Hollywood boys-club known as the Rat Pack. The Rat Pack indeed packed 'em in when they played the Sands or the Sahara in Las Vegas. And when one of the four had a solo engagement in Las Vegas or Hollywood, one if not all three of the others would often stop in to visit their "pallies"—sometimes even bringing along friends and "good luck charms" like glamorous actresses Shirley MacLaine and Angie Dickinson.

Dean's son Ricci recalled in his book on his famous father that when *The Dean Martin Show* premiered in 1965, there was nothing else like it on TV. He was understating the case. *The Dean Martin Show* was the most innovative variety show of the 1960s apart from *Laugh-In*—perhaps even including the Smothers Brothers. It would be the first truly sophisticated, hip variety show since the days of *Your Show of Shows*.

People used to seeing stiff, controlling hosts like Lawrence Welk and Ed Sullivan traffic-copping their shows found Dean's relaxed, sophisticated style to be like a breath of fresh air. His appeal was so strong that, according to the book *TV Facts*, in 1968 Dean's show was the only show to be listed in the Top 10 of both middle-American rural homes *and* the best-educated, wealthiest city viewers too.

Dean's show also commanded the respect of the biggest names in Hollywood. Stars who would have never even considered appearing on a lesser show, like his good buddy Frank Sinatra and movie stars like Gina Lollobrigida, David Janssen, Peter Sellers, and Orson Welles made regular guest shots—often unannounced and when you'd least expect them! The show was also must-see TV for radio personalities, stand-up comedians, and up-and-coming performers from coast to coast. One Hollywood radio and TV personality joked that when he started working years later at the KNBC Burbank lot where Dean used to tape, he practically "genuflected" at the very sight of Dean's old stage.

Two variety legends, Dean and Dionne Warwick (*right*); the Golddiggers (*below*) in all their glory.

The show's main set was a swinging '60s lounge that could have been pulled right out of the Playboy Mansion—complete with a "fire pole" Dino would slide down (in his tuxedo) from the upper balcony above. Of course, the central feature of the living room was the huge, wood-paneled wet bar, alongside the shag throw rugs and bean-bag pillows at center stage.

Dean said in a famous 1965 interview that he wanted his show to be "something a man could watch with his whole family—around the bar!" He'd start the show off with a breezy musical number like his signature "That's Amore," while talking directly to the audience as if they really were in his living room. Then he'd get the show started with a sketch here, a conversation with one of the guests there, or just banter with pianist Kenny Lane (usually taking one of his innumerable pratfalls off Ken's piano).

And there was one other part of the show that made it worth watching. Longtime producer Greg Garrison was often quoted as saying things like, "Here's an incredibly charismatic, handsome man in the prime of his life. Why not surround him with beautiful girls?" Why not indeed? And so the Golddiggers were born. Over the years the lineup of gorgeous girls would change occasionally, but *The Dean Martin Show* would provide a lifeline for many young actresses and girl singers trying to make it in showbiz. Dino would reward many with a high-paying, visible spot on the show as one of his girls, and they rewarded the show with their beauty, brains, and talent.

And there was the final secret of the show's appeal. Not until Benny Hill, or Cher's evening gowns, would another variety show be as frank and what's-the-big-deal about S-E-X. The 1960s were the era of the "Summer of Love" and the sexual rrevolution, but most TV shows still held to the old '50s values when it came to that taboo topic. Marlo Thomas and Mary Tyler Moore were the only single women on prime-time TV during Dean's era who even hinted they might be "more than friends" with their boyfriends. The only other shows of that era with as many "whoopee" jokes and innuendoes were *The Dating Game* and *The Newlywed Game*. And Dean's show didn't treat sex as "dirty" or juvenile—just as a fact of life, and a happy one to be enjoyed as often as possible!

Another aspect of the show that fascinated critics was that Dean rarely showed up for the show or attended production meetings during the week. Dean usually came in only on Sunday afternoon to spend the day taping the show, and maybe having a pro-duction breakfast or brunch on Monday to discuss the following week's show with Greg Garrison's inner circle. That was it.

But in a 1983 *PM Magazine* interview Dino dismissed the charges that this meant he didn't care about his show or didn't work hard on it. He explained that he would have a cassette tape made up of the songs to be performed and a shooting script of the comedy sketches each week. He would play them and read them over and over again, on the tape deck in his car, at home while relaxing, or in between working on other projects, until he had them down pat. Then, when he would walk in on Sunday night to do the show, he would have the songs and sketches nailed—leaving the cast to say, "He's a genius!" and wondering how he did it "no rehearsal." Dino had the last laugh. "I rehearsed all the time on that show—they just didn't know it!"

By the summer of 1970, Dean's show was the anchor of NBC's powerhouse Thursday night lineup, and the highest-rated variety hour on television besides *Laugh-In*. NBC negotiated what was reported to be the largest contract in the history of television for Dean's services, with a firm three-year commitment and a multimillion-dollar salary, complete with his and Greg Garrison's ownership of the show. The show continued to ride high atop NBC's Thursday night lineup of *Flip Wilson* and *Ironside* in 1970–71. The following year, ABC finally found success against it with *Owen Marshall, Counselor at Law,* but Dean still placed a strong second as effortlessly as he seemed to do everything else.

However, 1972 marked the end of Dean's twenty-three-year marriage to Jeanne Martin—and that would, in turn, mark the beginning of the end for *The Dean Martin Show*. Jeanne never looked back on the eventual end of her marriage as a sign of failure. Instead, she rightfully took pride in the fact that she had kept a marriage together under the glare of Hollywood for nearly a quarter century, with a millionaire husband who had dozens of real-life "golddiggers" at every corner that would be his for the asking. Not to mention having managed to raise her large extended family of stepchildren, plus her and Dean's own kids.

Jeanne seemed to indicate that the divorce was more about Dean being "married to his work" than any infidelities or indiscretions. Now that the kids were grown, Dean was serving up a full schedule of doing twenty-five to thirty episodes a year of the show, plus Las Vegas and Lake Tahoe live gigs, and an occasional motion picture or TV movie. Dean was around the house less and less, and the relaxed superstar didn't want to have to "work" at a marriage that had been a done deal for so long anyway.

The classic midlife crisis also reared its ugly head, as Dean started openly pursuing affairs with girlfriends half his age, which resulted in several short-lived marriages, all through the early 1970s. Dean also found himself hospitalized with ulcers and chest pains at times during the early '70s, and his hiatal hernia from back in the '40s hadn't gotten any better. His health scares made him only more determined to prove his virility and masculinity, and the results inevitably showed up in tabloids across America.

The swingingly sordid details of Dean's love life in the gossip columns only added fuel to the fire that Dean's show was the ultimate in male chauvinism to the feminists that were now zeroing in on it. The same news columns and critics that rejoiced over the show's innovations and freshness for its first five or six years now dubbed Dino "King Leer," and trashed the groundbreaking variety show as being sexist and sleazy.

Funny business was business as usual—
Dom DeLuise (*above*) and Cowboy Dean
(*right*).

Best pals Dean and Frank croon a tune on *The Dean Martin Show.*

Dean seemed oblivious to the criticism—when he downsized his large troupe of "Golddiggers" to only four regular girl singers, he rechristened them with an even more offensive moniker: "The Ding-a-Lings."

Sensing weakness, in early 1973 ABC moved a big gun against the established show, the new Karl Malden/Michael Douglas hit *The Streets of San Francisco*. It was no accident that they hit the *Streets* at 10:00 Thursdays, as NBC's San Francisco-set copper *Ironside* was on patrol from 9:00 to 10:00. By the end of the 1972–73 season, ABC had thrown the book at Dean's show, as millions of *Ironside*'s NBC loyalists sped over to ABC as soon as *Ironside* wheeled away.

NBC returned the compliment by moving Dean's show over a night to Fridays that summer. The nearly decade-old show still had enough oomph in it to put the hurt on ABC's strong Friday night lineup. Dino managed to knock off ABC's once-unstoppable *Love, American Style* by mid-season, stealing away almost all of the fans of that show's *Odd Couple* lead-in.

But Dean's show was still slipping, and when ABC moved the new *Six Million Dollar Man* and *Toma* (which would mutate into *Baretta* a year later) to Friday nights, it finally went into freefall. It also became obvious that with Dean making the show while simultaneously undergoing love-life issues and making the legal crime drama *Mr. Ricco* for the movies, the fifty-six-year-old performer had less time and energy left for the show.

Proving the old TV axiom that repetition equals success, NBC noticed that Dean's most successful shows were "special" episodes where he "roasted" a celebrity friend of his, à la the fabled Friar's Club "roasts" in Hollywood. NBC put more and more pressure on Dean and Greg Garrison to change the format to a "roast-of-the-week" show, with Dean serving as emcee while a celebrity colleague (preferably a big NBC star) would get "Martinized" by Dean and his comedian pals. By early 1974, it was clear that NBC had little enthusiasm left for continuing the program as the free-wheeling variety hour of song, dance, and sketches it had always been.

To put the final nail in the coffin, NBC developed a promising trio of brand new shows for the following year's Friday night schedule—*Chico & the Man*, *The Rockford Files*, and *Police Woman*. Those Friday night shows of 1974–75, led off by the legendary *Sanford & Son*, made up what was probably the best night of TV in all the 1970s, aside from CBS's still-unmatched 1973–74 Saturday comedy lineup. And by 1974, most of Dean's pallies on the NBC variety playground—*Laugh-In*, Flip Wilson, Sammy Davis Jr.—were moving away.

In May of 1974, after almost nine years on the air, *The Dean Martin Show* wished its fans a fond farewell. Dino himself went into one of the most active retirements in history, regularly appearing in Las Vegas, filming holiday TV specials, and continuing his side-splitting celebrity "roasts" regularly through 1978 (and sporadically into the '80s). His TV and movie schedule was far from reclusive, with guest appearances on everything from daytime shows like Dinah Shore's talk show to cameo shots in big-budget movies like *Cannonball Run*. He also made a notable (and appropriate) guest shot as a casino magnate in the 1978–79 season premiere of *Charlie's Angels*.

And when he wasn't working, the Commissioner of Cool could be found relaxing at the pool, watching TV, or reading Westerns. Or enjoying his favorite pursuit of all: golfing at the Riviera with close friends like Dick Martin, Don Rickles, Buddy Hackett, Bob Newhart, Monty Hall, Sammy Davis Jr., and Richard Dawson.

But despite his money and fame, in the late 1980s, TV's epitome of congenial class would suffer the worst of all fates. In the spring of 1987, Dean's son Dean-Paul died in a freak plane crash over the mountains in Southern California. The rugged World War II–generation patriarch tried to put on a strong face for his family and friends (including ex-wife Jeanne, with whom he had long ago reconciled and visited constantly). But it was obvious to all those who really knew him that much of Dean Sr. died along with his son.

A year later in 1988, the seventy-one-year-old entertainer left a tour with best friends Frank Sinatra and Sammy Davis Jr., citing exhaustion and ill health. But it was actually Sammy whose health was beginning to fail. Just a year and a half after that, Sammy Davis Jr. died of cancer in Hollywood at the age of sixty-four (on the very same day that fellow entertainment legend Jim Henson died of viral pneumonia and cardiorespiratory arrest.) Dean, who absolutely loathed hospitals, regularly visited his pallie Sammy toward the end, a gesture that Sammy's closest friends and family still remember today.

Dean's health and spirits took their final downturn after his longtime best friend's death. By the mid-1990s, tabloid reporters and TV magazine shows salivated over stories that Dean was near death himself, and took the most lurid and intrusive pictures they could of the seventy-something singer. Privately, Dean was enraged by their inexcusable behavior (as were Jeanne and Dean's adult children.) But ever the easygoing entertainer, Dean refused to allow the vulturous paparazzi the satisfaction of a person-to-person confrontation.

Dean did, however, keep more to himself, driving only to an occasional golf game and each night to his favorite Italian ristorante in one of his luxury sedans. "He would kiss his St. Christopher medal and thank God for a safe trip," when he returned home to read and watch TV, a longtime friend recalled.

(A considerably more sordid chapter in Dean's final days came to light toward the end of his life, when professional celebrity stalker and future Robert Blake wife Bonny Lee Bakely entered the scene. Bonny was undoubtedly the most literal "gold-digger" that Dino had ever met, and tabloids were rife with speculation about the nature of their relationship. Reported accounts of Bonny's reaction to Dean's death revealed, shall we say, a less than flattering side to her nature or compassion for others, especially her alleged temper tantrums when she discovered that she wouldn't profit the way she'd evidently hoped to.)

On Christmas Eve, 1995, Dean was on his deathbed at home in Beverly Hills talking with Jeanne. His longtime life partner in good times and bad, Jeanne could tell all too well that Dean was tired, sick, and rapidly nearing the end. "You don't have to keep fighting [for us]," she cried, and reassured him of the immortal place he had in the hearts of all his family. In the early morning hours of Christmas Day in 1995—the twenty-ninth anniversary of his mother's 1966 passing—Dean Martin died of congestive heart failure. He was seventy-eight years old.

The Chairman of the Board himself said it best, in his eulogy of Dean. "Dean was my brother," Sinatra stated simply. "Not by blood—but by choice!" Rosemary Clooney sang the recessional at Dean's funeral, as old and new Hollywood alike turned out to wish one of the most beloved entertainers of the century a final goodbye.

Despite the sad denouement to Dean's final years, the pleasure his very memory still brings to millions is the real referendum on the Dean Martin legacy. Unlike so many Hollywood families, Dean's children generally have only positive memories of their father. And that's not to mention the unique manner in which he lived his life. An old-world family man who still knew how to have a good time. An urbane sophisticate who was the epitome of "hip" and "in-crowd"—and yet was as unpretentious and down to earth as your next-door neighbor.

That memory will endure as an example of a man who truly knew how to "have it all." His son Ricci provided the final epitaph for his dad, which will be respectfully reprinted here as the final word on Dean and his 1965–74 NBC show.

"Now that's livin,' Pallie!"

## MEMORABLE MOMENTS

Were you watching when . . .

- Nobody in TV history could play the seen-it-all, dissatisfied wife the way that Audrey Meadows—Alice Kramden herself—could. In 1969, she played a middle-aged hausfrau sitting around the den who asked her husband (Dean), "Would you climb the highest mountain for me?" "Of course, dear," the smoking-jacketed Dean replied. Off he went (with footage of mountain climbers rappelling and ice-picking their way to the top), coming home to find his unimpressed wife still sitting in her chair.

   Audrey wasn't finished yet. "Would you swim the deepest ocean for me?" she sighed. "Of course, dear," Dean wearily gasped (only to be attacked by an "octopus" on his way back in the door). After several more, "Will you do [blank] for me," requests, Dino the Valiant Hero returned the last time—only to have Audrey to declare that she wanted a divorce. "Why?" Dean asked. She replied, "Because you're never home!"

- Dean interviewed everybody's favorite dingbat, *Laugh-In*'s Goldie Hawn, who announced that she was proud to be a founding member of the American Dumb People's Party. "Think about it," Goldie giggled. "Who causes all the trouble in the world? Smart people!" The "dumb" blonde continued, "I mean, look at the ecology, and pollution—who causes that? The people who build the automobiles on the road. And who causes the war problems? The senators and congressmen and scientists who build all the weapons," and so on. It was pretty obvious just how smart Miss Goldie was, and Dean's roaring, grinning comedy timing in the chat was as sharp as ever.
- The Golddiggers got their revenge one night for any "sexist" treatment from their maestro. Dean was in a giant magician's box, and the gorgeous gals thrust one sword into the box after another. Dean finally broke free, and thankfully there was no sign of blood or other damage to his immaculate tuxedo—until he took a nice drink of vodka and the water started squirting out of him from all over!
- On several other shows, Dean wrapped up his "goodbyes" with, "See ya next time everybody—I gotta go pee!"
- Johnny Carson appeared in the early '70s in the office of Dean the Hospital Administrator, as a patient named Cindy, with a problem that would have made Blue Cross turn blue. (S)he had received a sex-change operation by mistake! Completely ad-libbed, Johnny even motioned for Dean to pull "her" chair out for him, which Dr. Dino did. "Cindy" was inconsolable. "Now, when my husband and I want to have a good time, we go out to the bars to look at chicks!"

   Dean said he'd promise to see what he could do, but wanted to meet "Cindy's" husband first. Of course, in walked Ed McMahon, wearing a blond flip and eye makeup, pink chiffon dress, and Mother Marcus boobs!

## BLOOPERS AND BREAKUPS

- Early in 1969, Milburn Stone of *Gunsmoke* fame dropped by to play one of Dean's favorite word games—"Spoonerisms" (transposing the pronunciation of words while speaking). This time, it was to regale that classic story of "Findercella, and her Three Sisty Uglers." "No shit!" a perhaps really drunk Dean exclaimed, upon hearing the title. (It was bleeped, of course, but even amateur lip readers weren't fooled.) Both men doubled over, laughing so hard they could barely finish the sketch!
- What about the night when Dean slid down the "pole" into his living room set— only to go crashing down through the floor into the basement! And then, just when you thought it was safe, Frank Sinatra came up through the hole in the floor. "Don't worry! Dean's OK," Frankie reassured the fans. "He fell into the wine cellar!"
- Gina Lollobrigida had trouble understanding why baseball was America's

national pastime. "In Italy, the national pastime is love," the screen legend purred. When Dean tried to draw an analogy between the two "national pastimes," he was at a comical loss to 'splain to Gina why only men played America's national pastime and only with each other. . . . Thirty years before *Will & Grace*, the convulsing audience got the point!

- Charles Nelson Reilly played the Farmer and luscious Elke Sommer played his Daughter in a takeoff on the old chestnut with a swinging early '70s twist: Dean and guest star David Janssen were a dueling duo of travelling salesmen who *both* needed a place to sleep, with only the daughter's room available. . . .

- Peter Sellers guested late in the series run, as the client of NBC barbers Nipsey Russell and Dom DeLuise. In those pre–politically correct days of 1973, Sellers's scarf-wearing, swishy, temperamental Hollywood "star" was enough of a challenge to keep DeLuise and Russell from breaking up. But when Dean sashayed in, swatting Dom on the rear and mincing to his seat, the entire company lost it. "I used to think I was the token Black on this show," Russell said. "Now, I think I'm the token straight!"

- One of Dean's Golddiggers screwed up the lyrics during "Musical Questions" in 1969. The girl started singing her song with the wrong verse, and ever-absent-from-rehearsals Dean roared with laughter. "*She* made the mistake!" he exulted. "For once, *someone else* made the mistake! I didn't make the mistake!!" Taking it cool as ever, Dean restarted the sketch, "Don't worry, sweetheart," he smiled. "It'll just come out of your check!"

    Then, to finish, he said he was just joking, and that "After all, we all make mistakes—remember Hitler?" (The tete-a-tete in question, by the way, was that the lovely lady was to sing "I get no kick from champagne / Mere alcohol doesn't thrill me at all" to which Dino responded in song, "Two different worlds / We live in two different worlds.")

**Marquee names that tried the variety format—and failed!**

### Mary (The Mary Tyler Moore Hour)

*Network: CBS; On the air: September 24, 1978–May 6, 1979*

"The summer I found myself without the 'wedding ring' that was *The Mary Tyler Moore Show* would hit me with the same force I later felt at the ending of my [actual] marriage," Moore recalled in her 1995 autobiography. "I had nothing left." Mary had been working nonstop from the age of nineteen, from her early work on *Jimmy Durante* and *Richard Diamond: Private Eye,* to *Dick Van Dyke* and her own classic sitcom, with some moderately successful comedy movies like *Thoroughly Modern Millie* in between.

Now, after the 1977 demise of *The Mary Tyler Moore Show,* the forty-year-old Mare was suffering from a case of empty-nest syndrome. Her son Richie was grown and living with his father (Moore's first husband), and Mary spent most days at home "watching Jane, Goldie, and Sally make feature deals, and waiting like a jilted lover for the phone to ring."

It didn't. After a year, Mary had had enough of her "retirement," and started seriously talking with her husband, producer Grant Tinker, about pitching another TV show for her to star in.

At first, the idea of putting Mary into a prime-time variety show seemed like a no-brainer. Mary had studied ballet and classical dancing all through her youth, earning top grades, and had a relatively pleasant singing voice, not to mention her impeccable comedic timing and acting skills. CBS instantaneously "bought" the concept, and opened up a primo Sunday night slot at 8:00 for the fall, right after the number-one-rated *60 Minutes*. The show also booked top-flight guest stars like Lucille Ball, Bea Arthur, Dick Van Dyke, and Gene Kelly.

The 1978 *Mary* show assembled a to-die-for cast of supporting regulars that made even Mary's sitcom almost pale in comparison—Michael Keaton, Swoosie Kurtz, Dick Shawn, and a thirty-one-year-old stand-up comedian named David Letterman. Each cast member also had roles and routines that were specifically tailored just for them.

Sadly, what Mary had failed to realize was that, as she later put it, "the genre was fading away from the horizon … [with] the 'black cloud' of what would become MTV shutting off the sun." *Mary* lost so much of *60 Minutes'* audience that CBS yanked the show after only eight episodes had been completed—and only three telecast on the air! The show went into the CBS think-tank for emergency surgery, with the ultra-talented cast all fired on the spot, except for Michael Keaton.

(Meanwhile, CBS shifted proven hits *All in the Family* and *One Day at a Time* to the 8:00–9:00 hour on Sunday, and instantly went back into the "win" column the very next week.)

In early March 1979, the retooled show, now titled *The Mary Tyler Moore Hour,* premiered on CBS. Mary's producers and writers decided to gently get back at CBS for the astonishingly fast hiatus of the earlier program by making the new show a spoof of TV variety shows from behind the scenes. Mary was now cast as Mary McKinnon, the slightly aging and perplexed star of her own big-budget, Carol Burnett–style variety show, with Michael Keaton as her personal assistant and veteran character actress Joyce Van Patten as Mary's right-hand associate producer. (It was not all that different from the plot of the *Dick Van Dyke Show,* in which Rob Petrie worked as a writer for the fictitious Alan Brady variety hour.) But CBS didn't find anything funny about the "joke" on them, nor were the ratings any laughing matter. By the end of April, the network had pulled the plug.

Mary was "decimated" by the loss. Two years earlier, her show had been one of the most successful and prestigious sitcoms on television; now, she had to live down two spectacular failures within six months' time. (At least her variety show still looked good in comparison to other 1978–79 fare, such as *Supertrain, Whodunit,* and *David Cassidy: Man Undercover.*)

Showing the same spunk that made Laura Petrie and Mary Richards immortal, Mary promised to be back on the air with a good old sitcom—perhaps even as Mary Richards again—in the fall of 1980. But no sooner had *The Mary Tyler Moore Hour* been cancelled than Paramount Studios announced it would be filming a Robert Redford–directed adaptation of Judith Guest's 1976 best-seller *Ordinary People.*

Mary, a fan of the book, made a beeline to the studio to audition for the part of the superficially together mother who is trying to get over the death of her favorite son and the suicidal tendencies of his brother. To boost her clout, she even got her agent to book her on Broadway in the right-to-die drama *Who's Life Is It, Anyway,* where she replaced male lead Tom Conti—making it the first show in Broadway history where a lead character's gender was changed during the course of a play's run. (In a truly horrifying irony, Mary's younger sister had committed suicide by overdose in 1978. What's more, her twenty-four-year-old son would also die of a handgun accident in October of 1980—the same month that *Ordinary People* was released!)

Despite these knockout blows, Mary battled back to triumph in both roles, winning a Tony for the Broadway play and an Oscar nomination for *Ordinary People.* By the end of the year, with everything else that had happened, everyone forgot about *The Mary Tyler Moore Hour* (as well as Mary's plans for a new 1980 sitcom). Mary spent the '80s rebuilding her life in New York, finding new romance with a prominent New York cardiologist after her divorce from Grant Tinker was finalized in December 1980. She continued to star in occasional TV series and movies in acclaimed supporting roles, taking on a wide range of characters, from a too-sexy middle-aged mom in *Flirting With Disaster* to child-stealing social worker Georgia Tann in the Emmy-winning TV movie *Stolen Babies*.

More importantly, Mary now had a far greater achievement to derive happiness from. Despite all the odds and tragedies, she really had "made it, after all."

## Van Dyke and Company

*Network: NBC; On the air: September 20, 1976–December 30, 1976*

Dick Van Dyke left his biggest and best show after five years in 1966 to return to feature film roles, with which he had some clear successes, most notably in *Chitty Chitty Bang-Bang* and alongside Julie Andrews in *Mary Poppins*. When his film career started to bang-bang at the box office, he was back on CBS alongside Hope Lange, Richard Dawson, and Fannie Flagg in *The New Dick Van Dyke Show*, which ran until 1974.

With two successful sitcoms in recent memory, a third sitcom project was out of the question. But Dick's abilities as an actor, singer, stand-up comedian, and hoofer, not to mention his preternatural ability to take a pratfall, all pointed in an obvious direction: A variety show!

Allan Blye and Bob Einstein, who had worked on shows like *The Smothers Brothers* and *Sonny & Cher*, were brought in to helm the series, which would be NBC's only prime-time variety hour of the 1976–77 season. The show is notable for being Andy Kaufman's truly big break into television after years of showing his stuff on the L.A., San Francisco, and New York comedy club circuit.

Van Dyke's verve, likeability, and talent were such that the show beat out even the likes of *Carol Burnett* and *Saturday Night Live* for the Best Musical/Variety Series Emmy for the 1976–77 season. Unfortunately, NBC was up to its counterprogramming tricks again. They slotted the show against two established, wry-humored crime shows starring middle-aged men with a similar relaxed appeal, *Barnaby Jones* and *The Streets of San Francisco*. Furthermore, NBC was by late 1976 mired badly in third place, and the show had little or nothing in the way of a lead-in to support it—while its competition had the tsunami-wave strength of *Hawaii Five-0* and *Barney Miller*, respectively, in the hour before.

Dick Van Dyke went on to star in *The Music Man* in 1979 and '80 on Broadway and in a national tour. He made frequent high-profile guest shots on other TV sitcoms and dramas throughout the '80s (including as a corrupt judge on a memorable *Matlock* in 1986). And he tried a sitcom in 1988 but it was short-lived. But in 1993, the nearly seventy-year-old veteran finally found another worthy vehicle. He charmed his way into the hearts of an entirely new era as the quirky yet effective Dr. Mark Sloan in the long-running mystery drama *Diagnosis Murder*. For eight years, the occasionally suspenseful yet easygoing and often funny show held down the fort for all hospital-happy *ER* fans who weren't watching the NBC Thursday-night "must-see" sitcoms.

At age seventy-seven, Dick reunited with Mary Tyler Moore herself in a stunningly good PBS adaptation of the 1977 Hume Cronyn/Jessica Tandy stage play, *The Gin Game*. Even thought this show failed, America still loves Dick Van Dyke's company, and it's easy to see why.

## The Julie Andrews Hour

*Network: ABC; On the air: September 13, 1972–April 28, 1973*

ABC had its highest hopes for a successful variety show launch with this one since trying their hand with Pearl Bailey's show at the end of 1970. The network had gone all out to try to find the biggest and most proven star that they possibly could for the new series. Showing the same love affair with England that had previously brought ABC *The Avengers, The Persuaders, This Is Tom Jones*, and *Englebert Humperdinck,* ABC approached English impresario Sir Lew Grade (who would later launch *The Muppet Show*) for ideas on the new program.

By 1972, the era of flourishing, big-budget movie musicals were on the wane, replaced by rock operas like *Godspell* and *Pippin* or downbeat dramas like *Cabaret.* As a result, top musical star Julie Andrews found herself shopping for another venue for her considerable talents. Since big-name English and Australian stars were less snobbish about doing TV than their American counterparts, Julie was eager to do the show. Besides, one of her best friends was—and is—variety diva Carol Burnett, with whom she had done several TV specials in the early 1960s and on whose show she had guested several times.

The most prominent star of the departed *ABC Comedy Hour,* Rich Little, was brought on board as one of the *Andrews Hour* regulars, along with veteran movie comedienne Alice Ghostley (who would achieve her greatest fame as the stylishly dotty neighbor Bernice Clifton on *Designing Women* from 1986 to '93).

Unfortunately, television was no longer putting anywhere near the kind of thought and planning into variety-TV that had made earlier-launched shows the successes they were. The show was entertaining enough, but slotted in one bad time slot after another right from the beginning (certain that Julie's star power would bring in viewers), and it sadly lacked any distinguishing characteristics beyond Julie's obvious talent and style.

Julie returned to the live stage and made appearances in several of her husband Blake Edwards's movies in the following years, like *S.O.B.* and *Victor/Victoria.* And Julie is going strong even today, having made TV movies, Broadway appearances, and big-screen roles in movies like *The Princess Diaries,* while her 1960s musicals have stood the test of time to become cinema classics.

## The New Bill Cosby Show/Cos

*Network: CBS/ABC; On the air: September 11, 1972–May 7, 1973/September 19, 1976–October 31, 1976*

Bill Cosby has probably had more TV shows bearing his name (or some variation thereof) than any performer, other than perhaps Bob Newhart. From 1969 to '71, NBC had the star (fresh from the unexpected 1968 cancellation of the legendary *I Spy*) in a Sunday-night sitcom, where he played the coach of a high-school sports team. A year after that show's demise, CBS got the Cos in an hour-long variety show installed at the finish of their Monday-night lineup, along with costars Quincy Jones, Lola Falana, Foster Brooks, and Susan Tolsky. While it fared adequately, it failed to hold on to the ratings of the huge hits *Here's Lucy* and *Doris Day* the hour before, and didn't make it past the following May.

Then in 1976 it was ABC's turn, with the family-friendly *Cos*. The show was ostensibly aimed at children, but it managed to feature adult-friendly guests like jazz-rock superstars Chicago and several of Bill's jazz-musician buddies. However, the trumpets soon faded as the killer competition from *60 Minutes* and *Walt Disney* emptied the series out the Nielsen spit valve.

From 1977 to 1984, Cosby concentrated on making movies, doing stand-up, and filling his much-lampooned (and beloved) role as spokesman for Jello desserts. In 1984, with the monikers *The Bill Cosby Show, The New Bill Cosby Show,* and *Cos* already exhausted, NBC offered the imaginatively titled sitcom *The Cosby Show* a half hour of prime-time TV. The rest, as they say, is history.

But wait, there's more: In 1996, four years after the passing of *The Cosby Show*, Bill and costar Phylicia Rashad returned in—yes, you guessed it—*Cosby*—on CBS. While not quite as popular as the 1984–92 show, *Cosby* still proved a solid and beloved hit until its cancellation four years later in 2000.

## The Don Knotts Hour

*Network: NBC; On the air: September 15, 1970–July 6, 1971*

This show's behind-the-scenes Hollywood story was far more interesting than what went on the air.

In January 1970, Don Knotts informed his agent that nearly five years after he'd left behind his immortal character of Barney Fife on *The Andy Griffith Show,* he was ready to return to the small screen. Knotts had made several relatively successful comedy movies for Universal in the late '60s. But as Hollywood films finally got "with-it" in the countercultural era of *Easy Rider, Midnight Cowboy, They Shoot Horses Don't They, The Wild Bunch,* and *M\*A\*S\*H,* the childlike movies Knotts had been making didn't look long for the world. A weekly TV variety show seemed like the obvious choice for him, a format where the comedy legend could showcase all of his talents.

No sooner had he said it than CBS began throwing write-your-own figure contracts in his face, certain that with his movie-star name and universally beloved appeal from *Andy Griffith,* a Don Knotts show would lead to instant Top Ten status in the standings.

But there was one wee little snag: Knotts had signed an old-fashioned studio contract with Universal when he left the *Griffith* show, and he still owed them another year or two of projects to be chosen at their discretion. Since Universal concentrated its television arm in filmed dramas and sit-coms, the studio would have to release Knotts from his contract in order to allow him to do the variety show.

They were more than happy to oblige. "Don't worry, Don," the Universal execs smiled. They wouldn't do anything so mean and petty as to sue him for breach of contract, or stand in the way of his plans—that is, as long as they retained one right: Universal, not Knotts, would decide which network would get the rights to *The Don Knotts Show.*

CBS was willing to offer Knotts the moon itself in order to get him back on their schedule, but Universal had other ideas. They wanted to use the proposed series as "bait" to ensure that NBC would renew two on-the-fence Universal-produced shows, and give the green light to their heavily hyped new "Four-In-One" anthology series (which included *McCloud* and *Night Gallery* among others).

NBC accepted the deal even though in fact they were the most lukewarm of the Big Three networks toward a Don Knotts show, on the theory of continuing good business with Universal—and figuring that they were stronger if CBS didn't have Knotts. They slotted the freshman series against the huge hit *Mod Squad,* understandably thinking that Knotts had an entirely different audience. But CBS, smarting at the loss of "their" show, decided to go after what audience Knotts did have, by putting the fading yet still popular heartland favorites *Beverly Hillbillies* and *Green Acres* against the program.

Against that impossible competition, *The Don Knotts Hour* was doomed from the outset. There was also the fact that NBC always emphasized hip, with-it, urban comedy-variety shows (*Laugh-In, Dean Martin, Flip Wilson*), which made the Knotts show something of an orphan on their schedule. Most important, Knotts's self-deprecating, schleppy persona was a stark contrast to the Ed Sullivan or Lawrence Welk style of I'm-in-charge authority and command that were the trademarks of a successful variety, game, or talk show host.

Don Knotts returned to making movies (mainly for Disney) following the death of the show. And at the end of the '70s, he reintroduced himself to a whole new generation of fans as the hilariously garish, sex-starved leering landlord Ralph Furley on the classic sitcom *Three's Company.* And of course, Barney Fife is still on patrol in the eternal rerun-land of Mayberry on *The Andy Griffith Show.*

## Dolly!

*Network: ABC; On the air: September 27, 1987–May 7, 1988*
By 1987, country superstar Dolly Parton had already conquered stage and screen (*Nine to Five, The*

*Best Little Whorehouse in Texas*), live country music and the Grand Ole Opry, soft rock (her 1974 anthem "I Will Always Love You"), and television. The drop-dead-gorgeous Dolly had also expanded upon herself with a brand-new amusement park in her native Pigeon Forge, Tennessee—appropriately called Dollywood.

Meanwhile, ABC was looking for new programming to revitalize Sunday nights. For more than twenty years ABC had weathered television's deadliest competition (including *Bonanza, The Smothers Brothers, Mission Impossible, Columbo, Mannix, Kojak, Alice,* and *The Jeffersons,* to name but a few) on TV's biggest night with their Sunday night movie. By 1987 all three networks were running movies on Sundays while the upstart Fox network was getting rave reviews and reasonable ratings with their extraordinary and excellent new *Tracey Ullman Show.*

It was not lost on ABC's executives that the last network variety show to be a success, before Tracey, was hosted by a sexy young country and western singer (*Barbara Mandrell and the Mandrell Sisters*). ABC was so eager to get Dolly that they signed a record-breaking two-year commitment worth a total of $40 million dollars to get the show. The program itself was a fun and fancy-free collage from Dollywood, with Dolly riding amusement park rides, going down waterslides, and doing on-location song scenes in the breathtakingly beautiful hills and countryside. Dolly invited a wide variety of guests, and showed the fun, good ole gal sense of humor that she always had and the comedy timing that made *Nine to Five* and *Best Little Whorehouse* the smashes they were. And there were truly inspired moments on the show too, such as a 1987 three-way duet with Linda Ronstadt and Emmylou Harris (they had just recorded the bestselling album *Trio* earlier that year).

Nonetheless, ABC's Sunday-night schedule was the weakest of the big three at the time. CBS had *60 Minutes* and *Murder, She Wrote* to anchor the evening among retirees, while NBC's *Family Ties* ruled the ratings with young people. ABC was counting on a massive switchover at nine o'clock for Dolly's show, and unfortunately it just didn't happen. *Dolly!* finished a respectable forty-seventh in the ratings race, but that was an awfully expensive bust for the forty-million-dollar show. ABC quietly bought out Dolly's contract and returned to movies the next season.

(It's sad to contemplate the fact that barely a year after *Dolly!* went off the air in 1988, ABC *did* finally get a pair of winners on Sunday nights—*Life Goes On* and *America's Funniest Home Videos,* to which *Dolly!* show would have been the perfect companion. But hey, that's showbiz!)

# The Smothers Brothers Comedy Hour

## Vital Stats

**STARRING**
Tom and Dick Smothers

**ALSO STARRING**
Steve Martin, Rob Reiner, Leigh French, Bob Einstein, Pat Paulsen,
David Steinberg, Glen Campbell, Jennifer Warnes

**NETWORK**
CBS

**ON THE AIR**
February 5, 1967—June 8, 1969

**ORIGINATION**
CBS Television City, Stage 31

"Mom always liked you best!"

The Who (*above*) rock Tommy's world, while Pete Seeger (*right*) gives the finger to authority on *The Smothers Brothers Comedy Hour.*

Television networks have always wanted to have their cake (social relevance, critical acclaim, high quality) and eat it too (across-the-board appeal, freedom from threats, boycotts, and letter-writers). But few other shows in TV history suffered from TV Network Bipolar Disorder more than *The Smothers Brothers Comedy Hour*.

At the start of 1967, which would give us the "Summer of Love" and Monterey Pop, old reliable network CBS's biggest problem was their 9:00 to 10:00 time slot on Sunday nights. For the past five years NBC's *Bonanza* had so dominated the evening that every single show CBS had programmed against it had been canceled at the end of its season. The slot had been given the nickname of "The Kamikaze Hour," since what few households weren't watching the adventures of the Cartwright clan were more than likely tuning in to ABC's world-premiere movies. Making the problem even more frustrating was the fact that CBS's 8:00 entry, *The Ed Sullivan Show*, was winning its time slot, meaning that a huge portion of Ed's viewers were switching over to NBC at 9, avoiding what CBS had put in the spot.

Sunday and Monday nights, as the "family nights" at the beginning of the workweek, had been from television's inception its biggest night for business, with the highest total viewership across the board. Yet the only show that had managed to hold its own against *Bonanza* was *Perry Mason* in 1965–66. But by then Perry had been trying cases for the past nine years on CBS, and the network had already more or less made up its mind to cancel it anyway. The last-year scheduling move was more of a temporary stopgap to give CBS time to develop something for the future. By the end of the year, the network was surveying researchers, ratings experts, and critics from coast to coast in search of a scheme that could help them climb the mountain back to Sunday-evening superiority.

The network's research revealed a surprising thing. What the doctor ordered for Sunday nights at 9:00 would be a variety series with distinct appeal to a youth audience—people in high school, college, and in their twenties. It would draw off enough young viewers who'd grown up with, and perhaps in some ways "outgrown" *Bonanza*, and give the stodgy network a much-needed shot in the arm to revitalize the evening.

At the same time, the young comedy and folk-singing team of brothers Tommy and Dick Smothers had just finished a lightweight fantasy sitcom for CBS imaginatively titled *The Smothers Brothers Show*, a not-so-wonderful takeoff on *It's a Wonderful Life*, in which straitlaced New York book editor Dick found himself "living" with his recently deceased goofy brother Tom, now an inept "probationary angel" assigned to "help" (sitcom-style) the poor Earthlings down below. While happy to have the national exposure of a TV series, neither Smothers Brother was happy with the show's format. They wanted a show that would enable them to display a range of talents and abilities, instead of the constricted, repetitive weekly show.

The brothers were young, and they had recorded several folk albums that were very popular with young record buyers. CBS knew that it need look no further than its own backyard for the "stars" of the new comedy-variety show they were planning.

Tommy and Dick Smothers were also respected as stand-up comedians, which was what got them the CBS sitcom gig in the first place. Their comedy act was based on the eternal love-hate relationship between two brothers, and it was one of the funniest of the time. Wide-eyed Tommy would earnestly play his acoustic guitar, usually stumbling over some misheard lyric or going off in kind of a twenty-year-old's version of a Dick Martin or Jerry Lewis routine, never "getting it." Patient stand-up bass player Dick (who was actually younger, but always *seemed* older, as he was the more level-headed and thoughtful), would try to explain, in vain, until Tommy got so flustered and frustrated he'd cry out, "Mom always likes you best!"—or, when the two would get into a disagreement, "He started it!"

This memorable act was better in the seeing and hearing than in just the description: the two brought facial expressions and nuances of voice to the shopworn routine that made it usually seem fresh, and there was the obvious bond of young brotherly love between the two that set them apart from the standard comedy duo.

The idea for a musical-comedy show was a godsend to the Smothers Brothers. Here was a show that they could tailor-make to their own talents—singing, stand-up comedy, and sketch acting, with something new and fresh every week. The loose format of a star-hosted variety series meant something else: more creative control and a chance to write and perform their own material. And Tommy Smothers in particular was beginning to have an idea of just what kind of material he wanted to perform.

At the time, a recently divorced Tommy was sharing a bachelor pad in Hollywood with his fellow folkie and friend, guitar virtuoso Mason Williams. When Tommy came home and told his best friend that they had just gotten an offer for their own variety show opposite *Bonanza* on CBS, Williams was instantly electrified by the possibilities. At the time, neither he nor Tommy Smothers had much use for most of what was on the air.

"We'd watch TV and be appalled," Williams recalled in an interview for Doug Hill and Jeff Weingrad's landmark 1986 treatise on *Saturday Night Live*. "There was nothing on there for him, or me, or anyone else we knew to watch. . . . You could tell there was a revolution in the works, but it wasn't being reflected on TV at all, except maybe for Mort Sahl on PBS."

True enough, much of 1967 television was typified by escapist fare like the CBS country sitcoms, *Gilligan's Island*, and *Batman*. In contrast to today's TV scene, where the vast majority of sitcoms are about young adults, in 1967 only *That Girl* on ABC and *The Monkees* on NBC even came close to building their shows around young people. Furthermore, except for the risqué *Dean Martin Show* on NBC, all the major variety shows on the air in '67 were wholesome and uncontroversial shows like *Lawrence Welk, Ed Sullivan, Carol Burnett, Red Skelton, Danny Kaye,* and *Andy Williams.*

At first, the Smotherses decided to play by CBS's strategy, just to see if the show would have any staying power, or if it too would be gone in twenty-six weeks just like everything else in *Bonanza*'s way. But as the show got going, Tommy and Mason Williams opened a "shoebox" in their apartment (and later in the writers' wing of the show) that they started pitching ideas in, for sketches on the youth movement, government regulations, and 1967 society itself.

CBS demonstrated it had a bit of concern right from the get-go of just how young and unconventional the folk-singing fraternals might be. The new show opened with Ed Sullivan, in a taped remote from his soundstage in New York, giving a fatherly "introduction" of the "boys" and their new program. It came complete with a clip montage of the Smotherses' apple-pie upbringing, and campy family pictures of the dynamic duo as children and in their high school and college years.

The network seemed to know right from the beginning that they were walking the razor's edge. The network's programmers wanted—needed—a show with young stars to superficially "look" appealing to sixteen through twenty-one-year-old viewers. But the network most definitely did *not* want a show that would openly and honestly reflect the viewpoints of much of America's youth at the time.

CBS *should* have been thrilled with the results of the Smothers Brothers' twenty-week tryout in the spring of 1967. The show had succeeded beyond anyone's hopes, bringing in a solid second-place to *Bonanza*, scoring as the sixteenth most popular show on television in 1966–67. The show was succeeding in its mission of siphoning young adults away from *Bonanza* (and the ABC movie in particular), and had modernized and rebuilt the rest of Sunday night for the network. By the fall of '67, CBS would install a ten o'clock show after the Smotherses that would enjoy even more success and longevity: the hot CIA action drama *Mission: Impossible*.

But the success of *The Smothers Brothers Comedy Hour* was inextricably linked to the freshness and new viewpoints it represented, and the creative freedom that the show had—or tried to have. Even before the first show of the 1967–68 season had aired, controversy arose over the booking of folk singer Pete Seeger on the show's fall 1967 premiere. Interestingly, the Smothers Brothers tried to play by the rules with this one, coming to CBS program executives Michael Dann and Perry Lafferty ahead of time and asking their "permission" to book Seeger, who was blacklisted in the 1950s for suspected communist sympathies. Seeger had also attracted heavy controversy at the beginning of his career when, in the early '40s, the twenty-two-year-old singer had gotten in trouble with the law for openly resisting the draft of World War II.

Dann said that he had no legitimate reason to "deny" the Seeger booking and approved it. But the Hollywood press learned almost immediately of the upcoming booking, which was scheduled for the Smotherses' heavily hyped fall 1967 premiere episode. CBS was soon inundated with letters from outraged viewers, accusing them of "giving aid and comfort to the enemy," while conservative station managers sent in reams of TelExes and Western Union telegrams. While Dann was busy with bigger problems finalizing the fall schedule, the Standards department demanded that Seeger not sing his new folk hit, "Waist Deep in the Big Muddy" (a blistering indictment of the way the Vietnam War was being run), much to Tommy Smothers's disgust. Finally, following months of a real-life "You started it!" and a who-likes-who-best fight between Smothers and Standards, Seeger was finally able to sing the song, in early 1968.

More battles would be on the way; a 1968 "Salute to Mothers" that asked mom to think how much longer the Vietnam War would be drafting their sons when they voted for president later that year was especially controversial. All this *sturm und drang* took its toll on the show's staff. The program went through a total of at least six directors (including Tim Kiley, who had directed *The Ed Sullivan Show* before and would go on to mount *The Flip Wilson Show* shortly after).

Talented producers like Saul Ilson, Ernie Chambers, and Allan Blye often found themselves caught in the crossfire between the Smotherses themselves and the ever more recalcitrant CBS. Tommy Smothers responded by opening up writing jobs for several of his youngest friends from the comedy-club scene, including comedy legend Carl Reiner's twenty-three-year-old son Rob and a twenty-three-year-old stand-up comedian named Steve Martin.

Still, despite the myths, in actual fact a lot of CBS executives loved the *Smothers Brothers* show—even as the brothers grew bolder in their lampooning of the mismanagement of the Vietnam War, and with their love-letter invitations to rock and folk acts deemed too hot for TV. Many furtively egged on the brothers to take on sacred cows and make the show more cutting-edge and controversial. Some of the execs (especially the younger ones) did it because they were in general accord with the Smotherses' views. Many others did it simply for the pragmatic business reason of wanting a "hot" show on the air, one that was grabbing press headlines and generating its own publicity.

That was the irresistible force; on the other side was the immovable object, veteran CBS vice-president of standards and practices William Tankersley. Tankersley, a six-foot-tall Texas fundamentalist, was absolute in his convictions of what was (and wasn't) appropriate for the CBS airwaves. He was proud of his richly earned nicknames "Mr. Prohibition" and "Dr. No." And until movie and golden age TV producer Norman Lear came into the picture with *All in the Family,* Tankersley had nearly unchallenged power to veto and overrule items he felt were in bad taste or simply inappropriate for CBS's corporate image.

Tankersley was willing to make some concessions to social relevancy and grown-up subject matter in showcase hour dramas like *The Defenders* and *Perry Mason*. But for comedy programs, Tankersley favored broad slapstick à la Red Skelton, Danny Kaye, Carol Burnett, and the country comedies—and certainly not subjects that

Peacenik Pastor Dave (Steinberg) finds time to give a sermon in between counseling conscientious objectors and performing interracial and gay marriages.

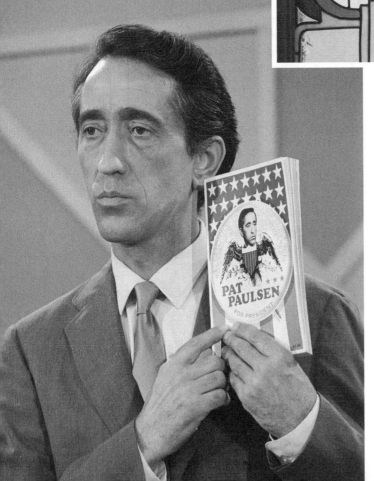

The Prime Minister of political comedy, Pat Paulsen, running for president in 1968.

could seriously offend large portions of the viewership, let alone be perceived as "making fun of" a war-torn America.

Even beyond his own personal tastes and beliefs, "Mr. Prohibition" had another, more pragmatic executive concern over the program. Ever since the tenure of James T. Aubrey Jr. as CBS's chief programmer from 1959 to '65, the network had emphasized its strength in the heartland of the South and Midwest, where its strongest and most loyal affiliates were. Most of these stations were owned by local radio operators, newspaper publishers, or theatre-chain owners who were pillars of their local communities.

They were also, by-and-large, ultra conservative—especially when compared to the counterculture of New York and San Francisco that the Smothers Brothers had such affection for. Many of them expressed their disdain openly and violently to Tankersley's department. They were shocked at seeing what they felt was almost the electronic equivalent of a draft-card "burn-in" week after week on their very airwaves, and on the "family night" of Sundays too!

(It's important to note at this point that men like Aubrey and his CBS successors, Mike Dann and Robert Wood, were sophisticated men whose own viewing tastes were the exact opposite of most of CBS's schedule at the time. Far from being friendly or folksy, Aubrey was the self-admitted model for Jacqueline Susann's amoral, womanizing studio chief in her novel *The Love Machine* and was widely considered the inspiration for the character of J.R. Ewing from *Dallas*. Program chief Dann once said off the record that he saw what little he cared to of prime time during his normal work routine, and wouldn't even recognize the shows from CBS's daytime schedule.)

Still, the Smotherses might have been able to hold the line against the CBS censors if it weren't for one other executive who dwarfed all of the others put together.

The man who held absolute power at CBS until his retirement in 1973, second only to that of CBS's de facto owner and Chairman, William S. Paley, was Dr. Frank Stanton. Dr. Stanton had started with the network in 1935 as director of research at the youthful age of twenty-seven. And he was as active in the Democratic party as his boss William S. Paley was with the Republicans. Before the McGovern candidacy in 1972 and Richard Nixon and Ronald Reagan's assumption of "the Silent Majority," the Democratic party was being torn to shreds from within—between young hippie voters on one hand, and pro-draft, WWII and Korea veteran, labor-union "hardhats" on the other. *The Smothers Brothers Comedy Hour* hit right to the very bone on this unfortunate and uncomfortable cultural revolution, and it embarrassed staunch Democrat Stanton terribly.

It made Stanton even more concerned when his close personal friend—none other than President Lyndon B. Johnson—entered the fray. Johnson was outraged enough at the Smotherses' lampooning of pompous, uncaring draft boards and stuffy

Pentagon officials. But when they started going after Johnson himself, all bets were off! One sketch that prompted a blackout on several Southern stations featured a vulgar, trash-talking President Johnson remodeling the White House itself into a down-home, countrified plantation complete with barbecues and ten-gallon hats. Another, aired shortly after Johnson's retirement in early 1969, had impressionist David Frye essaying a drunk and disjointed Johnson incoherently trying to justify his four-year war with no end in sight.

CBS programmer Michael Dann recalled in a documentary about *The Smothers Brothers Comedy Hour,* appropriately titled *Smothered,* that he would get irate phone calls from Frank Stanton more often than not on Monday morning, after the show had played the night before. Lyndon Johnson started tuning away from his favorite *Bonanza* on Sunday nights to keep his eye on what new barbs the boys were going to throw at him this time—often watching in the company of frequent White House guest Stanton himself! "How can you let them do this to me?" Johnson would ask, only half joking.

Not only that, but Lyndon Johnson also actually owned (in Lady Bird's name, for the sake of propriety with FCC regulators) the CBS TV and radio affiliates in Austin, Texas! The stations were amongst the highest rated and most visible in the Lone Star State, with the reflected prestige of being "the president's stations." And CBS was getting a bloodshot eye at the thought of the president publicly switching affiliations to ABC or NBC in retaliation.

Now the Smothers Brothers had three different "constituencies" to answer for in their political appeals: the execs who wanted the show hot and trendy for young viewers, scandal, and sensation; the somber, funereal viewpoint of Frank Stanton and William Tankersley's censorship bureau; and increasingly, the president of the United States himself.

Meanwhile, the show still managed to be exciting and refreshing to watch. Even some people who had no sympathy whatever for the hippie lifestyle tuned in just to see what they were gonna do *this* week. Hangdog, laconic, middle-aged comedian Pat Paulsen mounted a "campaign" for president of the United States, for one. This "alternative" candidacy was made even funnier when juxtaposed with the dog fights going on at the time as to whether it would be Bobby Kennedy or vice president Hubert Humphrey who would succeed a retiring Lyndon Johnson as the Democrats' nominee (not to mention the racist "third party" candidacy of Alabama Governor George Wallace, the reality of which was no laughing matter).

Then there was young stage and improv actress Leigh French, whose most popular character was hippie talk-show hostess Goldie O'Keefe, who invited you to "Share a Little Tea with Goldie." (Interestingly, her character made her premiere just one day prior to another Goldie's debut, on a brand new show called *Laugh-In.*) Goldie had household tips on getting rid of "roaches" before any unwanted visitors might see them, and a recipe for homebaked brownies that was so far-out you'd feel, like, wow, all day!

And finally, the show's most controversial act, a liberal young minister, who was totally out of the closet about his progressive views on religion, played by regular guest David Steinberg. (Rumor has it that Steinberg patterned the character after the ultra-liberal and openly gay minister Malcolm Boyd.)

Rock acts and folk singers were already getting some exposure on TV thanks to Ed Sullivan and an occasional *Hollywood Palace* or *Kraft Music Hall* concession, but the Smothers Brothers attracted guests like Jefferson Airplane and Simon and Garfunkel with regularity. And as rock music became the anthem of the Baby-Boom generation, the show was made all the more into appointment TV for young people by the bookings.

By far the most popular (and mainstream) regular music guest on the show was singer Glen Campbell, a young country vocalist who had a modern look and style, and helped erase the reactionary "hillbilly" stigma that the then-fringe music of country and western had. His songs "Wichita Lineman" and "Galveston" were all over the radio in 1968, after their debuts on the *Smothers Brothers* show. And by the time he got to his biggest hit, "By the Time I Get to Phoenix," Campbell's star was so strong that he was offered the role of a young deputy opposite John Wayne in 1969's Oscar-winner *True Grit*. The tongue-twistingly-titled *Summer Brothers Smothers Show* that replaced the regular *Comedy* Hour on Sunday nights in the summer of 1968 was hosted by Campbell. Its popularity was such that Campbell would have his own highly successful show on CBS by early 1969.

On the parent show by then, a lot of people—even the Smotherses, looking back—recall that they were a bit smug and self-satisfied, and not entirely sympathetic themselves, as the war jokes and political preaching became ever more the focal point of most of the routines. Years later, Dick Smothers even wondered if maybe the show's termination might have been for the best—there being nothing funny about things to come in the near future like Kent State or the bombing of Cambodia.

However, like a dog chasing its tail, by 1968, both the Smotherses and CBS were locked in a vicious no-win battle. The more that the brothers would want to book a rock act or do a political routine, the more relentlessly the censorship would come, making them insulted and ready to strike back in print, making CBS more determined to take revenge, and on, and on, and on. . . .

One of the reasons that lesser lights like the Standards and Practices department and letter-writing station managers had so much power within CBS at the time was that its top executive suites were a game of musical chairs. From the time CBS dismissed James "The Smiling Cobra" Aubrey in 1965 (he would later go on to head MGM for four years in the early '70s) until early 1969, CBS's presidents had come and gone, with none leaving any kind of substantial mark on the network.

But all that was about to change.

In early 1969, CBS appointed veteran station man and ad-sales executive Robert Wood to the job. Wood would later say to the *Los Angeles Times* in 1976, after taking an early retirement package at age fifty-one, that a lot of CBS's presidents and vice-presidents were "invisible"—that no one really knew that they'd been there after they were gone. And Wood was determined that "they'd know [he'd] been there" before his tenure was over.

While Wood was a conservative, Beverly Hills–raised country-club Republican, he also realized that the network was mired more deeply than ever in escapist, irrelevant fluff while America's most tumultuous era in a century raged around it. Wood knew that *The Smothers Brothers Comedy Hour* was one of the few breaths of fresh air on the CBS schedule, and one of the only CBS shows that came even close to NBC or ABC in younger viewers and city sophisticates.

But despite his desire to begin remaking CBS's schedule into a modern, up-to-date offering, by early 1969 the die was already cast for *The Smothers Brothers Comedy Hour*. Leigh French summed it up when she said that the fights weren't even about the quality of the scripts or the tired political controversies anymore. By the time Wood took over, "it became about *minding*," about putting the outspoken young comedians in their place and "showing them who was boss." The Smothers Brothers were making outside appeals to the FCC and running off at the mouth with Hollywood gossip columnists and underground political magazines, enraging breaches of decorum and authority in Wood's mind. Soon, Wood would "answer" the Smothers Brothers outspokenness in kind.

Meanwhile, Wood's second in command, CBS program czar Mike Dann and his colleague Perry Lafferty, had finally arranged for Tankersley's censorship department to be put in *its* place, and a "peace agreement" was starting to be implemented. In return for the relaxed rules, though, CBS insisted that the show be taped several weeks in advance of airtime, with the videotapes flown ("as if they were armistice documents," Dann later joked) by bonded messenger to CBS headquarters in Manhattan. This way, even if they didn't edit out the uncomfortable segments, the network would at least be prepared for what they were about to unfurl on the public, and could have press releases and soundbites at the ready when the Southern and midwestern stations inevitably fought back.

Ratings-wise, the show was still so popular with desirable viewers that CBS mounted a considerably less controversial spin-off of the show, giving Glen Campbell his own *Goodtime Hour*, which immediately established itself as a hit in February of 1969.

But fatefully, with the détente with Dann and Lafferty in place, and their old nemesis Lyndon Johnson finally forced into retirement, the Smothers Brothers went full throttle in their countercultural causes.

Two of the Smothers Brothers' most controversial guests: Harry Belafonte (*right*) and Joan Baez (*below*).

In the most infamous show of the new year, Joan Baez was their featured guest, and she dedicated a song to her husband, peace activist David Harris (who was serving a stiff jail term for aiding draft resisters at the time). CBS management was so shocked that it went back to its old ways, and deleted most of the "dedication." Tommy Smothers returned the favor by going to the National Broadcasters' Association and denouncing the network's actions, calling for greater creative control for actors and producers of TV series.

After the Joan Baez incident, any hope of restraining Robert Wood's tidal wave of wrath at the Smothers Brothers' defiance went right out the window. In March of 1969 CBS announced its 1969–70 schedule, with *The Smothers Brothers Comedy Hour* given a firm renewal on Dann and Lafferty's recommendation. But in early April, a videotape of one of the last planned shows of the 1968–69 season was delivered late to CBS's corporate offices in New York. A jubilant CBS attorney, who'd long wanted to stop the *Smothers* steamroller, reportedly leapt to his feet with glee. "We've finally got 'em!" he exclaimed.

Robert Wood couldn't have agreed more. On April 3, 1969, Wood announced that *The Smothers Brothers Comedy Hour* was cancelled due to breach of contract regarding the tape incident. The last show aired the following June. (In an interesting irony, Tommy Smothers successfully sued CBS on those same grounds of breach of contract. Tommy claimed that the so-called "late" tape was just a flimsy excuse to back out of the in-writing commitment CBS had made to the show's renewal, in their press release of the 1969–70 season. The jury—as well as the court of public opinion—agreed, granting the Smotherses close to a million dollars in damages.)

Following the sudden death of their CBS show, Tommy and Dick Smothers used their new time off to regroup and take in the enormity of what had happened to them. Many if not most entertainment trades expected NBC, or especially ABC, to snap up the show as soon as CBS had let it go. But ABC, who already had Johnny Cash, Englebert Humperdinck, the Lennon Sisters, and Tom Jones on their "youth-variety" plate, waited a full year before finally reinaugurating the Smothers Brothers' show and presented it as a summer replacement series. The network then made overtures to the Smotherses about installing them in a late-night talk show, to compete with NBC's Johnny Carson and CBS's Merv Griffin, both of which were doing double the ratings of ABC's *Dick Cavett Show*.

Fortunately for Dick Cavett, but unfortunately for the Smotherses, ABC changed their minds before the end of summer. No new variety shows would bow on ABC's fall 1970 schedule. Tommy Smothers then flew off on a solo effort, 1971's painfully of-its-time *Organic Prime-Time Space Ride*, in syndication for a year. In early 1975, NBC finally took its long-overdue crack at the duo with a short-lived variety hour slotted in *Laugh-In*'s old Monday night at 8:00 time slot. In 1988–89, the Smotherses marked the twentieth anniversary of their original effort on CBS with a limited series of shows and specials right back in their old homestead of Television City, stage 31.

The cancellation of the Smothers Brothers in 1969 was rightly viewed as a huge setback to cutting-edge comedy with bite and political satire on TV. However, the show's premature death probably did more than anything else to *help* the cause of modern, socially relevant television.

The backlash against the program's demise, and the controversy surrounding it, cast a public microscope on the inner workings of CBS's programming practices for the first time. When CBS elected to replace the show with the cracker-barrel comedy of *Hee-Haw* over the summer—combined with the fact that the overwhelming remainder of CBS's schedule already consisted of rural sitcoms—the snickering among influential TV critics went into maximum overdrive. By year's end, jokes were circulating that rechristened CBS as the "Country Broadcasting System." Snarkier wags opined that you really did "see B.S." on CBS.

Meanwhile, ABC's and NBC's salesmen were having a field day taking advantage of CBS's shortcomings among affluent, city-dwelling viewers and the youth market. The rival nets poked the discrepancy right in CBS's "eye," with young, trendy shows like *Partridge Family*, *Dating Game*, *The Music Scene*, *Laugh-In*, and *Mod Squad*.

Early in 1970, CBS called for a summit meeting of its top officials to deal with the crisis: network president Robert Wood, program chief Mike Dann, corporate vice-president Jack Schneider, station man Richard Jencks, and the Chairman of the Board himself, William S. Paley.

In an almost Shakespearean irony, the man who wielded the knife that killed *The Smothers Brothers Comedy Hour*, CBS prez Robert Wood, made it his priority to come up with a long-range plan to modernize CBS's image and attract a younger, more urban audience. As the 1970s got under way, the programming mission at CBS would be to win back sophisticated viewers and promote a newly relevant, up-to-date image.

Soon, old CBS standbys like *The Beverly Hillbillies*, *Green Acres*, *Petticoat Junction*, *Mayberry RFD*, *Family Affair*, and *The Jim Nabors Show* were out. *All in the Family*, *Sonny & Cher*, *M\*A\*S\*H*, and *Maude* were in, along with hard-hitting detective dramas like *Cannon* and *Kojak*, and several controversial Lily Tomlin specials. For most of the '70s, CBS not only featured shows with taboo issues like Vietnam, Watergate, urban crime, politics, sex, and religion—it led the way.

And it is not unreasonable to suggest that, if the Smothers Brothers hadn't forced CBS's hand, all those other groundbreaking shows might never have seen the light of day.

Even CBS itself recognized this fact. At their landmark studio complex Television City in Hollywood, it has always been a common practice to erect pictures of the stars that tape on each stage inside. When a star's show is cancelled, their picture is naturally taken down and replaced with whoever will be the next tenant—except for the Smothers Brothers. Only Carol Burnett was accorded the same honor. More than thirty-five years later, their pictures still stood at Television City, as a memorial to a show that was ahead of its time, died before its time, and changed the face of TV comedy for all time.

## MEMORABLE MOMENTS

### losses:

- Probably the most famous deletion from the show was the March 1969 episode where Joan Baez let loose on what she really thought of the people who'd locked up her husband, anti-draft activist David Harris. The edit was so sloppy that there was a noticeable gap in camera angles and in what Joan's mouth was "saying" as opposed to what was coming out over the sound.
- The show put together a fascinating think-piece of a musical sketch in 1968, where Harry Belafonte sang a Caribbean song about a carnival—while footage from riots were projected in back of him.
- A relatively harmless 1967 sketch about film censorship, featuring Tommy Smothers and Elaine May as movie critics, was also summarily axed from the show. This was the first incident where the program was edited not because someone actually said a dirty word or gave an obscene gesture, but because the *attitude* of the sketch, the *viewpoint* it represented, was offensive and challenging to the CBS powers-that-be. It wouldn't be the last.
- Even kindly old Dr. Spock was too controversial for CBS when he came aboard the Smothers Brothers stage. The sixty-five-year-old child-rearing icon was opposed to the war in Vietnam, and especially to the unfair way in which the draft was being applied, with rich kids and scholarship winners deferred from service while poor black and Latino men were being sent by the dozen. The interview that Tommy and Dickie did with the doctor ended up on the cutting-room floor.
- What on earth could be "obscene" or "controversial" about the simple wish "Please talk peace!" that Tommy signed off with on a "Salute to Mothers" in 1968? Even Lawrence Welk featured the moving hymn "A Prayer for Peace" on his patriotic 1970 Thanksgiving show! Once again, it was the 'tude that the Smotherses were sportin', not the actual words or actions, that felled this one. Broadcast Standards got out the red pen and scissors once again.
- Tommy Smothers once introduced a rock act by describing their sound as "mind-blowing," and CBS sure blew his mind when it wiped out the reference. In those days using words that even hinted at drug use in a rock context (as Jim Morrison learned in a famous 1967 Ed Sullivan Show appearance) were strictly forbidden.

## wins:

- After a protracted battle with Standards and Practices, legendary folk singer Pete Seeger was permitted to come on the show to sing his ultra-controversial hit, "Waist Deep in the Big Muddy." It was a song about an egotistical blood-and-guts commander, who could see well ahead that his troops were about to drown in mud and quicksand, and "the big fool said to 'push on'" anyway (ordering his troops to certain death). The song was a blatant metaphor for the way the Vietnam War was being run, and the relentless escalations that the draft boards would order, only for the ante to be matched accordingly by the North Vietnamese.

- Young (but prematurely gray-haired) comedian David Steinberg's most popular character on the show was his young liberal minister, whose take on religion made him worthy of excommunication to a lot of the Religious Right. His sermons (which look surprisingly respectful by today's standards) poked gentle fun at absolutist Bible literalism (the infamous "Moses and the Burning Bush" sketch), and the maverick young cleric had no qualms about performing interracial marriages, either. Plenty of Bible Belt affiliates were thrilled to see peacenik Pastor David get defrocked when the show went off in 1969, but his "sermonettes" stayed in the show right up to the last.

- The Jefferson Airplane sang their rock anthem "White Rabbit" despite the objections of censors who thought the song too drug-friendly (and who had little use for counterculture diva Grace Slick, who often "flashed" her audience, and had a fondness for leather S&M motorcycle outfits). Still, their psychedelic-color rendition of the song on the *Smothers* show rocked in every sense of the word!

- Mason Williams, wearing an artist's smock and sitting on the floor of a darkened set, read a haunting "poem" about censorship, holding a pair of stainless-steel surgical scissors for effect. It was perhaps the Smotherses' most blatant reference to their troubles with CBS; the network surprisingly displayed a much-welcome sense of fair play by allowing them to retain the segment.

- Mason Williams also featured in one of the show's most breathtaking features, when he played the debut of his 1968 acoustic-guitar hit, backed by symphony horns and strings, the awesome and aptly named classic-rock instrumental "Classical Gas."

- Toward the end there was an "Our Town"-like montage sketch with Steve Martin (as the husband in an interracial marriage) and a Southern sheriff, disgusted by the "pre-verts" that were taking over everything, among other characters set in counterpoint to "The Times They Are a-Changin'." While openly progressive, this memorable sketch, like *All in the Family* a year and a half later, transcended us-versus-them proselytizing. It was a moving state-of-the-union address on the stresses that change brought to both the right and left of the political "fence," as the '60s drew to a close.

## WHERE ARE THEY NOW?

- Tommy and Dickie continued their careers in casinos, resorts, and nightclubs, and made regular PBS appearances. Tommy also set up a vineyard north of San Francisco, where his not-too-far-away neighbors were people like David Clayton-Thomas and Raymond Burr, and became known as an expert yo-yo artist (appropriate, considering that a lot of people thought he was a yo-yo all along).

- Pat Paulsen, alas, lost his bid for the presidency, but had a short-lived ABC sitcom and made frequent appearances on shows like *Gong Show*, *Merv Griffin*, and *Sha Na Na*. Paulsen was much beloved by everyone on the Smothers Brothers' set, and after his death some thirty-odd years later, Tommy referred to him as the "color" in the *Smothers Brothers* show's "rainbow."

- Bob Einstein, who played tall, humor-impaired doofus policeman Officer Judy, went on to produce several other short-lived variety efforts and reinvented himself as inept stuntman "Super Dave" Osborne in several pay-TV comedy specials.

- Steve Martin, of course, went on to be one of the premiere stand-up comedians and comedy-movie actors of the 1970s and '80s, and hosted *Saturday Night Live* more than anyone else in history.

- Rob Reiner was barely out of work from the *Smothers Brothers* show before he became Mike "Meathead" Stivic on *All in the Family* from 1970 to '78. He went on to become one of the hottest movie directors in Hollywood, with films like *The Princess Bride*, *This is Spinal Tap*, *Stand By Me*, *When Harry Met Sally*, and *Misery*, to name a few.

- Leigh French appeared in lower-budget movies like *Halloween II* and worked steadily in voice-overs and commercials for many years.

- Jennifer Warnes, known as Jennifer Warren when she was a young regular on the show at barely twenty, went on to become a hugely popular singer in the late '70s and '80s, with hits like her Grammy- and Oscar-winning duet with Bill Medley, "Up Where We Belong."

# The mod squad

## ABC's Late-sixties Attempts at Flower-Power Variety

After conservative CBS "scooped" ABC with their groundbreaking 1967 Smothers Brothers effort, followed less than a year later by NBC's equally stereotype-smashing *Laugh-In,* ABC executives were in a bit of a panic. For all of the decade, ABC had built its reputation on being the youngest, trendiest network, with up-to-the-minute vitality and *American Bandstand*-era teen appeal.

But by 1968, ABC found itself with perhaps the stodgiest variety lineup of the Big Three, with only the venerable Lawrence Welk and the old-fashioned, Sullivan-style *Hollywood Palace* as clear hits. Their previous attempts at rock-music shows and youth variety in prime time, like the excellent *Shindig,* had been here-today, gone-tomorrow fads.

Prior to catching up with CBS and NBC in the mid 1970s (by which time most of ABC's variety efforts had disappeared), ABC was by far the least desirable network for an established star to use for a showcase. If a truly big name—a Sinatra or a Streisand—had expressed interest in having their own show back in 1968 or 1970, ABC was so far behind CBS and NBC, it's likely their business managers might not even have *asked* the third-place network. This left ABC able to draw only on the talents of up-and-coming performers who hadn't really "made it" yet, or performers heading toward the sunset of their careers.

There was one other little snag: ABC wanted youth-appeal shows, but they didn't want shows that would jeopardize their American Pie image of squeaky-clean, "Brady Bunch"–era suburban youthfulness. Bubblegum rock and teen idols, yes—but psychedelic Vietnam protests á la the Smothers Brothers, or the satirical swipes of *Laugh-In,* or the frank grown-up sexuality of Dean Martin? Not a chance!

In their late-'60s variety-show efforts, ABC tried to have its cake (youthful relevance, up-to-date performers) and eat it too (nonthreatening, upper-middle-class wholesomeness). It succeeded at neither. The following shows were the casualties.

## Operation: Entertainment

Network: ABC; On the air: January 5, 1968–January 31, 1969

Chuck Barris, who would later achieve pop-culture immortality in his own right hosting the hilarious 1976–80 *Gong Show,* produced this Vietnam-era effort—a sort of younger, more mod (and lower-budget) version of Bob Hope's wartime entertainment revues. The comedy and music show was shot and staged at various military bases, with a new guest-star host each week. Jim Lange, the host of Barris's firstborn property *The Dating Game,* frequently appeared, as did his *Newlywed*

*Game* counterpart Bob Eubanks (whose prior claim to fame was having been the L.A. DJ who brought the Beatles to Los Angeles). A group of skimpily clad young go-go girls, dubbed the Operation Entertainment Girls, added some new talent and sex appeal, while the Terry Gibbs band provided the backup.

## This Is Tom Jones

*Network: ABC; On the air: February 7, 1969—January 15, 1971*

Scheduled as a replacement for *Operation: Entertainment,* this glossy London-produced entry was considered quite a coup for ABC when it was released during the height of February "sweeps" in early 1969. CBS was also busy launching a high-profile variety hour that same month, tailored around another then-huge young pop star (Glen Campbell). Of course, a "competition" of sorts developed in the press, as to whether either, neither, or both young rock singers could successfully carry over to weekly TV.

After a successful tryout against the fading days of the 1968–69 season, and holding down its

Despite being opposite the powerhouse CBS sitcom *Gomer Pyle,* Jones's show took off, its target audience being the antithesis of *Pyle*'s elderly, country-oriented main viewership. It was also the closest of ABC's shows to a truly sophisticated, grown-up effort besides *Johnny Cash,* and the closest besides David Steinberg's *Music Scene* to targeting a rock-influenced, perhaps even counterculture-friendly audience. Most importantly, Jones was by far the biggest established "name" ABC had signed for a variety show, with top hits on the radio, a gigantic fan base (especially among young women), and sold-out concert dates.

After a successful tryout against the fading days of the 1968–69 season, and holding down its time slot over the summer, ABC shifted the show to a considerably more competitive Thursday-night berth. It was ideally placed from 9:00 to 10:00 (thereby allowing its viewership to switch over to NBC's similarly sophisticated *Dean Martin* at 10:00 if it chose to), with the youthful and up-to-date comedies *That Girl* and *Bewitched* providing its lead-in.

During the show's second season in 1969–70, *This Is Tom Jones* really came into its own. It was far fresher and younger than any show since the *Smothers Brothers,* and even faster paced. The Ace Trucking Company, an improvisational comedy group with four guys and a girl, joined on for more and more comedy sketches, with riffs on politcs, the counterculture, and swinging London. Each show kicked off with a hard-rocking opening number (often Jones's number-one hit "It's Not Unusual") with Tom's gyrating hips and cool moves going full throttle, and the shrieking young fans going out of their minds. The clear promise the show had and its young audience (many of whom had little use for most else on TV at the time) prompted ABC to approve two other cutting-edge series, *The Johnny Cash Show* and *The Englebert Humperdinck Show.*

Nonetheless, under heavy fire from NBC's *Ironside,* the show averaged a 25 percent share of the audience—which was fair considering the circumstances even in those three-network days, but also considerably less than the rock-star, *Laugh-In* size numbers ABC expected from the top-billed program. The show was shifted back to Friday nights at 10:00 in September 1970, capping off the first year of ABC's near-legendary Friday night schedule that included *Brady Bunch, Partridge Family, Nanny & the Professor, That Girl,* and *Love, American Style.*

But instead of being the show's second wind, the move proved to be its rapid downfall. Despite the star's being a marquee name and one of the top draws in Las Vegas, New York, and the Sunset Strip, the numbers just didn't add up for *This Is Tom Jones.* In January 1971 the show was removed from the ABC schedule as quietly as it had loudly burst on the scene two years before. While fans cried foul, what wasn't known at the time to the general public was that this was merely the first step in ABC's changing of their entire scheduling strategy. By the following September, ABC would eliminate every variety show and nighttime game show remaining on its prime-time schedule.

## (Jimmy Durante Presents) The Lennon Sisters Hour

*Network: ABC; On the air: September 26, 1969–July 4, 1970*

*"Da luffly"* Lennon Sisters left their longtime patron Lawrence Welk in early 1968, after a dozen years as his show's most popular act. The young girls who had first appeared on Mister Welk's show on Christmas of 1955 were all grown up and understandably wanted to have more direct control of their careers, as well as free time to choose from the options available to them.

Welk also was initially displeased with the young ladies' choices in music to record in their later years. Like most women of their age, the now young-adult Lennons were enthusiastic about doo-wop, the Beach Boys, and the Beatles. The fashion-conscious foursome also wanted to wear the miniskirts and pantsuits that were all the rage in the late '60s, and even semiscandalized some of Welk's oldest viewers when they sang a number wearing modern bathing suits in his 1965 color premiere. In many ways, though, Lawrence Welk still thought of the Lennons as "girls"—not young women—and he felt that these weren't exactly the kind of things that their audience would accept from them.

After a year of occasional TV specials and personal appearances in shows and revues in Vegas and Tahoe and across the country, the Lennon sisters landed back at ABC in 1969. The networks offered them their own variety hour to do with as they would. But there was a catch. To broaden the show's appeal and give the young gals the chemistry of an established old pro to play off of, the network signed seventy-six-year-old vaudeville legend Jimmy Durante to costar in and "present" the program.

*The Lennon Sisters Hour* proved to be all of what the Lennons had hoped for in their final year with Welk—modern soft-rock songs as well as the old favorites, big dance numbers, up-to-date fashions, creative control, and Carol Burnett–style comedy skits with guest stars. And of course, the interplay between salty old-timer Durante and the sweet young Lennon ladies.

But while the girls gave all of their considerable talents, the over-the-top camp classic just never achieved the recognition or cachet of the NBC and CBS shows. To start with, the show was scheduled on Friday nights, a hard place for a new show to get a foothold. ABC tried bolstering the program at mid-season by slipping the Lennons in right behind their old maestro Lawrence Welk. Scores improved somewhat, but slotted against the final days of heartland fave *Petticoat Junction,* followed by pistol-hot detective drama *Mannix* over on CBS, a passing grade just wasn't gonna happen. On Independence Day 1970, *The Lennon Sisters Hour* faded away.

Years later, the Lennons revealed an especially shocking and poignant postscript to the story of their 1969–70 show during a 1993 interview on fellow variety-show queen Vicki Lawrence's daytime talk show. The ladies told Vicki that starting late in their tenure on the *Welk* show, an obsessed fan (whom they later found out had a history of severe mental illness) began sending them obscene messages and sexually harassing "fan" letters.

The girls initially wrote the man off as just another weirdo of the type that stars have to put up with. But in August of 1969—just days after the Manson atrocities in Beverly Hills—the stalker managed to follow the ladies' father, Santa Monica Chamber of Commerce president William Lennon, to his country club, where he had a golf date. He approached the elder Lennon in the parking lot and picked a fight with him. Then the madman drew a gun and shot William Lennon point-blank.

Despite frantic efforts to save him, the fifty-three-year-old Lennon died later that day. (The gunman, who escaped at the time, committed suicide a few days later.) Almost unbearably tragic, too, was the fact that Lennon's son, sixteen-year-old Dan Lennon (the younger brother of the girls), was working as a caddy at the country club and horrifiedly witnessed his father's murder.

The fact that the four ladies were even able to continue with their normal lives, let alone star in a nationally televised show that was taping (at that very time) for nearly a year, is a testament to the unique talent and strength of the Lennon sisters. Surely nothing could have made their father prouder of them.

## The Music Scene

*Network: ABC; On the air: September 22, 1969–January 12, 1970*
Many, if not most, in the industry expected that ABC would steal away CBS's Top Thirty *Smothers Brothers Comedy Hour* as soon as CBS cancelled it, the show being a much more natural fit for ABC than for conservative, pre–*All in the Family* and *Sonny & Cher* CBS. But that didn't happen until a year later. The net came close, however, when it signed *Smothers Brothers* regular David Steinberg

to host an unusually formatted music show that premiered that fall of 1969. The show would be paired with a "groovy" take on the old *Gilligan's Island* theme of stranded castaways, called *The New People* (except in this case the castaways were all sexy, mod young people in the thirty-and-under category). It also had a forty-five-minute running time, rounding out the 7:30–9:00 Monday hour.

The twenty-six-year-old, handsome, and irreverent Steinberg was an ideal host choice for the program, especially considering that the young comedian was a trumpet enthusiast himself. (He was going to show his stuff as a jazz musician in a planned Smothers Brothers sketch, but the show was cancelled beforehand). As well as being musically literate, Steinberg was the anchor of a troupe of young comedians that would appear in "runner" sketches interspersed throughout the show—a group that included a young, up-and-coming comedienne named Lily Tomlin. The show also had one of the youngest production teams in Hollywood, with twentysomething producer Stan Harris in charge of the program along with producing partner Ken Fritz.

ABC showed either unbelievable chutzpah (or unbelievable stupidity) in scheduling the fresh-man series smack opposite *Laugh-In,* in the vain hope that it would siphon away younger and hip-per viewers from that show. Making things even more absurd, the youthful duo's lead-out on Monday nights was the glitzy nighttime soap opera *The Survivors,* perhaps the one show on all tele-vision guaranteed to repulse hippie viewers even more than the CBS country sitcoms. *The Music Scene* had its volume turned down permanently in December of 1969—which was highly unfortu-nate, since the show was unquestionably the best and most unvarnished TV presentation of the acid rock and hardcore jazz/R&B of the late '60s, outside PBS and BBC specials. Janis Joplin appeared in a particularly memorable, harrowing performance with Big Brother and the Holding Company, belting out her incomparable versions of "Summertime" and "Try Just a Little Bit Harder."

The show's rapid failure was not a referendum on the talent it contained. Just a few weeks after production ceased, Lily Tomlin was given an audition by none other than *The Music Scene*'s arch-nemesis *Laugh-In,* and the rest, as they say, is history. Steinberg went on to a highly successful career in comedy clubs and Vegas, writing, and in occasional TV appearances. And producer Stan Harris had several pick-up writing and producing jobs after, and was picked less than three years later by producer Burt Sugarman to be the show-runner of his far more successful and influential *Midnight Special* on NBC from 1972 to '81.

## The Englebert Humperdinck Show

*Network: ABC; On the air: January 22, 1970–September 19, 1970*
Premiering the same night as ABC's Johnny Cash variety show (immediately following Cash at 10:00), this show was actually the surer bet of the two to succeed in the minds of most TV indus-

try insiders. It had the extra added value of having its costly budget partially defrayed by London production for British TV. And more importantly, it could feed off both Cash's 9:00 audience and that of Cash's competition, NBC's similar-appeal *Kraft Music Hall.*

Most important of all, sixties crooner Humperdinck was a sexy, suave performer with across-the-board appeal, as opposed to the edgy, controversial persona of the Man in Black. But that may have been the show's fatal flaw. In a year that boasted a minimum of one variety show per night each and every night of the week, *The Englebert Humperdinck Show* had little to recommend it above the crowd. The young folk-rock fans and hardcore country enthusiasts who had made the Cash show appointment TV likely found little simpatico with the glitzy, shagadelic Humperdinck affair.

After a very strong start, the show began slipping more and more in popularity each week. By the end of the season, most of its viewers had already said "aloha" to the series, returning to its formidable *Hawaii Five-0* competition. A switch to Saturday nights following Lawrence Welk was to no avail, as the Lennon Sisters' variety show had already failed in the time period. The same Saturday that Englebert departed, a young lady named Mary Richards threw her hat in the air for the first time. And from that point on until *The Love Boat* sailed in 1977, ABC would be forced to essentially concede Saturday nights to CBS.

# The Carol Burnett Show

## Vital Stats

**STARRING**
Carol Burnett, Tim Conway, Harvey Korman,
Vicki Lawrence, Lyle Waggoner

**ON THE AIR**
September 11, 1967–September 8, 1979

**NETWORKS**
CBS (1967–78), ABC (1979)

**ANNOUNCER**
Ernie Anderson

**MUSIC AND DANCE**
The Harry Zimmerman Orchestra (to 1971); The Peter Matz
Orchestra (1971–79); The Ernie Flatt Dancers

**ORIGINATION**
CBS Television City, Stage 33

"I'm so glad we had
this time together."

"Cootchie-cootchie!" Carol as Charo (*above*); getting hip with Sonny and Cher . . . and Harvey (*left*); and as CBS's most talented cleaning lady (*below*).

This was TV's quintessential variety show. Other ones, like *Lawrence Welk* and *Ed Sullivan*, ran longer; others, like *Laugh-In* and *Dean Martin*, had higher ratings; and others still, like the *Smothers Brothers* and *Saturday Night Live*, were hipper and more socially relevant. But no other variety show in the history of television is remembered as fondly as *The Carol Burnett Show*. For nearly twelve years, Burnett's show was the ultimate in "appointment" variety TV, with an unparalleled supporting cast of comedy blackbelts like Harvey Korman, Vicki Lawrence, Lyle Waggoner, and Tim Conway.

And just as her longtime Saturday night neighbor Lawrence Welk often referred to his cast as a "Musical Family," the Carol Burnett crew was far more than just a faceless repertory company to her thirty million fans. They were a part of America's family too—Vicki, the kid sister; Lyle, the "golden boy"; Tim, the crazy uncle; and Carol and Harvey, the mature but unpredictable couple.

Carol Burnett was born on April 26, 1933, in San Antonio, Texas. Her childhood was a turbulent one—both of her parents battled alcoholism as the South and Southwest faced the twin devils of the Dust Bowl and the Great Depression. As a little girl, Carol moved in with her grandmother, who lived in an apartment just north of the fabled intersection of Hollywood and Highland in Los Angeles. Carol's grandmother was enchanted by the then relatively new medium of the movies, just then entering its golden age, and she shared her love affair with her granddaughter.

Carol later recalled that it wasn't unusual for the two of them to see as many as five or six shows per week at the many movie theatres that studded Hollywood Boulevard. Carol drank in the world of classic films as a much-needed escape from the depressing apartment and her early life's challenges. From the musicals of Fred and Ginger and Mickey and Judy, to the dark film noir and suspense of Alfred Hitchcock, to the sophisticated adventures of Bogey and Bergman, Carol was there—and taking mental notes. By the time she finished high school in the film capital of the world, Carol had no question in her mind that she too wanted to be an entertainer. And she was developing the skills and talent to back it up.

In the middle 1950s, the aspiring actress moved to New York, which was then the live-TV capital of the world, in addition to being the center of radio and theatre. Carol's specialties were physical and musical comedy, and she knew that the Broadway of the 1950s was the ultimate testing ground for those skills.

After years of hard work, in 1958, Carol finally received her big break, singing the bizarre novelty number, "I Made a Fool of Myself over John Foster Dulles" on Jack Paar's *Tonight Show*. Guest shots on other shows followed, most notably on Ed Sullivan's and Steve Allen's, after which she was spotted and hired as a regular on Garry Moore's CBS variety show.

In addition to becoming the most popular performer on the Moore program (often eclipsing even Garry Moore himself), Carol met a handsome, thirtyish production staffer on the show named Joe Hamilton. Romance soon blossomed, and the two were married in 1962. Garry Moore was unrestrained in his praise of Carol's talents, and Carol would consider Garry her mentor and one of her closest friends until his death in 1993.

"She has simply got to be a star," Moore explained, in a 1961 *TV Guide* interview. "She's wholesome . . . she's cute . . . and she's disciplined. She's got a glimmering, but no real idea of just how important she's become." Garry saw to it that his new young find had the best agents and frequent exposure on other shows, including Sullivan and Paar, and on Moore's other series, the Goodson-Todman game show *I've Got a Secret*. (Even while she was busy with her own series, she would also occasionally visit Moore on his final show, the 1969–78 version of *To Tell the Truth*.) Carol also became a virtual regular on the even more popular *Password*, and became a best friend of host Allen Ludden and his wife, comedy legend Betty White.

Despite all this exposure, in 1963 Carol went on record in *TV Guide*, saying that she would "NEVER do a regular TV series. Period. Once you've been a [sitcom] character, you're that character for *life*. They'd probably name me Gertrude or Agnes, and that's all I'd be forever."

But while Carol was allergic to the idea of a repetitive sitcom format, her highly rated variety specials (including one with her best friend Julie Andrews) and enormously popular guest appearances on other shows convinced CBS that Carol was just too good to let go. Carol and Joe were offered a development deal with CBS for their TV specials, and CBS saw to it that it included a relatively standard (under the circumstances) clause—one that would eventually change the course of both of their lives.

It said that if they exercised their option, CBS would commit to thirteen weeks of a prime-time show Carol would star in, the concept of which would be dictated by a meeting between herself and the network. The clause was just an enticement to keep Carol within the CBS stable of stars, lest she be tempted to entertain offers from NBC and ABC or from movie studios. But it had a deadline for action that was fast approaching by the time the calendar turned to 1967.

While CBS still wanted Carol primarily for a *Lucy*-style situation comedy, Joe Hamilton approached the network with a compromise. He wanted to take advantage of the tremendous opportunity for them to have their own TV show, and he felt sure that he could convince Carol to do a weekly series—but only if it gave her the chance to utilize all of her talents, from singing and dancing, to stand-up comedy and audience participation, to the sketch comedy that had been her first love from the Golden Age of Television.

It would be a prime-time variety hour, starring Carol and a company of regulars, with weekly guest stars, that Joe would own and produce for the network. Despite CBS's reservations about a woman carrying a prime-time variety hour—

only Dinah Shore had accomplished that successfully up to then—the network finally agreed.

With a growing family plus the mortgage on a brand-new house in ultra-posh Brentwood, Carol didn't need much convincing to take the deal. Assured of her creative control and a freewheeling variety format, Carol "pressed the button" in her contract faster than the timer switch on an electric clothes dryer. CBS kept its word and set aside a dream Monday-night time slot following *Lucy* and *Andy Griffith*.

On Monday, September 11, 1967, *The Carol Burnett Show* premiered with Carol and a small repertory company of regulars—Harvey Korman, Lyle Waggoner, and an eighteen-year old theatre arts major and "Miss Fireball" named Vicki Lawrence, along with guest star Jim Nabors of *Gomer Pyle* fame. Nabors would launch a tradition of being the first guest star on the first show of each new season for the rest of the series' run.

Other stars who guested so frequently that they were virtual regulars were Tim Conway, Ken Berry, Betty White, Eydie Gorme, and Steve Lawrence. (Conway became a full-fledged regular in 1975.) Right from the very first, Carol facilitated a familiar, family atmosphere on her show, with her audience Q&A sessions and her open, friendly approach.

Each week, the show would tackle a new set of comedy skits and sketches, from Carol's famous parodies of classic movies and TV shows, to one-time-only skits and character studies. But also, over the next several years, the show would introduce a company of running characters and sketches that would become some of the most valuable players in television's comedy hall of fame.

From 1967 to 1971, Carol capped off CBS's unstoppable Monday-night lineup of *Gunsmoke*, *Lucy*, *Mayberry RFD*, and *Doris Day*. Then Carol spent a year and a half kicking off CBS's Wednesday night schedule, until *Sonny & Cher* took over the real estate at Christmastime. As 1972 ended, Carol was switched to the time slot where she would achieve her greatest fame and success—Saturday nights at 10:00. There she would wrap up what many people believe—to this day—was the best single lineup of television shows ever.

Two of the most influential comedies in the history of television started the evening off, back-to-back. *All in the Family* opened Saturday night at 8:00, followed directly by *M*A*S*H* at 8:30. Mary Tyler Moore's legendary sitcom turned the world on at 9:00, followed by the buttoned-down mind of Bob Newhart (and Suzanne Pleshette) at 9:30. And at the pinnacle of it all was Carol—her comedy timing and musical variety by now refined to an art form. Some of the trendiest sophisticates even admitted that it wasn't even all that hip to go out on Saturday nights anymore, with this first incarnation of true "must-see TV."

By the fall of 1975, *The Carol Burnett Show* was the longest-running prime-time network show still on the air besides *Walt Disney*, and it was at the height of its popularity. This was both a blessing and a curse. Half a decade earlier, there had been sixteen prime-time variety shows on the networks, not to mention three prime-time game shows. Now, there were only six variety hours in prime time, and that included the non-network *Lawrence Welk Show* and *Hee-Haw*. At the 1975–76 Emmy Awards, *The Carol Burnett Show* was the only musical/variety show nominated in its category—except for a brand-new show that had premiered on NBC late-night in the fall of 1975.

*Saturday Night Live* swept the Emmy award categories for writing, acting, and music in 1976. The new, hip, rock-and-roll show revitalized the variety-show genre, and its late-night time slot gave it the freedom to tackle issues and book rock-star guests that were definitely "not ready for prime time." With the variety-show format on the decline, Carol began to feel the pressure on her popular series.

Other performers might have been tempted to call it quits right then, and merely rest on their laurels. Instead, Carol rose to the challenge of the newer, younger shows to prove that her show could still keep its title as the leader of the league. In the fall of 1976, NBC broke ratings records with the network television premiere of the movie masterpiece *Gone with the Wind*—and Carol and the crew took advantage of the golden opportunity.

Carol's takeoff on the film classic, "Went with the Wind," would be the show's most-remembered moment, and deservedly so. Dinah Shore guested as goody-two-shoes Miss Nellie (who blew a kiss goodbye in her death scene, after finally knocking her nasty sister-in-law down the staircase), and Harvey gave a flawless impersonation of Clark Gable as "Ratt" Butler. Tim was cast as "Brashley" Wilkes, and Vicki played the hysterical maid. It's hard to choose the funniest moment of the skit, filled as it was with laughter: Carol takes the punch meant for "Brashley" and tumbles down the staircase in a hoop skirt, "Starlett" makes her dramatic entrance down the stairs in her "curtain rod" dress, and many more. The skit ranks alongside even the classics from *Lucy* herself as one of the funniest moments in all television history.

A year after the *SNL* sweep, in 1977, Carol reclaimed her crown as the gold standard of comedy/variety, with several sweeping Emmy wins despite firm competition from deserving variety title-weights like *Saturday Night Live*, *SCTV*, and *The Muppet Show*. But the victory among her peers was balanced by the winds of defeat on several other important fronts.

By 1977, the immortal CBS Saturday-night lineup (which Carol had helped anchor since 1972) was coming apart at the seams. Mary Richards had already thrown her hat in the air for the last time. Bob Newhart and Bea Arthur were getting ready to announce that 1978 would see the end of both of their shows. And *All in the Family* and *M\*A\*S\*H* had been moved to keep other nights nailed down for CBS. Without the benefit of her former dream lead-ins, Carol's show began to struggle in the ratings.

Some of Carol's great classics: Queen Elizabeth meets Tim's "Hollow Hero" *(top)*; Mama's Family in 1974 *(left)*; and silent-film star Nora Desmond, with a face that puts words to shame *(bottom)*.

The newly top-rated ABC network was also making inroads with their brand-new romantic comedy *The Love Boat,* which began soundly sinking the Burnett show just a few weeks into the new season. By Christmastime, Carol was switched to a Sunday night time slot, as *Kojak* left Sunday night patrol to shoot it out with *The Love Boat* and *Fantasy Island* for its last few months on the air. The ratings instantly shot upward. But CBS had dominated Sundays for years, and it was no secret to Carol that the network had no plans of using one of their choicest time slots just to keep a decade-old show alive.

In June of 1977, Carol's longtime righthand man Harvey Korman had to leave the show on a fulltime basis in order to begin filming the Mel Brooks comedy classic *High Anxiety,* along with Brooks, Madeline Kahn, Dick Van Patten, and Cloris Leachman. (Fortunately, Dick Van Dyke, whose NBC variety series had just been canceled, agreed to come on board for the final season.)

Last but not least, Carol was just plain exhausted. After eleven years of singing and dancing and backbreaking physical comedy sketches, the forty-five-year-old Carol wanted to have some time for herself to concentrate on her family.

After discussing the situation with her husband and business partner Joe, Carol made a decision. In early 1978, Carol walked into CBS Television City to Stage 33, which had been her second home for nearly eleven years. She made an announcement: When the twenty-four episodes of the 1977–78 season finished taping, *The Carol Burnett Show* would go off the air. The decision stunned Tim Conway (along with the rest of Hollywood). "Well, she's crazy," he half joked, trying to lighten the mood. "We can commit her, and then do the show after she gets out!"

For the last episodes, CBS moved the show once again, this time to one of their most problematic time slots, Wednesday nights at 8:00 (a time slot that Carol had actually held down in 1971–72 despite stiff competition). It remained there until the fall shows premiered in September. That coming Sunday, a new, controversial, and sexy five-part miniseries would be riding to the rescue—about a rough-hewn, fractious family of oil barons in the contemporary South, which CBS was hoping to spin off into a weekly series. It was called *Dallas.*

On March 29, 1978, Carol Burnett sat down on the floor of Stage 33 and, on a darkened set, sang her theme song, "I'm So Glad We Had This Time Together," for what many thought would be the last time. It capped off a two-hour special that aired from 9:00–11:00 that night, replete with classic clips and bloopers from her earlier shows. Appropriately, the comedienne who had forged an unequalled respect and rapport from her studio audience (to say nothing of her home viewers) sang the song directly to them, looking her audience face to face. The bittersweet lyrics had their truest meaning that night, as Carol bid a fond farewell to her viewers, and the show, after eleven unforgettable years.

But, as one famous reference guide noted, "that wasn't quite the end." Reruns of the show kicked off CBS's Wednesday night lineup for the rest of the summer. And by early 1979, Carol was reconsidering whether semiretiring from TV had been a wise decision after all. By that summer, Carol was back, this time on ABC, starting off their Saturday-night lineup with *Carol Burnett & Company*. Vicki Lawrence and Tim Conway remained, along with Craig Richard Nelson (not to be confused with actor Craig T. Nelson) and veteran character actor Kenneth Mars (the nutty Nazi in the 1967 movie *The Producers*). Announcer Ernie Anderson also returned—appropriately, since he was the longtime voice of ABC's flagship Los Angeles station KABC-7.

However, by 1979 TV had newer kids in its comedy campground, such as *The Love Boat*, *The Dukes of Hazzard*, *Three's Company*, *Soap*, and *Diff'rent Strokes*. The growing cable-TV industry was already rife with plans for music-video channels, and Carol's own personal crises (such as a rocky marriage to Joe Hamilton and eldest daughter Carrie's battles with substance abuse) had only gotten worse. The show that Carol had evidently hoped would keep her busy and lift up her spirits ended up only sapping her strength—which she needed now more than ever.

On September 8, 1979, just one week shy of her show's twelfth anniversary, Carol finally said goodbye for real. And what a goodbye it was! Oscar nominee (and future winner) Sally Field was her last guest, and the show hit one home run after another. It featured probably the funniest *As the Stomach Turns* parody ever (with Sally as a Miss America on the run for refusing to give up her title, Vicki as the butch bitch from the pageant out to get her, and a cross-dressing Ken Mars as a female fashion consultant). All that, plus a musical salute to "Palimony" (this was during the trial of actor Lee Marvin and his "divorcing" life partner Michele Triola), and a music-video spoof with a liberated, singing Sally walking out on her hippie boyfriend (Tim).

Very few shows can claim the luxury of going out on top. But when Carol Burnett's show said its final "so long" that night in 1979, it did just that.

Carol spent the 1980s on the Broadway stage and making movie appearances. Just before closing up shop in 1979, she made the landmark TV movie *Friendly Fire* with Ned Beatty, based on the true story of a couple who lost their son in Vietnam. In 1982, she was an outrageous Miss Hannigan in John Huston's big-screen adaptation of *Annie*, only to make a riveting dramatic turn in the TV movie *Life of the Party: The Story of Beatrice*, about a real-life recovering alcoholic who started a sobriety program for women. She also made frequent appearances on her favorite show, *All My Children*, as carnival runner Verla Grubbs.

By the end of that year, a spin-off of sorts of *The Carol Burnett Show* was also launched on NBC, based on the show's most popular sketch. *Mama's Family*, starring Vicki Lawrence (as well as frequent Burnett guest Ken Berry) ran on NBC and in first-run syndication all the way into 1990, enjoying top ratings and cult appeal from start to finish.

Starlett O'Hara (*right*) says hello in 1976;
Carol (*above*) says goodbye in 1979.

Also in 1990, Carol Burnett was lured back to network TV once again. Carol became one of the few performers to make a three-network trifecta, this time slotted on NBC's *Golden Girls*-anchored, powerhouse Saturday night lineup. In *Carol & Company*, Carol headlined a half-hour comedy anthology, with Terry Kiser, Richard Kind, Anita Barone, Maegan Fay, and future HBO stars Peter Krause (*Six Feet Under*) and Jeremy Piven (*Entourage*).

Taking note of the success of *Carol & Company*, CBS made Carol an "offer she couldn't refuse." A one-hour variety show, just like the old days—but supposedly modernized for the '90s audience. Ironically, it replaced the program that had replaced *The Carol Burnett Show* on CBS back in 1978, *Dallas*, which had just ridden off into the sunset in May 1991.

Unfortunately, the new and improved Carol Burnett show of 1991 didn't even come close to equaling *Dallas*'s Friday night scores, which had already been on the decline. Even more tellingly, it failed badly in its assigned mission to dent the ratings of ABC's "TGIF" Friday night family comedies. The show was off the air by Christmas.

Carol had also been dealt a horrible blow earlier that year. Even following their divorce in the early 1980s, she and husband and partner Joe Hamilton had remained close, and Carol was devastated when Joe passed away after a lengthy battle with cancer in 1991. A decade later in January 2002, Carol would have to cope with the ultimate tragedy, when her daughter Carrie Hamilton passed away at age thirty-eight, also from cancer.

Carrie had survived her battles with substance abuse to build a successful career as an actress in her own right, and was collaborating with her mom on the play *Hollywood Arms*, based on Burnett's memoirs of her early years as a theatre actress and stand-up comedienne. In a bittersweet triumph, Carol continued with the play, knowing it was what Carrie wanted, and launched it to rave reviews on Broadway.

Back in 1991, CBS had had hits with two *Ed Sullivan Show* retrospectives (the first of which was hosted by Carol herself). They were among the highest-rated TV specials of the year on any of the four major networks. No sooner was the "new" Burnett show cancelled than CBS inked a deal to produce a big-budget, full-bore, two-hour look back at the glory days of the 1967–79 classic.

In January of 1993, *The Carol Burnett Show Reunion* reunited Carol, Harvey, Tim, Lyle, and Vicki (who by then was hosting her own syndicated 1992–94 talk/variety show), on the same CBS stage where they had taped a decade and a half earlier. The ratings and public acclaim went through the roof.

Nearly nine years after the first retrospective—and almost thirty-five years after the first show—in November of 2001, *The Carol Burnett Show*'s appeal was still undiminished, as shown when CBS aired yet another Carol Burnett retrospective, which racked up almost Super Bowl–strength Nielsen numbers, with an audience of well over thirty million.

Syndicated and cable reruns of the show continue to be successfully distributed, as they have been ever since 1977. Among family variety shows, only *The Lawrence Welk Show* and *The Muppet Show* can claim an equal track record or as durable a fan base.

But that's no surprise for Carol's legions of fans across the United States and Canada. It's just more proof that we will always be "so glad we had this time together!"

## WHAT A BUNCH OF CHARACTERS!

There were . . .

- The "Old Folks at Home"—who reminisced about their lives from the twin rocking chairs on their porch.
- Stella Toddler, the accident-prone, skirt-wearing, droopy little old lady who'd "been hurt a lo-ott."
- Tim's equally oft-injured Little Old Man, who would occupy the unlikely occupations of fireman (where he gave a choking Harvey mouth-to-mouth while muttering a love song), house-calling doctor (he used stuffed animals from his pediatric practice to "reward" Harvey for taking an injection like a man, after threatening to "spank him on his banky-wanky" if he didn't), and in a delicatessen skit that was even more hilarious than intended, when Harvey accidentally split his pants.
- Mother Marcus, the elephantine Jewish mama with watermelon breasts, played to the hilt by Harvey.
- Funt and Mundane (Harvey and Carol), the Burnett show's homage to the legendary theatrical couple Alfred Lunt and Lynne Fontanne. (Lynne Fontanne, who died at the age of ninety-five in 1983, was reportedly a huge fan of the Burnett show and the F&M sketches.)
- Heavy-accented Boss Tudball (Tim), and his slinky-skirted, gum-chewing, nail-filing, empress-of-inefficiency secretary Missus Wiggins. (Rumor has it that Carol patterned Missus Wiggins's vacuous, vapid style of speech and reaction after *Sesame Street*'s Big Bird.)
- Tarzan (Lyle) and Jane (Carol).
- "As the Stomach Turns"—prime-time TV's funniest soap opera until *Mary Hartman, Mary Hartman; Soap;* and *Falcon Crest* came along.
- Nora Desmond—The Greatest Silent Film Star of Them All, according to her butler, Maxx (Harvey).
- Vicki's immortal Mama Thelma Harper, and her daughters Eunice (Carol) and Ellen (frequent guest star Betty White), and Eunice's husband Ed Higgins (Har-

vey). Vicki was all of twenty-five years old when she invented the unforgettable Mama, with nothing more in the way of makeup than an old dress, granny glasses, and a gray wig. Sometimes they were joined by hearing aid–wearing Mickey Hart (Tim), Ed's assistant at the hardware store he managed, who somehow managed to be even dimmer than Ed was (which was no mean feat).

- The shows often opened with an animated cartoon of Carol as the CBS Cleaning Lady, with her trademark denim uniform and rainbow-colored cap, and the letters C–B–S (to help spell *Carol Burnett Show*, as well as the obvious). Carol often played the cleaning lady in skits—a cross between Lucy Ricardo and the mother feline in *Cats*, who would sing her way through the floor washing, vacuuming, and laundry while dreaming of making it big on the stages she cleaned.

- It would appear the cleaning lady lived her dream of achieving fame after all— she would (in cartoon form) open each episode in the later years, as well as open and close every *Carol Burnett and Friends* rerun from 1977 onward. She even got to sing a live duet with Ray Charles! (And needless to say, in the early to mid-'70s, many people *did* indeed think CBS stood for *Carol Burnett Show!*)

## WHERE ARE THEY NOW?

- Carol Burnett spent the rest of the '90s doing musical comedies on the Broadway stage and making guest appearances on top sitcoms, most notably as the mother of Helen Hunt's Jamie on *Mad About You*. Her status as a pop-culture icon was by now firmly enshrined in the TV pantheon, to say nothing of her costars.

- Harvey Korman continued making movies with Mel Brooks, including the Leslie Nielsen vampire spoof *Dracula: Dead and Loving It!* He and Tim Conway have teamed up time and again for appearances in Vegas, on talk shows, and on *Hollywood Squares*. The duo also made an uproarious guest shot as a dueling comedy team on Dick Van Dyke's *Diagnosis Murder* in 1998. In 2003 at age seventy, Tim helped launch a new—and of course, short-lived—variety format on the WB Network.

- Lyle Waggoner achieved his greatest fame starring alongside Lynda Carter on the TV show *Wonder Woman*, and he made innumerable guest shots on shows like *Love Boat* and *Murder, She Wrote*. In semiretirement from his showbiz career, Lyle takes it easy sailing on his boat, travelling, and playing sports.

- Vicki Lawrence, of course, hit the sitcom jackpot with *Mama's Family*, which ran from 1982 to 1990 on NBC and in first-run syndication and proved to be almost as popular as the Burnett show itself. She also became one of the game show world's few female hosts, starring in the daytime version of *Win, Lose, or Draw*.

    Just two years after those two shows concluded, Vicki launched a highly enjoyable daytime talk show, *Vicki!*, which ran in syndication. Despite successful ratings, the show ended after just two years in 1994, following a bitter power struggle over interference from the show's distributor on the program's direction. And by 1994, the fact that talk TV was more exemplified by Geraldo, Jerry, Ricki, and Jenny spelled "the end" for her rival series. But the undaunted Miss Fireball rebounded to write her autobiography and continued to make frequent TV and musical-theatre appearances.

## FUN FACTS

- Carol Burnett first discovered Vicki Lawrence when theatre-major Vicki wrote her a fan letter in early 1967, during her senior year of high school, enclosing a snapshot of herself and noting correctly that "a lot of people think we even look alike." Unbeknownst to Vicki, this was at the same time that Carol and Joe Hamilton were looking for a young actress to play Carol's "kid sister" in some sketches. Vicki "nearly passed out" when Carol called her soon after and came to a local play that Vicki was starring in. The rest is showbiz history.
- Vicki Lawrence titled her autobiography *Miss Fireball* after the name of the youth talent pageant she'd won back then.
- The fact that most people think Tim Conway was in every episode is just another example of what a beloved icon he is. In fact, Tim didn't become a full-fledged regular until the end of the 1974–75 season, although he did make frequent guest appearances right from the start.
- As a young man, Harvey Korman was a door-to-door salesman before getting his first break in show business.
- Carol's famous ear-tugging began as a not-so-secret code of saying an on-air "hello" to her beloved grandmother, who proudly never missed any of her grand-daughter's TV, film, or stage work until the day she died.
- A rumor circulated in 1975 that Carol had presided over a "marriage" between her close friends Rock Hudson and Jim Nabors. (It was jokingly denied by all parties concerned.)
- Carol Burnett became a hero to the entire entertainment community in 1981, when she won a multimillion-dollar judgment (all of which she donated to charity) against the *National Enquirer*. The story they ran claimed that Carol had started a loud, nasty fight in public with Henry Kissinger in 1976 at a party while intoxicated. The daughter of alcoholics, Carol was also battling to keep her daughters away from drugs in the disco world of 1970s Hollywood. She decided not to take the gratuitous insult lying down—to the eternal gratitude of countless other harassed Hollywood stars.
- Carol was and is one of the biggest fans of ABC's *All My Children*. In 1976, she made a guest appearance as a hospital patient named Mrs. Johnson, and in 1983, after retiring from her weekly show, she became a semi-regular as Verla Grubbs, the long-lost daughter of character Langley Wallingford.

## QUOTABLE QUOTES

- "AHHH-EY-YAHEE-YAAH-YE-YAHEE-YAAAAAAWH!" (Carol's famous "Tarzan yell")
- "Missus Ah-Wiggins-ah?"
- Some of Mama's Words of Wisdom: "Eunice, you got splinters in the windmills'a yer mind!" "Is this your time of the month or somethin'?" Mama's response when Eunice says, "Well, hey, Mama—I'm gonna get me a job!": "Well hey—I'll believe that when I see it!" (During a spirited game of "Sorry"): "SORRR-EEYYY!"
- "MAAAXX???" The way Nora Desmond, "the greatest silent-film star of them all!," would greet her butler.

## AMERICAN MOVIE CLASSICS

Who can forget the fractured film follies or terrific TV spoofs of *The Carol Burnett Show*? Carol's takeoffs on classic films of the '40s, '50s, and '60s were the most popular feature of her show, and Carol's favorite as well. Here are a few of the many highlights:

- In the show's most famous sketch of all—1976's "Went with the Wind," "Starlett O'Hara" (Carol) descends the bomb-battered steps of Tara, to greet "Ratt Butler" (Harvey). Starlett's wearing a dress fashioned from the window curtains—with the curtain rod still in place—giving Carol shoulder padding that would make Sylvester Stallone look like a sissy! "Starlett—that gown is gorgeous!" Ratt exclaims. Starlett demurs, "Why thank you . . . I saw it in the window, and I just couldn't resist it!"
- In 1971's "Lovely Story," everything seems to be going great for our two newly-weds until wife Carol develops a "slight cough." "Don't worry, honey," husband Harvey sobs to reassure her. "I'll get you the best doctor money can buy!" The very next instant, a doctor (Lyle) bursts in the door. "Who are you?" asks Harvey. Lyle responds spot-on, "I'm the best doctor that money can buy!"
- In "Sunnyset Boulevard," Carol plays the eccentric movie queen Nora Desmond, assisted by her creepy bald butler Max (Harvey). Despite her makeup and jewelry, Nora's age showed all too well in the form of two very prominent, sagging, swinging, and drooping parts of her anatomy (in real life, they were two sacs filled with oranges at the bottom!) Accident-prone oldster Stella Toddler had the same condition.
- In "Slippery When Wet," Carol sang in an elaborate water ballet sequence at the pool of a Beverly Hills mansion, with waterfall in back—gurgling and burping her way through the song, and even hitting her head on the side of the pool!
- Only a rerun of *Dynasty* could outdo the bitch-slapping, chandelier-swinging brawlfest that ensued in Carol's version of "A Star Is Born!"

Still fabulous after all these years—Carol and Co. celebrate their twenty-fifth anniversary in 1992.

- In one of many film-noir spoofs, Steve Lawrence, playing a "fatally" shot private dick, is narrating his final case into a tape recorder before he goes on to the big sleep—only to realize at the very end of the sketch that there wasn't any tape in the machine!
- TV wasn't immune from satiric swipes on the Burnett stage, either. Some of the funniest moments ever were Carol's spoofs of TV commercials, where a beleaguered middle-class housewife faces off against singing toilet bowls, foul mouthed wall ovens, intruding next-door-neighbors—and in the funniest moment, a chorus of spokespeople who tear off her dress, singing "Look for the Union Label!"
- In the final "As the Stomach Turns" from 1979, Sally Field's Miss America does not want to surrender her crown for the new 1980 winner and hides in Carol's living-room closet from a bull-dyke pageant inspector (Vicki) out to get her. Vicki finds her, though, and drags the screaming Sally out, in front of a dress-wearing fashion adviser (played by Ken Mars). Carol stammers, "Why, she came out of the closet!" To which the fashion adviser adds, "Just like me!"
- And there were so many more—"From Here to Maternity," "Mildred Fierce," "Pillow Squawk," and on and on . . .

## BLOOPERS AND BREAKUPS

- One of the most infamous examples of the cast making each other laugh and break character was the famous "Dentist's Office" sketch with Harvey and Tim. Tim based the sketch—where an intern dentist (Tim) accidentally injects himself with novocaine while trying to operate on a patient (Harvey)—on an actual incident that happened to a friend of his who'd recently finished dental school. Tim's dentist friend told him that he had accidentally poked the very tip of his syringe through the cheek of his patient, where it hit his other hand and paralyzed it for several hours! This was perhaps the first sketch where Tim completely and totally broke up Harvey (who was supposedly in "agony" as an abscessed-tooth patient)—but it certainly wouldn't be the last!
- After ten years of breaking everyone else up, Tim Conway finally met his match in 1977. During a "Mama's Family" sketch, Tim's dimwitted Mickey Hart was telling a shaggy-dog story (which was totally ad-libbed on Conway's part) about seeing two "Siamese elephants"—attached at the trunk—at a freak show. Instead of being able to lift their trunks and go "Wheeeee!" they could only muster up a "geschnorkle!" After Mickey finished, Eunice asked Mama if she had anything to say . . . and grouchy Mama drawled, "You sure that lil' asshole is finished?" The entire cast (and half the audience) was on the floor.
- Carol was singing in a spoof of Mickey Rooney–Judy Garland musicals (this one set on a farm) when the live horse in back of Carol showed what it thought of the goings-on, as it lifted its tail and relieved itself—right on camera!

- Carol actually sprained her ankle when she tumbled down the stairs during "Went with the Wind." But being the trouper she was, she went right on with the show.
- Carol couldn't stop laughing during a death scene (*she* was the one dying) set in a hayloft with Lyle and Harvey. Harvey wept "Look at her, a minute ago, she was laughing and dancing . . . and she's still laughing!" He finally covered Carol's face up with a bale of hay!
- Harvey was playing the hapless customer of Tim's Little Old Man (who was running a delicatessen in this one), and Harvey's pants came off halfway through the sketch! Instead of the baggy boxers dictated by TV standards at the time, Harvey was wearing the workout briefs he wore in real life, and ended up "flashing" the entire studio audience!
- In the audience that same night was none other than Harvey's acting idol, Sir Laurence Olivier! ("Lord Larry," as Carol called him, found the sketch hysterically funny.)
- An audience member raised her hand during the Q&A session and Carol called on her—only she didn't want to ask Carol a question. She was asking permission from one of the pages to leave the studio and go to the bathroom!
- Carol played "Mary Worthless" in a takeoff of comic-strip busybody Mary Worth—in a sketch where everything that could go wrong *did* go wrong (props falling over, forgotten lines of dialogue, and the usual breakups). "Don't be surprised if you see me in your neighborhood," warned "Mary" at the end. And then, after a double-take, "As a matter of fact—*be* surprised—'cause I'm never doing *this* sketch again!"

## AUDIENCE PARTICIPATION

It was appropriate that Carol taped her show on the same stage that was the home of CBS's equally legendary "Come on Down!" game show *The Price Is Right*. No other show in television history got more mileage out of its studio audience—Phil Donahue, eat your heart out!

- "Are you going to be on the air next season in an [earlier] time?" asked one older member of Carol's audience. "I sometimes end up falling asleep during the show!"
- One woman actually asked Carol—with a straight face—"What do you use to clean the floors?" Carol fell apart at the unlikely question. "Now, I think that's just a little too personal, don't you?" she said.
- Carol finally got the answer about the floor-cleaner from a page, and she asked the woman, "Do you have vinyl floors at home you wanted to clean?" The woman nodded, and Carol asked which rooms. "All over," the woman yelled. "So you have vinyl . . . aaaaalllllll over your houusse?" Carol wrinkled. The woman yelled, "No—just on the floors!"

- A middle-aged *Maude* look-alike named Terry McAnn got up to belt out a bravura rendition of "You Made Me Love You" alongside Carol, after another audience member pointed at Terry and asked Carol if "that lady" was Bea Arthur!
- One adolescent audience member wanted to read Carol a poem he'd written. "I'm in love with a beautiful girl, but there's a catch, oh brother! The girl I love, this glorious girl—is old enough to be my mother!"

## MUSICAL MEMORIES

What do Bing Crosby, Ella Fitzgerald, Peggy Lee, Karen Carpenter, Mama Cass Elliott, Loretta Lynn, Perry Como, the Pointer Sisters, Steve Lawrence, Eydie Gorme, Sammy Davis Jr., Sarah Vaughan, and Ray Charles have in common? If you answer that they all sang duets with Carol Burnett, you're right!

# Tim Conway

TV's greatest variety shows have had stars that have come and gone. And some people—Jo Anne Worley, Vicki Lawrence, Ruth Buzzi, Harvey Korman, Jo Ann Castle, Martin Short, and Gilda Radner, to name a few, are almost synonymous with the glory days of the old format.

But Tim Conway is perhaps in a class by himself. His career covers the entire groovy gamut of our spectrum, from the mid-1960s to the end of the line fifteen years later. His luxury cars have the personalized license plate "13WKS"—which is how long most of his many solo series have lasted. So here's our affectionate tribute to the ups and downs (and downs again) of TV's most successfully unsuccessful personality, and a campy comedy genius for all time.

Tim Conway was born on December 15, 1933, in the appropriately named town of Chagrin Falls, Ohio. After a stint in the army just after the Korean War had died down, where the land-bound Tim bravely "defended" his stateside barracks, the quirky young comedian started his career in local radio.

Tim was discovered by fellow comedy black belt Rose Marie just before she herself achieved her greatest fame as wisecracking writer Sally Rogers on *The Dick Van Dyke Show*. (Of course, Sally herself worked for a fictitious variety hour, *The Alan Brady Show*, on that show.) The vaudeville and Vegas big-band era comedienne and future queen mother of the *Hollywood Squares* thought that what was "coming out of the sound booth" during her radio interview was "funnier than what was on the air!"

Rose's husband, the late West Coast jazz legend Bobby Guy, was equally convinced of Conway's talent, and pressured Rose to sign Conway to her management. It was a testament to the talent of all three people that within just a few years, Conway had landed the plum role of Ensign Chuck Parker on the CBS sitcom *McHale's Navy*.

After his three-year tour of duty on *McHale's Navy* ended in 1966, Conway kept a high profile with guest shots, comedy writing, and club appearances. And late in 1969, CBS green-lighted a filmed half-hour sitcom, *The Tim Conway Show*, to follow *Get Smart* in its final season on Friday nights. Premiering in late January 1970, this would prove to be the first show to bear Conway's name—but it certainly wouldn't be the last.

*The Tim Conway Show* found Tim reunited with his old buddy from *McHale's Navy*, Joe Flynn. The two played best friends and co-owners of the "Anytime Anyplace Airlines" (whose company fleet consisted of one commuter plane). In a fate that was unfortunately prescient of so many more things to come, the series found itself near the bottom of the ratings heap. (CBS program chief Mike Dann bore it an especial enmity, referring to it as "that Tim Conway crap that nobody likes" in an interview with *Variety*'s Les Brown.)

However, Dann's boss, CBS chief Robert Wood, was busy revising CBS's schedule for the following season, beginning to shed the old-fashioned shows that had personified the Eye network for the past half-dozen years. With Jackie Gleason, Red Skelton, and *Petticoat Junction* gone (all of which were still winning their time periods), CBS's development department was left with a Grand Canyon–sized hole of slots to fill.

And with the Sunday night hit *Mission: Impossible* moved to help anchor Saturdays, CBS prescribed a new variety hour to keep the momentum of *Ed Sullivan* and *Glen Campbell* going and siphon off as many middle-American *Bonanza* viewers as possible from the previous hour on NBC. The network wanted a show headlined by an entertainer young enough to be relevant and compatible with the handsome and youthful Campbell—but not a risky, satirical, counter-culture performer like Richard Pryor, the Smothers Brothers, or Mort Sahl. Despite Dann's initial objections (and those of his number-two man, a young executive named Fred Silverman), *The Tim Conway Comedy Hour* arose from the ashes of Conway's sitcom that fall.

Joining Conway was perhaps the most impressive cast of regulars outside of *Laugh-In* on television at the time—Sally Struthers, McLean Stevenson, Art Metrano, Bonnie Boland, Bruce Belland, and Dave Somerville—along with the Jimmy Joyce Singers and Tom Hansen Dancers. Not to mention a junior writer named Barry Levinson, and voice-over legend Ernie Anderson as announcer. (Of course, Ernie also announced Carol Burnett's show, and was the voice of ABC's Los Angeles flagship KABC-7—as well as the father of future film director Paul Thomas Anderson.)

Conway knew going in that CBS largely regarded the show as a temporary time-filler until they could develop something "better," and he was all too aware of how shockingly fast CBS pulled the plug on Leslie Uggams's Sunday-night show the year before. With his usual sense of humor, Tim kicked off his show in the sweltering summer of 1970 with a big-time, snowy "Christmas special"—predicting that his show wouldn't last long enough for the real thing.

Of course, he was right.

*The Tim Conway Comedy Hour* proved to be a smashing success for almost everyone connected with it—except its star. Singer Bruce Belland moved behind the camera to work for Ralph Edwards and spent the next two decades producing the nighttime game-show giants *Cross-Wits, Name That Tune,* and *People's Court.* McLean Stevenson immortalized Col. Henry Blake on *M\*A\*S\*H* less than two years later, and went on to a similarly unsuccessful-yet-successful career with several sitcom vehicles (most notably 1979–80's embarrassing *Hello, Larry*) until his death from a heart attack in early 1996.

Barry Levinson became an Oscar-nominated film director and Emmy-winning producer of *Homicide: Life on the Streets*. And Sally Struthers hit the biggest home run of all when—just as CBS handed the *Tim Conway Comedy Hour* its walking papers, Norman Lear handed the twenty-two-year-old actress the role of Gloria Bunker Stivic in *All in the Family*.

Conway spent the next five years guest-starring on other shows and making family feature films for Disney alongside his fellow comedy legend and friend Don Knotts. He appeared on *The Carol Burnett Show* so frequently that he was made a full-fledged regular by 1975 and stayed with Carol, where he enjoyed his biggest and most memorable success, until the show closed up shop in 1979.

Just six months after Carol called it quits, Tim was back on CBS again, in yet another *Tim Conway Show*, premiering in March of 1980. The show was positioned at the starting gate of CBS's Saturday night lineup, leading into the final episodes of the venerable *Hawaii Five-0*. CBS needed a big-time show to anchor what was once one of their strongest nights. And with Dionne Warwick, Marilyn McCoo, and Barbara Mandrell already committing to other series, the network understandably felt that despite his previous solo track record, nobody else available in 1980 knew more about variety TV or sketch comedy than Tim Conway.

And for once, to the surprise and relief of all, the show actually succeeded! At first . . .

*The Tim Conway Show* managed to perform fairly well in its spring tryout. Even when it was downsized from an hour to a half hour by September, CBS further strengthened the show by positioning the red-hot sitcom *WKRP in Cincinnati* ahead of it. For the first time in his TV career, it looked like Tim Conway finally had a hit he could count on.

NBC and ABC had other plans. NBC took their biggest risk of the year by programming their new Barbara Mandrell variety hour squarely against Tim's show—the only other network variety show still on the air by the end of 1980. To the surprise of the industry, Barbara not only soundly beat Tim's show, she also closed in hard on the once-unbeatable *WKRP*, dropping the sitcom from a top 25 finish in 1979–80 down to the 30s and 40s on the ratings staircase.

Soon afterward, ABC applied the death blow. Fearful of losing the momentum of their *Love Boat/Fantasy Island* duo, they positioned *Charlie's Angels* at 8:00 p.m. Saturdays for the February "sweeps." It would've been hard even for someone who looked like Tom Cruise to compete against *Charlie's Angels* or the *Mandrell Sisters*, let alone both. Just one year after it had begun, *The Tim Conway Show* ceased production the first week of March in 1981.

Tim tried again in 1983 on ABC, with the sitcom *Ace Crawford, Private Eye* (a spoof of hard-boiled detective fiction and macho private-eye shows like *Magnum, P.I.* and *Vega$*). But he found his most successful niche in home videos, appearing as the pint-sized "Dorf" in several spoofy how-to videos (the *Dorf on Golf* ones being especially successful). He also continued to be a regular guest of shows like *Love Boat* and *Diagnosis Murder,* and did several stage and theatre shows with his longtime best friend and comedy partner Harvey Korman. And in 2003, at age sixty-nine, Tim Conway returned to a sort-of variety TV format on the WB, in the comedy series *On the Spot.* It was gone in—you guessed it—less than thirteen weeks.

# Rowan & Martin's Laugh-In

## VITAL STATS

**STARRING**
Dan Rowan and Dick Martin

**MOST VALUABLE PLAYERS**
Ruth Buzzi, Judy Carne, Goldie Hawn, Arte Johnson,
Henry Gibson, Jo Anne Worley, Chelsea Brown, Alan Sues,
Dave Madden, Teresa Graves, Janice Pennington,
Jeremy Lloyd, Pamela Rodgers, Byron Gilliam, Ann Elder,
Lily Tomlin, Barbara Sharma, Johnny Brown, Dennis Allen,
Richard Dawson, Patti Deutsch, Sarah Kennedy, Moosie Drier,
Donna Jean Young, Willie Tyler & Lester

**ON THE AIR**
January 22, 1968—May 14, 1973

**ANNOUNCER**
Gary Owens

**MUSIC**
Ian Bernard

**ORIGINATION**
KNBC Studios, in Beautiful Downtown Burbank

"Sock it to me!"

**R**OWAN & MARTIN'S *Laugh-In* was not only *the* TV variety show of the 1960s—it was *the* definitive TV show of the late '60s, period. The show was justly acclaimed for revolutionizing the pace of television, the national vocabulary, smashing the barriers against political satire on TV, and launching dozens of careers.

Dan Rowan and Dick Martin started their comedy act together in the smoky nightclub scenes of post–World War II Los Angeles, New York, and Las Vegas. Suave, debonair Dan Rowan was the "straight man" of the act, while boisterous, irrepressible Dick Martin was the ace goofball of the duo. The two men were making semi-regular TV appearances on specials (or "spectaculars," as they were known back then) by the late '50s, and they had become one of the biggest draws in nightclubs and casinos across the United States.

At the same time that Rowan and Martin were building their careers on stage, two maverick TV producers were building names for themselves in two of the most memorable variety shows of the early 1960s. After earning his stripes in the talent-management end of the entertainment industry, a thirtysomething veteran of the Hollywood nightlife named George Schlatter was appointed to produce *The Judy Garland Show* on CBS in 1963–64. Garland's show was as great as one would think it would be, with showstoppers every episode and guest stars like Frank Sinatra stopping by. But someone as unrestrained in her fiery intensity as Garland simply wasn't meant to host a regular series in the "cool medium" of weekly TV, as ABC would discover for themselves a few years later with Johnny Cash.

Judy's show also offended CBS management at the time, and they relentlessly censored it. (Judy wanted to pay tribute to recently slain President John F. Kennedy, and a network exec even nixed that, on the grounds that it wasn't appropriate!) The show was cancelled after only one year, in 1964.

While George Schlatter tried to keep *The Judy Garland Show* focused despite the fact that Judy's emotional tornadoes had grown as strong as the ones that had blown her out of Kansas, another producer was working on a show that was equally ahead of its time—and headed for an equally premature end.

After waging a battle to get a show on the air that wouldn't be seen until Norman Lear tried to launch *All in the Family*, Ed Friendly finally succeeded in bringing an adaptation of one of the U.K.'s most popular and controversial hits to the American screen. It was called *That Was the Week That Was*, and after a protracted fight, it finally made it to air in late 1963. In many ways, the show was *Laugh-In* before *Laugh-In* and *SCTV* before *SCTV*, a topical spoof of current events with sketch comedy and a "newsmagazine" format that was way ahead of its time. *TW3* would be cited as an inspiration, if not the main inspiration, for virtually every groundbreaking comedy revue that followed it, from *Monty Python* to *Saturday Night Live* to *SCTV*.

*That Was the Week That Was* also boasted a stunning cast of regulars including Alan Alda, David Frost, Caterina Valente, Phyllis Newman, Nancy Ames, and Buck

Henry, along with Burr Tillstom's Puppets and the Skitch Henderson Orchestra. While almost everyone at NBC privately acknowledged that the show was top-quality, the consensus of the executives that cancelled it was that show was too disjointed, too fast, and just too unlike anything else on television at the time. Its weeks were over by May of 1965.

Flash-forward now a year later, when Dean Martin's longtime pallies from the casino circuit, Dick Martin and Dan Rowan, were handpicked by Dino to take over his show's spot on NBC in the summer of 1966. *The Rowan & Martin Show* proved to be a huge summer hit, and NBC started looking for a format to develop for the dynamite duo.

All of the elements were now in place. All that needed to happen was for these four talented men to be brought together to unite their energies and visions. When it happened, in Hollywood during 1966 and '67, it would prove to be a cosmic smash of creative energy that would revolutionize comedy forever.

The format was essentially a carryover of *That Was the Week That Was*—only the team had learned its lessons from that show's eventual failure. The new program would be more free-form and not held hostage to news-of-the-week jokes and skits. Instead, it would be a generalized satire of American culture itself, from the hardhats to the hippies and everything in between. "There was a bubbling kind of unrest into which the Beatles, Lenny Bruce, and *Laugh-In* came, and kind of focused attention on how crazy it all really was," Schlatter said, looking back on the show in a *Los Angeles Times* piece in 2003.

The show would have a central star (or two stars in this case), like *Judy Garland*, but the show wouldn't revolve around them or put them in every single segment. And with color TV having become the mainstream by 1967, George Schlatter wanted to use every available videotape, computer, and camera technology to make the show look like no other.

Everyone knew they had a winner with the new program, and when Schlatter went about assembling a supporting cast of crazies for the show, he decided to make it as large as his budget would allow. Following the formula of *TW3* (and also of *The Lawrence Welk Show*, when one looks back at it), the show wouldn't rely just on big-name guest stars to carry it. Instead, the show would have a "family" of fifteen or twenty regulars who would do two or three minimal-rehearsal skits or sketches per show, and keep it moving at lightning pace.

While other shows like *Ed Sullivan* and *Hollywood Palace* were making $25,000 and $50,000 multi-episode deals with rock bands and stand-up comics, George Schlatter chose a different approach. He asked stars to come in for union scale, stand before the camera for one minute—and get a pie in the face or a bucket of water dropped on them. And that was it! Many stars were fascinated by the idea, and others were good sports. Most complied. (And after the show really took off, even the likes of John Wayne, Bob Hope, and Burt Reynolds were waiting to have *Laugh-In* sock it to 'em!)

One major star came on the show for a "quickie" segment with Judy Carne that took just a couple of minutes to do, and of course, no extra "takes" or big rehearsals were required. The star finished his bit and turned to George, saying, "OK, when do we do the real thing?" "You've just done it!" George laughed. "That was it!"

It's a good thing some of the one-liners and walk-ons could be dispensed with easily, since *Laugh-In* was a hard enough show to produce. The show was taped assembly-line style with several "quickie" skits and jokes shot one after another back to back, which would then be spliced apart and edited into the finished show in various intervals. There were a lot of bloopers, too—"but we were the first to leave the bad stuff in!" laughed Dick Martin. Why not? *Laugh-In* would do anything for a laugh.

NBC's program counsel didn't know what to make of the completed pilot. Half the counsel was as excited as Schlatter and Friendly were, certain that *this* was that one show in a million that really could live up to the hype of Doing Something New and Different On Television. The rest of the committee were afraid of and put off by the show—for the very same reason! Finally, NBC programmer Mort Werner prevailed over the counsel with the nerve-wrackingly anticipated swing vote.

It was a "yes." "Oh for God's sake, it's just one hour [on the schedule]," Werner said. "Let the boys do what they want."

On September 9, 1967, *Rowan & Martin's Laugh-In* aired on NBC as a prime-time special, with most of the show's first-year cast in place. America had truly never seen anything like it before—but they definitely wanted to see it again! The show shot straight to number one, guaranteeing it a mid-season berth on NBC's schedule. The network notified Schlatter and Friendly to start crewing up immediately to start production in December of 1967 for a January 1968 launch. As 1968 started, so would NBC's new *Laugh-In*.

But it wasn't all sunshine and daisies just yet. The show was given what was potentially the worst time slot in all of television: 8:00 p.m. Mondays, against CBS's impenetrable *Gunsmoke* and Lucille Ball. New cast member Judy Carne remembers a high-level NBC executive telling her, "Listen, have fun, honey—because your show's not gonna make it!"

On January 22, 1968, at 8:00 p.m., TV screens across North America saw quintessentially over-serious announcer Gary Owens standing in front of an old fashioned pipe-microphone, somberly whispering, "What you are about to see is entirely true," while the word "FALSE" flashed onto the screen. And with that, he opened the show with the biggest and best battle-cry until *Saturday Night Live* came along: "Get ready America! Here comes *Rowan & Martin's Laugh In!*"

The show opened with a groovy go-go music theme song called "The Inquisitive Tango," as the psychedelic-colored "joke wall" burst open up to reveal the cast. Dan

Rowan and Dick Martin were dressed for success in their formal tuxedos, while the young supporting cast of crazies wore the latest in mod '60s fashions and hairdos.

Dean Martin's show and *The Smothers Brothers* were the only other programs of 1968 even remotely like the new *Laugh-In*. In the straight arrow variety-show world of Lawrence Welk and Ed Sullivan, *Laugh-In* came across like a freewheeling season pass into the hottest L.A. and Las Vegas parties. Indeed, a regular feature of the show was a mod, swinging party that might just as well have been filmed in Austin Powers's living room. Cocktails and cigarettes (and who knows what else) were conspicuously consumed on camera, while young go-go girls danced in wicker "cages" and on furniture, as the men wore scarves, double-vests, and Beatles wigs.

The show that that one NBC programmer had assured Judy Carne wasn't gonna make it had made it all right—straight to number one within eight weeks of the first telecast. When Sammy Davis Jr., guest starred to lay down the law as a jive-talkin' judge, America said, "Here Come Da Judge," giving the show a colossal 50 percent share of the U.S. viewing audience. By the time Greenwich Village performer Tiny Tim appeared, with his stringy black hair and shaky male-soprano voice, strumming his ukulele and singing "Tiptoe Through the Tulips" as Dick Martin bugged his eyes out at the sight, *Laugh-In* had become the television time-capsule for the late '60s.

In all this madness, Schlatter and Friendly managed to maintain just enough of a sense of order to *Laugh-In* to keep it ready for prime time. Each episode would have one or two main guest stars, in addition to the spot-on cameos, and have a topical "theme" to the main content. The show would also have several more regular segments that viewers could look forward to in addition to the quickies and interruptions and one-liners.

After the Party, there would also be "Ladies and Gents—*Laugh-In* looks at the News!" It would be kicked off by all the girls in the cast dancing and singing the song, "What's the News, Across the Nation?" dressed in one outrageous set of costumes after another (warring Indians, geisha girls, W. C. Fields look-alikes, pixie Tinkerbells, the Supremes, Richard Nixon look-alikes, and so many more). Then Dick would come out onstage and deliver a series of one-liners about the news of the day, after which Goldie would stammer, stutter, and giggle her way through introducing Dan to give "The News of the Future."

Sometimes there'd also be separate features (or, as Alan Sues's outrageously gay sportscaster would call them, "Featurettes!" as he jingled his pride-and-joy "tinkle" bell and rolled his eyes faster than the spinning teacups at Knotts Berry Farm). And let's not forget Rona Barrett's worst rival, "Kissy Kissy," played by Ruth Buzzi—a sleazy socialite of a gossip columnist who had more "dish" than Julia Child when it came to the world of Hollywood. Kissy took unashamed wink-wink enjoyment perverting even the most innocent stories into something salacious. ("Hey Kissy—this just in—Steve McQueen won his last tennis game with Ali MacGraw." Kissy: "It can

From Beautiful Downtown
Burbank—Gary Owens
(*above*) and Dan and Dick
(*left*).

now be reported that Steve McQueen brutally beat his young wife in public, at the Riviera . . .")

And there were other smaller, recurring features: "A Poem, by Henry Gibson," where Henry would read a peace-and-love poem in front of a huge painted flower, and "The Flying Fickle Finger of Fate," where Dick and Dan would "sock it to" one pretentious institution after another. The Pentagon, the pesticide and pharmaceutical industries, pushy teachers' unions and radical college professors, oil companies, health insurers, book censors, and even TV execs themselves all "got the finger" from *Laugh-In*.

Of course, the most iconic segment starred Judy Carne as the lovable "Sock It To Me" girl. "And now folks—it's Sock It To Me time!" she'd smile—and get splashed in the face with a bucket of water, her wig pulled off, or fall through a trap door. Most of the guest stars would also receive the same treatment. (Barbara Feldon of *Get Smart* fame even had her dress ripped off!) A close second would be Arte Johnson's Dirty Old Man, with the apropos name Tyrone F. Horneigh, who would chase after Ruth Buzzi's frumpy, hairnetted Gladys Ormphby—usually at an otherwise peaceful bench in Central Park. "Do you believe in the hereafter?" Tyrone might ask of his unrequited love. "Of course I do," Gladys would say, scrunching herself up to avoid the assault, as Tyrone laughed, "Good—then you know what I'm here after!" The outraged, sterile spinster would then wail on Tyrone's you-know-where with her heavy purse, in a fighting frenzy that Miss Piggy must have taken notes on in her karate classes. Arte also gave us Wolfgang, the German soldier still fighting World War II in 1968 from his vantage point behind a potted plant, who would cap off the show with "Veh-lee intelestink."(He often adding that in his taste, it was also "shtoopid.")

The transitions between segments and sketches were psychedelic "breaks" with go-go dancing girls in bikinis. Goldie, Teresa Graves, Chelsea Brown, and future *Price Is Right* queen Janice Pennington were the most popular go-go girls—with their bodies painted with peace signs and "graffiti" like "Danger—Curves Ahead!" Or sometimes there'd be Jo Anne Worley dressed in a feather boa and evening gown singing "When you're down and out . . . lift up your head and shout . . . I'M DOWN AND OUT!!!" or padded to look pregnant and ruefully belting out, "I *Should* Have Danced All Night. . . ."

By 1969, *Laugh-In*'s fame was so far-reaching that there were plans for *Laugh-In* themed diners, serving such delicacies as "Bippyburgers," "Pickle Fingers of Fate," and "Here Come Da Fudge" ice cream sundaes. Not only that, but there was also the cinema classic *The Maltese Bippy* (yet another groovy spy takeoff, starring Dan and Dick), and the daytime game show *Letters to Laugh-In*, hosted by Gary Owens, both in 1969.

But the biggest score for the *Laugh-In* gang—and an omen of things to come— came at the end of the year, when the Walter Matthau–Ingrid Bergman comedy/drama *Cactus Flower* was released. The best-remembered character in the movie was played by that daffy dynamo Goldie Hawn—who had gotten the breakout role largely due to her *Laugh-In* fame. Goldie was perfect as the carefree, kooky, sexy, much younger girlfriend of swinging bachelor Matthau (who was really in love with his longtime office manager, the refined and reserved Bergman).

The comedy of manners was warmly received by both the critics and at the box office, and Goldie had found a vehicle where she could show a full range of emotions and her considerable skills as an actress. In January of 1970, Goldie won a Golden Globe award for her supporting role in the movie—and the best was still yet to come. Just three months later, that giggling girl from the joke wall walked home with Hollywood's highest honor: the Academy Award.

After Goldie's Oscar triumph in the spring of 1970, Goldie's mother recalled in interviews that her twenty-five-year-old daughter was offered "the moon" by NBC to stay on the show. But the packed TV taping schedule and the big-budget movie offers that the film industry was now socking to Goldie just didn't mix. By season's end, Goldie had decided to go-go-go away from the *Laugh-In* fold.

Despite NBC's displeasure, there weren't many hard feelings as far as Schlatter or Rowan and Martin were concerned; their giggling Goldie had grown up and was ready to leave the *Laugh-In* cuckoo's nest for bigger and better things. But what they didn't realize was that Goldie's exit started a new trend that began unraveling the threads of television's top-rated show.

Other Hollywood movie agents and TV packagers had already been keeping an eye on the *Laugh-In* loonies even before Goldie's Oscar win. Now they zeroed in on the show like a swarm of buzzards spying fresh prey. As soon as the networks approved a new half-hour sitcom, or when a Las Vegas casino was looking for a headliner, *Laugh-In* was *the* go-to place to find your stars.

The handshaking agents and deal-making offers (many of which, predictably, didn't deliver anything near what they promised) took their toll on the *Laugh-In* cast. By the end of 1970, only Arte Johnson, Ruth Buzzi, Henry Gibson, and Gary Owens remained of the original group of *Laugh-In* loonies.

However, after finishing 1969–70 at number one once again, the series still managed to be a musclebound thirteenth place by the end of the following season. And the fact that the show's more visible regulars were being pursued by every movie producer or booking agent in Hollywood only confirmed how red-hot the series was. *Laugh-In* had become the Mecca for young comic actors and stand-up comedians coming out to Hollywood.

One of these new people would make perhaps the biggest impact of all on the show. While Goldie would certainly be missed, there was fortunately another young comedy queen on the rise who would seamlessly take over the center spotlight on the *Laugh-In* stage. Early in 1970, *Laugh-In*'s other most famous alumna would join the cast.

Lily Tomlin was on the phone arranging an audition for George Schlatter as soon as she got the word that the ABC rock-music show she had been starring in, the David Steinberg–hosted *Music Scene*, was being cancelled. After a rise in her career from the job on Steinberg's new show, the thirty-year-old comedienne had just bought a car and was shopping for a house or nice apartment. The show's cancellation proved a tremendous blow. Ironically, *The Music Scene* had been slotted against *Laugh-In*, as ABC had hoped that it would damage *Laugh-In*'s tremendous popularity amongst the high school and college-age set. It didn't.

Schlatter hired Tomlin almost immediately, after watching her Swiss-watch comedy timing and her unforgettable characters: wisecracking five-year-old Edith Ann and nasty, "omnipotent," phone operator Ernestine. After seeing the bring-the-house-down response Ernestine got in her first sketch on the show, Schlatter took Lily aside, and told her, "Ernestine's going to be *huge!*"

He was right. The following year, Lily released a comedy album titled *This Is a Recording*, with Ernestine's primped-up, laughably contemptuous face on the cover. It soared straight to the top of the charts.

Despite the on-the-floor hilarity of the 1971 album, Ernestine was really best seen as well as heard. One thing Ernestine managed to slip by the NBC censors in her proof that she could do "anything" she wanted was Tomlin's use of the middle finger when she dialed the phone numbers on Ernestine's switchboard. After beginning each of her cranky calls with "A gracious good afternoon," Ernestine would connive, cajole, and con one poor "customer" after another. And when anyone dared to disagree with the Martha Stewart of telecommunications, Ernestine shot back, "We can do anything—we're the Phone Company!" (It was appropriate that Ernestine worked for a public utility. In 1969 and 1970, half of America started Monday nights off with *Laugh-In*—and darn near the other half rode off into the sunset with *Gunsmoke*. As a result, Gary Owens revealed in a 2003 interview at the Museum of Television and Radio, people were so addicted to their Monday-night must-see TV that phone and water usage were reported to go down as much as 25 to 30 percent during the 8:00–9:00 hour.)

Besides giving today's generation of pushy telemarketers the ultimate role model, Tomlin brought on more characters, like the old-money matron the Tasteful Lady. She brought the entire house down when, after delivering a lecture on manners and etiquette Gloria Vanderbilt would have approved, the Tasteful Lady sat down in a regal antique chair. Twenty years before Sharon Stone in *Basic Instinct*, Lily's legs went full-width in her skirt, as she inadvertently "whomped" down on a giant whoopie cushion. ("How humiliating," she replied.)

And then there was the lady who could never, you know, make an issue of—it's like this, where you see, she tried to make a point, but she—well, she just couldn't, you know what I'm saying, like make the thing get to—well, because of her speech impediment and all that—a conclusion.

George Schlatter also raided the treasures of another variety show that had sunk at the end of 1969, *The Leslie Uggams Show*, bringing on full-size African American comedian Johnny Brown, along with his friendly smile and clever comedy. Red-haired Barbara Sharma, attractive Ann Elder, and the tall, skinny, dour young comic Dennis Allen also joined the show in the fall of 1970.

As 1971 began, *Laugh-In* was still near the top of the heap. While other variety shows feared for their lives, with the FCC's prime-access cutback rule that started network prime time at 8:00 instead of 7:30, *Laugh-In* had no such worries.

In the fall, Richard Dawson came on board after his long stint as one of *Hogan's Heroes*, while original cast member Henry Gibson got ready to leave. By the end of the 1971–72 season, *Laugh-In* was still a hugely popular audience draw, still in the Top 25 of the ratings. But it was clear that the show was slipping considerably below its number one ranking just two years earlier in 1970.

Furthermore, comedy-variety TV was then starting to give way to the newly re-energized sitcoms of the early 1970s. When *Laugh-In* went into production in 1967, half-hour TV sitcoms were typified by programs like *Run Buddy Run*, *My Mother the Car*, *Gilligan's Island*, and *The Beverly Hillbillies*. But by 1972, shows like *All in the Family*, *The Odd Couple*, and *The Mary Tyler Moore Show* had transformed half-hour comedies into the most sophisticated and with-it fare on the air. Newer, post–*Laugh-In* variety shows like *Flip Wilson* and *Sonny & Cher* borrowed the parent show's avant-garde camerawork, first-rate production techniques, and edgy comedy. For the first time, *Laugh-In* was no longer at the head of the class in hip variety.

And just as would happen a decade later with *Saturday Night Live* and *SCTV*, Hollywood movie studios and talent agents continued to draw off *Laugh-In*'s stars with movie deals and headline-billed Vegas and comedy club tours. Goldie Hawn, of course, was pursuing her movie career. Jo Anne Worley left in 1970 for live Vegas headlining, musical theater, innumerable talk and game shows, and holiday specials. Teresa Graves left for film work and her later starring role in *Get Christie Love!* By the end of 1971, Arte Johnson had also left the fold. And even though Lily Tomlin stayed with the show through the 1972–73 season, everyone knew that like Goldie before her, she was just too huge a star in her own right to be held to a weekly variety show as a second-billed performer for much longer.

In the fall of 1972, *Laugh-In* tried to arrest the decline by going through the most radical revamping of its format ever. By then, George Schlatter had exited the show after a protracted power struggle between his end of the production team and Rowan and Martin themselves. The show introduced a whole new cast of young people dubbed "The Burbank Quickies," with puppeteer Willie Tyler & Lester, future *Match Game* and voice-over regular Patti Deutsch, sexy Sarah Kennedy, and established comedienne Donna Jean Young coming on board. (Jo Anne Worley revealed in a 2003 interview that Donna Jean and she had the same agent, and the agent was actu-

Don't call us, SHE'LL call you—Ernestine (Lily Tomlin, *above*) in 1972; Funny girls Goldie Hawn and Ruth Buzzi (*right*) in 1968.

ally pitching Donna Jean to George Schlatter when *Laugh-In* sent out its original casting call in 1967. Fortunately for Jo Anne, she and her friend Barbara Sharma found out about it and got to George first—and happily, all three ladies got to make their memorable marks on *Laugh-In*.)

But for a show that had made an institution of oft-repeated catchphrases and regular routines, the gradual attrition of the original and most popular players took too big a toll. No more Henry Gibson and his fractured "poems"? No more Alan Sues giving the sports report with his beloved "tinkle"? No more Arte Johnson's nutty Nazi peering out from behind a potted plant, or dirty old man Tyrone Horneigh? Was this really *Laugh-In* anymore?

By the time the series finished taping at the end of January 1973, the handwriting was pretty much on the wall. When NBC announced their fall schedule that spring, two sitcoms (neither of which would prove successful) were in *Laugh-In*'s place. On May 14, 1973, the joke wall closed up for good, as *Rowan & Martin's Laugh-In* faded to black.

Even despite the declining ratings and the dizzying cast changes, NBC might have had second (or third) thoughts about canceling the show. It wouldn't be until three years later that they would have another dominant show at 8:00 on Mondays. (Interestingly enough, that program was *Little House on the Prairie*, which had been transferred from the Wednesday night lineup. It was also produced by Ed Friendly's production company—the same Ed Friendly who owned *Laugh-In* alongside George Schlatter.) And by then, NBC was in a third-place rut that it wouldn't emerge from until 1984.

After the original *Laugh-In* ended, the cast members (and Dan Rowan and Dick Martin) went their separate ways. Dick Martin made frequent appearances on *The Match Game* and was one of the foremost sitcom directors of the '70s and '80s. Dick regularly directed installments of his good friend Bob Newhart's shows (both of them), as well as several *All in the Family* and *Archie Bunker's Place* episodes. Dan Rowan made similar TV appearances, although less frequently.

By 1977, with shows like *Saturday Night Live* and *SCTV* flourishing, NBC decided to take a second look at *Laugh-In* and commissioned George Schlatter to create a limited summer series of *Laugh-In* specials. Dan Rowan and Dick Martin weren't involved in them, and Rowan and Martin sued Schlatter for the short-lived revival, claiming that he didn't have the right to revive the *Laugh-In* name and format without their consent or cooperation. (While Schlatter and Friendly had been the ones most responsible for the show's format, it was formally titled *Rowan & Martin's Laugh-In*.) A settlement was reached in Rowan and Martin's favor in September 1980, after which Dan Rowan more or less retired from showbiz, moving to and spending most of his time in France.

Despite the temporary rift, the entire *Laugh-In* community was united in their grief when Dan Rowan passed away at the age of sixty-five in 1987. Rowan had maintained a long friendship with novelist John D. MacDonald, who had died just nine months earlier. Shortly before their tragic ends, the two men had decided to publish a memorable compilation of letters written to and from each other, titled *A Friendship*. (Rowan's first jobs in show business were as an apprentice scriptwriter and editor in the movies, before being drafted into World War II.)

Five and a half years later, after the blockbuster numbers CBS had generated with their Ed Sullivan retrospectives of 1991, the whole crew reunited once again for a top-rated NBC special celebrating *25 Years of Laugh-In* in early 1993. It too went straight to the top of the ratings, with commentary from virtually all the remaining *Laugh-In* loonies, even Goldie and Lily.

*Rowan & Martin's Laugh-In* may seem inescapably rooted in the late '60s and early '70s, but that's because—more than any other mainstream TV program of the time—it truly *defined* the culture of the late '60s and early '70s. From flower-child hippies in Berkeley and Woodstock to cocktail-swigging Greatest Generationers in Las Vegas; from bra-burning feminists to stay-at-home housewives; from teenage kids to their giggling grandparents both wondering how they could get away with *that* on television. *Laugh-In* was one of the few things—if not the *only* thing at times—that everyone in the United States and Canada could agree on.

And despite today's soundbite heavy, MTV-style media, which makes *Laugh-In* look downright sedentary in comparison, the show is almost as relevant now as it was thirty-five years ago. "We did jokes about the Pentagon, oil companies, employment, and the economy," George Schlatter remarked in an interview with the *Los Angeles Times* in 2003. "And we [still] have the same problems. The things we made fun of on *Laugh-In* remain unsolved today."

## FUN FACTS

- Virtually everyone alive at the time in North America remembers the night in September 1968 when presidential candidate Richard Nixon appeared in a "quickie" and gasped, "Sock it to ME?" Nixon and *Laugh-In* head writer Paul Keyes were close friends, and Nixon's media consultant was Roger Ailes, an ex-producer of *The Mike Douglas Show* (one of *Laugh-In*'s best television friends). That explains that booking—but what wasn't as widely known was that George Schlatter tried his damndest to get Nixon's rival, Hubert Humphrey, to appear on the show for balance's sake. Humphrey didn't think doing a cheap TV variety show would be becoming to his image, though, and declined the offer. History wrote the final verdict on which man made the better decision.

- In January 1969, newly inaugurated President Richard Nixon called George to "thank" him for his part in Nixon's election. "Say," Nixon baited, "I hear that your nickname around there is C-F-G." "Uh, er, um—yes," Schlatter stammered, the color draining from his face. "It uh, stands for, Crazy *Funny* George." "No," Nixon slyly corrected, knowing what it truly meant. "I hear it stands for Crazy F———g George!"

- Jo Anne Worley and her husband, Roger Perry, had just moved into a lovely home in Toluca Lake near Bob Hope's residence when she was tapped to costar with Bob in an NBC holiday special. Jo Anne later recalled that when a page told Hope that Jo Anne was one of his new neighbors, Bob told the page to "Tell Jo she can come on over and borrow a great big cup o' money!"

- Both Mike Douglas in his talk-show memoir *I'll Be Right Back* and Peter Marshall in his autobiography *Backstage with the Original Hollywood Square* recalled that "*Laugh-In* was [their] single biggest talent pool."

- Shortly before *Laugh-In* premiered in 1967, Gary Owens was having dinner with Schlatter and Friendly at the Smoke House in Hollywood. When Gary went in to use the men's room, he noticed freshly installed acoustic ceiling tile in there, and as a joke, put one hand over his ear and imitated an old-fashioned radio announcer. George went to the bathroom at the same time, and caught Gary "in the act," and told him, "From now on, that's how we want you to do it on the show!"

- *Laugh-In* proved that it was in on the joke when it came to its rivalry with TV's other biggest topical controversy baiting variety show of the '60s. On the last *Smothers Brothers Comedy Hour* in June of 1969, Dan Rowan stepped in to cohost the show with Tommy Smothers (an under-the-weather Dick Smothers took the week off, not knowing it would be their last show).

## QUOTABLE QUOTES:

- "Sock it to MEEEE???"—37th president of the United States, Richard M. Nixon
- "Here come da judge!"
- "Look THAT up in your Funk & Wagnalls!"
- "You bet your sweet bippy!"
- The Flying Fickle Finger of Fate!
- "What's the news, across the nation? We have got, the information! In a way—we hope will am-use—you'se! We just love, to give you our viewwwwws . . . (LA-DA-DE-DAH!) Ladies and gents—*Laugh-In* looks at the newwwwwws!"
- "I LOVE my Tinkle!"
- "Easy fo' YOU to say, honey!"
- "And dat's da truth!" (PFFFTT!)
- "Do da name Ruby Bogonia strike a familiar note?"
- "One ringy dingy . . . two ringy dingies . . ."
- "We can do anything! We're the Phone Company!"

## BURBANK QUICKIES

- "My boyfriend is so radical, he thinks honky-tonk is a Chinese bigot!"
- "Boris says capitalism doesn't work. But then again—neither does Boris!"
- "My girlfriend and I went to a wild masquerade party. She went as Goliath, and I went as the Sistine Chapel. By midnight, she was stoned and I was plastered!"
- *Flying Nun* star Sally Field on the phone at the Party: "Mother Superior—come quick! I'm trapped with a group of weirdos in here and they're ALL flying!"
- "My fellow students in college were so envious of those astronauts who landed on the moon. I mean, to stay that high, for that long. . . ."
- Judy Carne to Sammy Davis Jr. "What's black and white and has two eyes?" The answer: "You and Moshe Dayan!"
- "Executioners get severance pay."
- "Barbara Eden [as "Jeannie"] can't stay away from the bottle!"
- "The government says that we can take off $600 for each of our dependents. So this year, I'm writing off the entire population of South Vietnam!"
- "If Shirley Temple Black married Tyrone Power, she'd be Shirley Black Power!"
- Dan Rowan's interview with Tim Conway and Cher (as a Native American princess): "Poc-ahontas?" Dan points at Cher. "Yes, I do," smirks Tim.
- Ernestine, on the phone with the Chairman of the Board: "Hello, is this Mister Sinatra's residence? Oh . . . are you his secretary? Oh—you're his Girl Friday! Well, what about Saturday and Sunday, sweetie?!"
- "Hello, Mister Sinatra, this is Ernestine Tomlin of the Phone Company. I'm calling about an unpaid bill—and I was wondering, what you're going to Doobie Doobie Do about it?!"
- "Well Mister Sinatra, I'd love to do it Your Way—but it's against Phone Company policy!"

## IN THE NEWS (ACROSS THE NATION)

- "News of the future, 20 years from now, 1988. President Ronald Reagan denied reports that he was running again for Governor of California!"
- "News of the future, 20 years from now, 1989. There was dancing in the streets today as the Berlin Wall finally came down . . ."
- (Remember—in 1969, no one [except Dan Rowan, perhaps] knew that Reagan would indeed *be* president in 1988, or that the Berlin Wall *would* come down in 1989!)
- "Recently, a Frenchman named Pierre Cosette took part in an experiment to prove that DDT was safe, by living off nothing but DDT pills for three weeks. All went well until yesterday morning, when while putting on his pants, his fly died!"

## MEMORABLE MOMENTS

- Remember the red-haired "Farkel Family"? (Especially Sparkle Farkel, played by Ruth, who'd flash her bloomers doing a somersault across the living room floor and yell, "Hi!!!")

- And how about Judy Carne and Arte Johnson in their uproarious "Robot Theatre" sketches—as husband and wife robots who tried but never could quite master the ways of being a "normal" human being—although they were blissfully unaware of this fact. "Here's some nice Chinese dinner," Arte might say, missing Judy's plate and plopping it right down in Judy's lap. "Mmm-mmm," Judy would smile, stabbing a fork into Arte's arm, thinking it was the food. Then she'd tie her bib (it was really the tablecloth), causing the whole table's contents to fall down around her, and so on. . . .

- Or the show's kiss-off to that not-so-wonderful year 1970, with big musical numbers "saluting" the dubious accomplishments of the year (the Beatles breaking up, Nixon invading Cambodia, bra-burning women's lib rallies, etc). The show also featured a time-out from the quickies and skits for a Q&A on the news with conservative commentator William F. Buckley and the *Laugh-In* cast.

- *Laugh-In* also took time out from the fun and games one other time, in one of the series' best and most thought-provoking sketches, where Dan Rowan played an army commander trying on his old uniforms, with Frank Sinatra's "September of My Years" playing in the background. "When I was seventeen," Dan remarked in the mirror, in his WWII uniform, "I was just about to be shipped off to World War II." Slow fade. "When I was twenty-one . . ." Captain Dan recalled, "we were just getting ready to fight in Korea." Another slow fade. "When I was thirty-five . . . the reserve units were just being sent into Vietnam." Final fade, as we find Dan putting on his Captain's uniform, with sound effects of bombs going off in the background. "Well, I've got to go now," he sighed wearily. "They're playing my song again!"

## WHERE ARE THEY NOW?

- After her Oscar triumph in the spring of 1970 for *Cactus Flower*, Goldie Hawn went on to become one of the biggest movie stars of the 1970s and '80s. She scored big alongside *Saturday Night Live* superstar Chevy Chase in 1978's *Foul Play* and hit it out of the park with her most successful movie, the funny feminist comedy *Private Benjamin* in 1980. Starting in the early '80s, Goldie got involved with fellow big-screen heavyweight Kurt Russell, and the handsome couple are still one of Hollywood's hottest as of this writing, some twenty-five years later. Goldie also gave birth to a daughter in 1979 named Kate Hudson, who became a huge star in her own right with her turn as the sweet hippie groupie Penny Lane

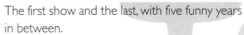
The first show and the last, with five funny years in between.

(a character who bore a striking resemblance to Goldie in her *Laugh-In* era), in Cameron Crowe's 2000 Oscar-winner *Almost Famous*.

- Lily Tomlin's career was equally successful, as she headlined some of the funniest and riskiest TV specials in history for CBS in the mid-'70s. Their success enabled their producer, a young ex-*Laugh-In* writer named Lorne Michaels, to get the job of executive producer on a new NBC show called *Saturday Night Live*. Lily starred alongside Jane Fonda, Dolly Parton, and Dabney Coleman in 1980's sidesplitting office comedy *Nine to Five* and mounted the Broadway stage show *The Search for Signs of Intelligent Life in the Universe* with her longtime life partner Jane Wagner. Lily fought for gay and lesbian rights and AIDS funding in an era when stand-up comedy was known for its homophobia, and she opened the doors for others like Ellen DeGeneres and Lea DeLaria to have successful careers. In recent years, Lily has showed no signs of slowing down, starring on Candice Bergen's *Murphy Brown* for its final two years in the late '90s, making independent movies like 2006's *A Prairie Home Companion*, and playing the role of President Bartlet's secretary on the Emmy-winning drama *The West Wing* from 2002 to 2006.

- Teresa Graves went on to achieve her greatest fame as the star of ABC's 1974–75 police drama *Get Christie Love!*, where she played TV's first ever sexy, liberated black policewoman. The show was very successful and ABC wanted to renew it, but the devoutly religious Teresa soon tired of the rape and murder stories and "jiggle" scenes, and asked to be released from the program. Teresa retired from show business afterwards, living modestly off of her performing money and caring for her mother, until a tragic house fire claimed her life in 2002.

- Dave Madden played avuncular manager Reuben Kincaid on ABC's 1970–74 blockbuster *The Partridge Family*, and played roles in several sitcoms as well as doing regular voice-over work in TV and radio commercials.

- Jo Anne Worley became one of the queens of celebrity-talk and game shows in the 1970s, and regularly headlined Vegas and nightclub tours. She also worked regularly in the touring theatre, especially in comedy and musical roles.

- Arte Johnson became a regular on the equally outrageous and of-its-era 1976–80 *Gong Show*, and made several appearances on other variety shows in the '70s.

- Richard Dawson became a regular on *The Match Game* immediately after *Laugh-In* was cancelled. He of course went on to achieve true stardom as the host of the wildly successful *Family Feud* from 1976 to '85.

- Henry Gibson had a relatively successful movie career, particularly in Robert Altman's groundbreaking films of the 1970s, including *Nashville* and *The Wedding*. In 1999, Henry played the part of a foppish, aging gay critic and barfly named "Thurston Howell III" (yes, just like *Gilligan's Island*) in Paul Thomas Anderson's superb comedy-drama, *Magnolia*.

- Chelsea Brown moved to Australia following a costarring role in the short-lived 1970 ABC medical drama *Matt Lincoln*.
- Gary Owens hosted the first year of the nighttime *Gong Show* in 1976–77 (Chuck Barris took over for the rest of its run into 1980) and continued his career as one of the most visible and influential radio personalities of the twentieth century.
- Ruth Buzzi was a regular on Dean Martin's specials and "roasts," made talk and game show appearances and guest shots on programs like *Carol Burnett* and *Sha Na Na*, and continued acting in sitcoms and specials into the 1980s. In the early '90s, Ruth became a semi-regular on the kids' equivalent of *Laugh-In*, the immortal *Sesame Street*.
- Alan Sues went on to do numerous personal appearances in comedy, game, and live stage shows throughout the Los Angeles and Beverly Hills area.
- Judy Carne struggled with a horrible substance-abuse problem in the 1970s, which reached its nadir when she was arrested for possession in 1978, as tabloids in both London and Los Angeles moved in for the kill. Proving that the spunk and verve that she showed off on *Laugh-In* was no accident, Judy fortunately overcame her addictions and had the courage to share her private struggles with the public, to prevent others from enduring the horrors she had. Judy continued her career in the UK and showed America that she was alive and well in *Laugh-In*'s 1993 NBC reunion.
- George Schlatter produced the 1975 *Cher* show and the huge 1979–84 forerunner of "reality TV," *Real People*—which, like *Laugh-In* a decade earlier, was NBC's highest rated series of the late '70s and early '80s. George also helmed "The American Comedy Awards" in the 1990s, which were replete with hilarious moments (most notably Jamie Lee Curtis and John Lovitz grabbing one another on-air) and salutes to the legends of comedy from both past and present. His old partner Ed Friendly enjoyed equal success as the executive producer (along with Michael Landon) of *Little House on the Prairie*, which also spent most of its 1974–83 run on Monday nights at 8:00—and almost invariably won the ratings too.

# Black and Blue

## Short-Lived Variety Shows with Bronze Stars

The years between the 1957 cancellation of *The Nat King Cole Show* and the 1970 birth of *The Flip Wilson Show* (both on NBC) were the very height of the civil-rights movement in America. However, TV's lukewarm treatment of black stars, while not as openly bigoted and hostile as it was in earlier years, still left a great deal to be desired. Here are some shows that could have, should have, and perhaps would have become great hits—if only . . .

### The Leslie Uggams Show

*Network: CBS; On the air: September 26, 1969–December 14, 1969*

"What better way to shut everybody up," recalled a rueful Leslie Uggams, in a 2002 TV Land documentary about African Americans in television, "than to give a little Chocolate Bunny her own variety show?"

What CBS wanted to "shut up" was the controversy surrounding their preemptive cancellation of the Smothers Brothers in June of 1969. Matters weren't helped any when CBS replaced the groundbreaking, countercultural, youthful Smothers show with the near-antithetical *Hee-Haw* that summer.

Leslie Uggams was only twenty-six years old when CBS signed her for her own big-time variety hour in September of 1969, but even at that age she'd had plenty of practice. Leslie started singing professionally at age nine and was a regular on Mitch Miller's CBS showcase, *Sing Along with Mitch*. The young singer was also a favorite guest on the talk- and game-show circuit, had plenty of variety show experience under her belt (plus musical comedy on Broadway), and was beloved by black and white fans alike.

With African American actors like Bill Cosby, Sidney Poitier, Nichelle Nichols, Diahann Carroll, and Gail Fisher finally smashing the old stereotypes, many industry observers predicted that Uggams's show couldn't fail. But defeat was about to be wrestled from the jaws of victory.

True to Uggams's fans, *The Leslie Uggams Show* featured a master blend of singing, dancing, comedy, and top talent in its Sunday night hammock in between *The Ed Sullivan Show* and *Mission: Impossible*. The young urban viewers CBS was starting to court as 1969–70 progressed regularly tuned in, even against heavy fire from NBC's *Bonanza*. Among African American households, it was appointment TV—especially since NBC's Bill Cosby was installed in the 8:30–9:00 slot directly leading in to Leslie's CBS show. And the not-yet-thirty-year-old entertainer more than held her own amidst the pressure-cooker circumstances.

The show had a regular feature that opened the door enormously for future black family comedies like *Good Times*, *The Cosby Show*, and *Family Matters*. The weekly sketch about a young, lower-middle-class black family trying to make it was called "Sugar Hill," and it featured future *Laugh-In* and *Good Times* regular Johnny Brown along with Leslie.

Despite this promise, CBS wanted instant gratification in the ratings with the brand-new, unestablished show, just as they had had with the Smotherses (but without any of that pesky hippie baggage). By December, CBS moved its proven Glen Campbell hit into the coveted Sunday-night berth. The network could have easily moved the Uggams show to a different time slot—Campbell's old one, for example—in order to give the brand new program time to build.

But according to Leslie Uggams, that was the least of CBS's concerns. "We were never there to succeed," she recalled, and the network's actions seemed to prove her right. "We were only there to take the heat off."

## The Pearl Bailey Show

*Network: ABC; On the air: January 23, 1971–May 8, 1971*

Barely a year after CBS canned Leslie Uggams, ABC thought they had finally hit a winner for their ailing Saturday night schedule when they signed Pearl Bailey for a big-budget, razzmatazz-filled hour to begin airing in January 1971. The show seemed to have everything going for it (besides the obvious fact that it starred one of the most talented and versatile jazz singers in history.) Veteran Oscar and Emmy awards-show producer Bob Finkel, who had previously worked for Andy Williams and Perry Como's shows, was brought in to run the new program. The show was assigned a then-state-of-the-art stage at the Hollywood Palace theatre, complete with money-is-no-object sets, video effects machines, and outrageous designer costumes.

To further protect the new show, *Lawrence Welk* was moved back an hour to provide the program with an established, musical-variety lead-in. The show's unimpressive 8:30 competition was only the aging *My Three Sons* and NBC's Saturday movie. Plus, African American stars were finally "hot" that year in the minds of network executives, taking note of *Julia* and the stratospheric success of NBC's top-rated *Flip Wilson Show*.

However, ABC's love quickly turned to hate when the divine Miss Pearl's show failed to become The Next Big Thing overnight. While the program drew a healthy number of viewers each week (especially for a brand new effort), having a show that was merely "successful" wasn't enough. ABC wanted a hit—a *big* hit—or else.

In the end, perhaps nothing could have rescued the Pearl Bailey show anyway. ABC chief Elton Rule had decided to build the fall 1971 schedule around movies, mysteries, and sitcoms. He reportedly felt that, with even the likes of *Laugh-In* and *Dean Martin* beginning to slip in the ratings, the TV variety show had no future. Rule's management was quoted as saying that in their opinion game, talk, and variety shows had "no prestige."

They meant it, too. At the end of the 1970–71 season, ABC wiped out each and every variety program and nighttime game show on their prime-time schedule. Thankfully, the premature cancellation of Bailey's show and the ups and downs of Hollywood didn't keep the indefatigable entertainer down for long. As she herself might have put it in her famous 1968 anthem, "That's Life"—at least in show business. And until the day Pearl Bailey died of a heart attack in August 1990, at the age of seventy-two, what a glorious life she had.

## The Richard Pryor Show

*Network: NBC; On the air: September 13, 1977–October 20, 1977*

What could have been—and *should* have been—the most talked-about and influential show of the 1977–78 season was totally wasted amidst typical Hollywood power plays. That fact was all the more ugly because Pryor's was such a refreshingly un-typical show.

Once again, just as with *The Smothers Brothers, Nat King Cole, Saturday Night Live,* and *Laugh-In,* network TV wanted to have its cake and eat it too. On one hand, they wanted a show with the illusion of "hip" and "in-crowd" appeal with a marquee name to carry it. Enter Richard Pryor, the preeminent stand-up comedian of the 1970s, whose appearances on NBC's *Saturday Night Live* had set the ratings needle to "tilt."

On the other hand, the network wanted a show with broad enough audience appeal to bring in top ratings—controversial enough to generate headlines, sure, but nonthreatening enough so as not to cause any real problems with letter-writing viewers or Bible Belt station operators.

They didn't get their wish. Combining Richard Pryor, who had Las Vegas and Hollywood movie star clout (and wasn't shy about using it), and NBC's intractable broadcast standards department was like putting nitroglycerin in a blender.

In an era when shows like *Charlie's Angels, Three's Company, Soap,* and *Dallas* were outrageous enough to provoke threats of sponsor boycotts and Religious Right action groups, *The Richard Pryor Show* photon-torpedoed the limits of what was acceptable to the prime-time censors. NBC's standards and practices division relentlessly overruled the program and wiped out enough scripts to make the Smothers Brothers look practically indulged by comparison. Even Pryor's attempts to satirize the controversy surrounding his show were bleeped. One show's opening had Richard bragging that he "didn't have to give up anything" to get his show—only to reveal him (in a body stocking) emasculated. NBC deleted it on the spot.

Indeed, one wonders if NBC really wanted the show to succeed in the first place. The net-

Richard Pryor reacts appropriately after seeing what NBC has planned for his show.

work scheduled it against two of the most popular programs on television—ABC's unbeatable combo of *Happy Days* and *Laverne & Shirley*. Moreover, Pryor was assigned the completely unacceptable 8:00 to 9:00 p.m. "family hour" for his show, instead of an infinitely more appropriate and sophisticated 9:00 or 10:00 berth.

On the black-tempered set of the Richard Pryor show, by the late fall of 1977 the tension level had become white hot. NBC pulled the show, "with regrets," within six weeks.

## The Redd Foxx Comedy Hour

*Network: ABC; On the air: September 15, 1977–January 26, 1978*
Toward the end of the 1976–77 season, after five and a half years on the air—four of them as the number-one rated show on NBC—Redd Foxx came into his Burbank studio lot and announced, "That's it—no more *Sanford & Son.*"

As soon as the announcement hit the trades that Redd would be leaving *Sanford*, ABC offered Foxx a supremely lucrative deal for an hour variety show, with most of his regulars from *Sanford & Son* (LaWanda Page, Slappy White, Whitman Mayo) along for the ride. Also boding well for the show was that ABC assigned it a far more appropriate (10:00 p.m.) time slot than NBC had given Richard Pryor and promised relaxed rules with regards to censorship. Redd was also given the title of executive producer of the show, although the real day-to-day responsibility fell to variety veterans Allan Blye and Bob Einstein.

In one notable segment from the series that made note of the fates of other black starring variety shows of the time, Redd was shown reading a *TV Guide* and saying to himself (aloud), "Let's see . . . Cosby ain't on . . . Flip ain't on . . . Richard ain't on . . . Sammy ain't on . . . On TV, I guess it must be White Night!"

Despite the talented cast, when the show failed to topple its entrenched *Barnaby Jones* competition in the rankings, ABC lost its patience, and quick. Just as with Pearl Bailey before, ABC didn't want a merely successful show—they expected top-rated, *Sanford & Son* numbers right from the start. Disgusted by the show's premature cancellation, Redd left for Las Vegas and stayed there for two years, until a then-desperate, third-place NBC offered him, "Money—LOTS of money," to reprise his best-known role in *Sanford,* from 1980 to '81.

Redd made intermittent appearances on TV and in films throughout the '80s until making a full comeback in 1991 alongside costar Della Reese in *The Royal Family* on CBS. Sadly, just as Fred Sanford kept waiting for the heart attack that would take him home to be with his departed Elizabeth, Redd was felled by an all-too-real attack on the set of the new show. He died in October 1991, at the age of sixty-nine.

"Redd was a gift," said Della Reese, who would go on to play tough-mama angel Tess on CBS's *Touched by an Angel* from 1994 to 2003. LaWanda Page recalled in an E! Network interview that, at Redd's funeral, she wanted to tell Redd that he "ain't got no business being in that coffin!" Then she smiled and said that if Redd could have heard her say that, he'd have probably just laughed and replied, "Oh shut up, bitch!"

# the flip wilson show

## VITAL STATS

**STARRING**
Flip Wilson

**ON THE AIR**
September 17, 1970—June 27, 1974

**NETWORK**
NBC

**ANNOUNCER**
John Harlan

**MUSIC AND DANCE**
The George Wyle Orchestra; The Jack Regas Dancers

**ORIGINATION**
KNBC Studios, in Beautiful Downtown Burbank

"What you see is what you get!"

A trio of singing superstars (*clockwise from left*): Ella Fitzgerald, Perry Como, and Bing Crosby.

TELEVISION'S BEST BLACK-HOSTED variety series started at the top in 1970 and ended that way four years later. While *The Nat King Cole Show*, also on NBC, was TV's first influential African American–starring variety show, it was cancelled despite high ratings after only one year in 1957. Several bigoted NBC affiliates had blocked the show, and threatened to opt out of the NBC "family" if it wasn't canceled immediately. And it wasn't just because Nat's show had merely starred a black performer; there had been others before it, like *Amos & Andy* and *Beulah*. *The Nat King Cole Show*'s unforgivable sin was showing a black man interacting with whites as an *equal*, with some white guests even looking up to and respecting him.

That was just too much to take for some in 1950s America. Unfortunately, the furor the show aroused would haunt the networks every time an influential black movie or singing star wanted to do a series. For the next ten years, African American performers would be completely locked out of star stature in being asked to host their own shows. Meanwhile, the truly biggest African American comedians—Redd Foxx, Richard Pryor, Rudy Ray Moore, Nipsey Russell, Slappy White—found their biggest fame in black casinos and clubs on the "chitlin' circuit," and released X-rated "party records."

*The Flip Wilson Show* changed all this. It was the perfect comedy-variety complement to an era when performers like Sidney Poitier, Bill Cosby, Diahann Carroll, Dorothy Dandridge, Harry Belafonte, and Sammy Davis Jr. were finally forcing the networks and studios to recognize the vitality of African American life. Along with Diahann Carroll's *Julia*, its success was responsible for a near-Renaissance in shows made by and for African American audiences. It was the first black-starring show to reach number one in the weekly ratings on a regular basis. (In its first season, it was the second-highest-rated show on all television, behind only *Marcus Welby, M.D.*) Following on Flip's heels, programs like *Sanford & Son*, *Good Times*, *The Jeffersons*, *What's Happening*, and *Benson* would emerge as hits during the '70s. The day *The Flip Wilson Show* reached numero uno, it finally shattered the glass ceiling for black equality in television—at least for a time.

But that wasn't the show's main accomplishment. What made *The Flip Wilson Show* unique was that it was the first show in television history to star a black man who based his comedy on black society and culture, without denigrating or apologizing for it. Les Brown of *Variety* said, in an almost comically pretentious summation of the show, that Flip's best-known characters (like Geraldine Jones, Sapphire, and Reverend Leroy) were "so distinctly Negro, they had no credible counterparts in white society." John Leonard's rave review in a fall 1970 issue of *Life* magazine said essentially the same thing.

Today, minority stars and costars are commonplace on top-rated hits like *Law & Order*, *CSI*, and *ER*, and there are many African American–starring comedies. But back in 1970, to have a black man who based his characterizations on ghetto life—

without mocking it in a vicious, self-hating way or glorifying the ugliest stereotypes—was unique on television.

Clerow Wilson was born on December 8, 1933, in Jersey City, New Jersey. Proving the adage that comedy comes from tragedy, there was nothing funny whatsoever about the future comedian's early life. Born at the height of the Great Depression in the "black bottom" of New Jersey, Wilson's formative years were spent trapped in a nightmare world of poverty and child abuse; he was raised for virtually all of his childhood in foster homes and orphanages.

At the age of sixteen, Wilson dropped out of high school, and soon he enlisted in the air force. He was ready to break free from the social-service system that had held him captive for all of his young life. The dynamic youth was eager for the opportunity to become a man in his own right and to pursue his lifelong love of flying.

He got it—but the circumstances were just as harsh as the worst foster home. No sooner had Wilson signed up than the communists invaded South Korea. By the time Wilson was eighteen in 1952, he found that his best outlet for surviving the horrors of war was doing stand-up routines and impressions for his fellow soldiers. While Wilson hadn't completely decided on a showbiz career after the army, he started putting on shows and involving himself with the USO all through his service in Korea. And he found to his encouragement that his take on wartime life was a breath of funny fresh air for the many servicemen who roared with laughter at his routines.

The irrepressible youth was nicknamed "Flip" by his predominantly black service buddies, after his flippant, irreverent comedy riffs—and it stuck. (It was also a lot slicker a moniker than *Clerow* for a stand-up comedian, no doubt.) After his service was completed, the restless youth who had been given no direction in his early life had finally found his calling.

Flip decided to strike out on his own in San Francisco, where he landed once he returned from the war. Flip worked odd jobs while trying to gather together nightclub and stage acting gigs in the black theatre, including as a bellhop at a luxury hotel, where he pestered the hotel manager until he was allowed to play a walk-on role in one of the hotel's dinner shows. And once he got on the stage again, Flip Wilson never turned back.

It was during this era that the twentysomething comedian created and defined the characters that would make him famous. What set Flip Wilson apart from almost every other stand-up comedian (besides Jonathan Winters and maybe Uncle Miltie himself) was that he didn't just stand up and do a monologue. He created and transmogrified himself into several different characters and personas. Watching Flip Wilson perform was like watching a sort of sane *Sybil* or *Three Faces of Eve*. One minute Flip would be Flip (or his alter ego, well-adjusted young black man Freddie Johnson); the next minute, he'd turn into a sexy swinging single gal named Geraldine Jones right before your very eyes. Geraldine loved her extremely jealous boyfriend

"Killer"—but not so much that she stayed especially faithful to him. "What you see, is what you get!" Geraldine would tease, flirting with her hands sashaying on her hips, as the crowd roared. And of course, whenever the impulse-control challenged Geraldine gave in to her latest whims, it would never, ever be her fault. No—"the Debbil made me do it, honey!"

Later characters included Herbie the Ice Cream Man, as bossy and protective of his meager position as any power executive; pigtailed honey child Sapphire; and, by the time the variety show came around, Danny Danger, Detective. But besides Geraldine, Flip's best-loved character was the designer threads–wearing, convertible Eldorado–driving Reverend Leroy, an irreverent takeoff on "name it and claim it" black prosperity preachers, whom Flip had based on a high-living minister he knew from his youth growing up.

By the mid-'60s, the thirty-year-old comedian was finally starting to play in "white" clubs and casinos as well as on the all-black "chitlin' circuit," and had caught the eye of the talent bookers for *The Tonight Show*. Flip's first appearance was a smash, and his Carson appearance caught the eye of the man who would give him his biggest and most lasting break—none other than Ed Sullivan. Sullivan's audience flipped for Flip's first appearance, and Sullivan soon started signing Flip for so many future appearances he became almost a "regular" on the program. Other shows, like *The Hollywood Palace* and *The Kraft Music Hall,* soon followed suit, as did Dean Martin's show and *Laugh-In*.

By now, thanks to the exposure, Flip was commanding top prices and standing-room-only crowds in Hollywood and Las Vegas comedy clubs and showrooms. In 1968, Flip starred in a special for NBC that proved to be one of the highest-rated and best-received variety specials since the first *Laugh-In* special in September 1967. That left NBC with simply no reason not to take that last step off the diving board and give the talented young comedian a regular weekly home.

NBC had had bad luck with half-hour sitcoms all through the 1960s. Sure, there was *I Dream of Jeannie* (and later, *Julia*). But while CBS struck ratings gold with their country-and-western comedies and ABC with their suburban kid-coms, NBC's luck with the lucrative format was notoriously poor. But the network still managed to boast the most sophisticated (and often the flat-out funniest) comedies on the tube, thanks to their commitment to stylish, unique comedy variety—*Laugh-In* and Dean Martin in particular.

Newer crime shows, like NBC's own *Ironside* and CBS's *Hawaii Five-0* and *Mannix* were considerably more sophisticated than a lot of the good-guy bad-guy shoot-'em-ups of the past. And that's not to mention the issue-of-the-week "relevance" shows, like *Marcus Welby* and the soon-to-launch *All in the Family*. The grown-up subject matter of these shows neccessitated the later 9:00 and 10:00 slots, leaving the early-evening "family hour" the most challenging hour of the day for NBC to program.

The network needed to find something relatively wholesome for the many children who'd be tuning in—but still sophisticated enough for its target audience of citified adult viewers—if it wanted to combat the entrenched comedies and kiddie-actioners on the other channels at the start of the broadcast night.

So, as the fall 1970 season approached, NBC decided to start almost every evening of the week off with a comical "checkerboard" of their spécialité d'house, refreshing comedy-variety series. Mondays would start off with a supposedly more sophisticated half-hour version of *The Red Skelton Show*, followed by the top-rated *Laugh-In* from 8:00–9:00. Tuesdays would have Don Knotts in a new show, while Saturdays would kick off with a revised Andy Williams show, and Sundays would, as always, lead off with the *Walt Disney* anthology.

One gaping hole stood to be filled on Thursday nights, as the slot's previous occupant, *Daniel Boone*, was about to hang up his saddle. The leadoff hour was not to be entrusted to a newcomer or amateur, with such muscle-weights as *Bewitched*, *Family Affair*, and *The Jim Nabors Show* on the other sides of the dial—or else the whole night might collapse. And Thursdays were NBC's most profitable night, with *Ironside* and Dean Martin completely owning the later hours of the evening.

By then, Flip's longtime business manager, the late great Monte Kay, had made it a deal breaker that Flip be given a firm pre-commitment to an NBC show for 1970 (or else no more top-rated specials and guest appearances). The network realized that of all the shows and performers they had sewed up for that fall, Flip Wilson alone was the best qualified to take on the challenge of leading off Thursday nights. Flip's easygoing, Cheshire Cat style of comedy was a far cry from the sticky-sweetness of *Family Affair* and the "gaw-all-ee!" cornpone of *The Jim Nabors Show*, his principal opponents for the hour. Yet his broad comedy and friendly image was made to order for a family show. After Monte Kay selected veteran producer Bob Henry and former *Ed Sullivan* and *Smothers Brothers* director Tim Kiley to helm the series, the fearsome foursome began working out a format that would be befittingly unique and set apart, just as the show and its host would be.

Those who worked with him said that Flip Wilson had one of the least obtrusive egos in all Hollywood (though Flip himself acknowledged that he could be very difficult, especially around the interviewers and paparazzi that pestered him at KNBC studios.). But there was one exception.

Flip Wilson would be THE star of *The Flip Wilson Show*. Period. No more pandering to the bigoted viewers who couldn't get over Nat King Cole—the ground rules were set from day one. It would be Flip's way, or the highway—take it or leave it. Unlike all of the other variety programs on the air in 1970, Flip refused to surround himself with a supporting cast of backup players, go-go girls, and singing troupes. The show would revolve around him alone, and the few guest stars he invited onto his program each week. Each episode would open with a Johnny

Watching Geraldine was never a drag. Here she flirts with Muhammad Ali (left) and Bill Cosby (bottom).

Carson or David Letterman–like monologue with the camera (and the hooting and clapping audience), with Flip taking full advantage of his abilities as a stand-up comic.

And really, a "supporting cast" on *The Flip Wilson Show* would have been unnecessary. Flip Wilson was *his own* supporting cast, by himself, what with characters as diverse, popular, and memorable as Geraldine, Rev. Leroy, Sapphire, Freddie Johnson, Herbie the Good Time Ice Cream Man, and Danny Danger, not to mention the one-shot characters he played in other sketches and skits.

And of course, Geraldine was so popular and so surefire that "she" practically became a costar of the show in her own right. Flip would sashay out on stage in micro-miniskirts and stiletto heels or go-go boots, wearing Geraldine's "flipped" wig and makeup, and let the audience see what they were gonna get!

While it may belabor the point in this day and age, there is no overstating how nervy and groundbreaking that move was for a black performer back in 1970. Only two years earlier, Petula Clark had made headlines for merely holding Harry Belafonte's hand during a prime-time special. Roles that would be taken for granted today—such as Nichelle Nichols' competent, intelligent Lt. Uhura on *Star Trek*, Gail Fisher's efficient and playful secretary on *Mannix* (many fans assumed she was Mannix's partner on and off duty), and Diahann Carroll's nurse *Julia*—were considered controversial to some at the time.

Now, an African American performer was demanding full star status, plus creative control, format approval, and financial ownership of his own prime-time network show. And what's more, he got it!

While discrimination would still raise its ugly head in Hollywood over the three decades since, Flip's all-or-nothing gamble set a fabulous, right-on precedent for African American comedians, actors, and singers. Many if not all who've come after have benefited from it.

Flip also demonstrated his savvy business sense, making it a deal breaker that he and his manager Monte Kay *own* the show. This meant that he and Kay's production company would sop up the gravy of the immense profits, rather than just NBC alone. Since it stayed in the Top Thirty from first week to last, this move would make both of them wealthy men.

A unique touch to the show (which Tim Kiley had experimented with off-and-on during the Smothers brothers' tenure) would be the way they shot the entire program "in the round." Flip Wilson's studio brought new meaning to the phrase "center stage." It was uniquely custom-made and configured to Flip and Tim Kiley's specifications. Instead of the usual audience-at-one-end/stage-at-the-other theatrical setup, the audience was spread into four quadrants surrounding a center stage where the action was. More often than not (even in sketches with elaborate backdrops and scenery) real-life audience members would be seen laughing, nodding, and sometimes even pointing or waving at the camera while the sketch went on. Talk about "suspension of disbelief"!

But that intimacy was just another trademark of the Wilson style that set his show apart. Having come from a background in small comedy clubs and intimate jazz bars, Wilson wanted to literally let his audience in on everything and make them a part of the show. The effect carried over to the home viewers as well. Watching at home, forty million TV viewers felt like they were personal guests at Flip Wilson's "house," which made him all the more welcome in ours.

Following a big publicity buildup, *The Flip Wilson Show* premiered on NBC on September 17, 1970, to rave reviews and strong ratings among both black and white households. The stakes couldn't have been higher. If Flip's show succeeded, the glass ceiling that had trapped minority performers in the ghetto of second-rate, embarrassing roles and characters would finally be shattered. But if it failed . . . it could effectively ruin the chance for other African American singers and comedians to have their own shows and the full support of a network for years to come.

Not only was the series premiere a hit—Flip's new variety show succeeded even beyond the wildest dreams of NBC. It blew its ABC and CBS competition out of the water from the get-go. By November 1970, NBC raised the price of commercials by half and doubled them from their original price in January 1971. By then, Flip had even toppled *Laugh-In* as the network's highest-rated variety hour. The show that had premiered less than six months earlier against entrenched competition was now well on its way to being the number one show on television—an almost unheard-of achievement for a brand-new show, let alone a black one. When the annual ratings were released that May, only *Marcus Welby* topped *Flip* in the rankings.

Just nine months after it first aired, the number one show on NBC—the number two show in all of television—was *The Flip Wilson Show*.

Flip's show, along with *Sonny & Cher,* set the standard for TV variety in the early 1970s. Almost no one—not even the likes of Paul McCartney, Lucille Ball, Aretha Franklin, or Bob Hope—turned down an invite to appear on Flip's center stage. Not only did it use the latest in production techniques, but its full-color photography, top-grade videotape, and A-list guest stars masterfully blended with the early TV–era intimacy of the round stage and the skimpy sets. From mod to old-fashioned, from black to white, from young to old—*The Flip Wilson Show* synthesized the best of both worlds.

After his show was ensconced at number one, Flip asked NBC to do just a touch more remodeling, which they happily agreed to do. Flip was known for keeping his own counsel, and wanting to go over the sketches and layouts of the show in private, where he could think them through and rehearse them himself, without being interrupted or interfered with. The network built him the best dressing room on the NBC lot, which was so large and sumptuous it was converted into an office suite after Flip retired and *The Midnight Special* took over the wing.

Aretha Franklin (*above*) and Lily Tomlin
(*left*) join in the fun.

TV'S GROOVIEST VARIETY SHOWS

After Flip's show sailed through two seasons as TV's clear variety leader, in 1972 both ABC and CBS tried to squeeze the hit show for all it was worth. ABC moved a big gun, *The Mod Squad*, against it, hoping that it would (as one of the few shows with a co-equal black character) draw off young urban black viewers. Meanwhile, CBS counterprogrammed the urban, minority show with the charming and high-quality Depression family drama *The Waltons*.

Flip busted *The Mod Squad* before the season was out, and finished the season in a virtual tie with the clan on Waltons mountain. By the following season, *The Waltons* were winning the time period, but Flip's show was still a muscle-strong second. In some ways, that made the show even more valuable to NBC. Now that CBS had made gains for the evening in a time slot they had been taking for granted, NBC needed Flip's show more than ever, to keep the night from collapsing entirely.

And NBC really wanted to keep the show going for the 1974–75 season. In 1973, their league-leader *Laugh-In* closed its joke wall for good, and Dean Martin's nine-year-old show retired less than a year later. Flip was NBC's great hope to keep them in the sophisticated-variety business that had been their biggest trademark for the past decade.

But Flip Wilson had other plans. He didn't want to do the show forever, only to watch its innovations and freshness gradually fade. By 1974, he had already earned a king's ransom from NBC in his four years on the air, especially since he co-owned the series. Flip's comedy records had been bestsellers for years, and he could write his own figure at any upscale comedy club or casino resort in the country.

Most importantly, at the time Flip was going through a very painful and public divorce, and consolidating a relationship with a new girlfriend. As such, the forty-year-old comedian began to rearrange his priorities. For four years, The *Flip Wilson Show* had taken first place in his life, with its demanding rehearsal schedules and A-list guest stars needing the proper treatment. Now, the comedian who had been shuttled from one foster family to the next in his early life of Depression-era bleakness was ready to refocus that same energy on his family and children.

The mellow entertainer had been prudent with his earnings, too, and while he provided a good deal of well-earned luxury for himself, he had lived moderately by the outrageously glitzy standards of Hollywood, Beverly Hills, and Brentwood. Flip had no need to work any longer, and decided to take some time off from the spotlight to concentrate on raising his children. Flip wanted to make a point of being the father to them that he had never had when he was growing up.

Around the same time, Flip also began studying the work of Eastern philosopher Kahlil Gibran, author of the legendary philosophy treatise, *The Prophet*. Flip became something of an expert on Eastern philosophy and mysticism, as well as his philosophy of life from being raised in the black church. To NBC's grave dismay, in the spring of 1974, Flip Wilson announced that *The Flip Wilson Show* was going off the air.

As it turned out, NBC was correct in their near-desperation to keep Flip Wilson on their schedule. For a full decade, until another equally influential African American centered comedy, *The Cosby Show*, moved in to the same berth in 1984, NBC would never have a successful challenge to CBS's dramas and ABC's sitcoms on Thursday nights at 8:00. And it would be another fifteen years, until Keenan Ivory Wayans's *In Living Color* on Fox, before another black performer would star in a successful sketch comedy show.

Flip Wilson downsized his profile for the remainder of the '70s, but fortunately he didn't disappear. He made an appearance on Cher's first solo show in 1975, but left before the taping of the episode was even completed. He also regularly made the talk- and game-show circuit, doing numerous episodes of Johnny, Mike, Merv, and *Hollywood Squares*, and some Vegas and comedy-club gigs. He even guest-hosted an episode of *The Midnight Special*.

Less than seven years after the demise of his show, Flip made headlines all over again—but not in a way he'd have wanted to. In 1981, Flip was arrested at an airport for possession of narcotics. (Flip served no jail sentence and the affair was speedily resolved.) But from then on, the already private comedian kept an ever-lower profile.

Flip's TV appearances in the 1980s were sporadic at best. In 1984, he hosted a short-lived revival of the 1950s game show *People Are Funny*. And in 1985–86 he teamed up with Gladys Knight for the situation comedy *Charlie & Company*. (Unfortunately it was smashed by *Dynasty* and barely lasted the season.) He also found himself the target of several "palimony" lawsuits by live-in girlfriends who wanted support after the relationships came to an end.

But in late 1997 and early 1998, Flip Wilson was back in the news again—for the worst possible reason.

Just before his sixty-fourth birthday, Flip Wilson was diagnosed with cancer. There were already malignant tumors speading across his liver and kidneys. While as private a person as Flip would have no doubt preferred to keep the news of his illness and treatment to himself, in the tabloid-TV world of 1998, he knew that just wasn't gonna happen. Resigned to the media hype, he showed the same kind of class and good sportsmanship he had shown on his own show, giving upbeat interviews to reporters where he claimed that the disease was being beaten back into remission every day. He rarely got snapped outside the doctor's office or hospital without wearing a genial smile or giving a knowing thumbs-up.

But despite his unfailing optimism and bravery, there was just nothing funny about having cancer. By the fall, Flip was confined to his Malibu Colony beachcliff home. And on November 25, 1998, Flip Wilson passed away, just two weeks short of his sixty-fifth birthday.

While it could have run for years longer, by calling it quits when it did, *The Flip Wilson Show* left the airwaves at the height of its popularity, and at the top of its

Nobody ever confused Big Bird (*left*) with a soul brother, but Bobby Darin and Johnny Mathis (*above*) were another story.

game. It was as fun and as fresh on its last day in 1974 as it had been on opening night. Unlike the vast majority of TV shows, Flip's show never "jumped the shark." And the *Flip Wilson Show,* and Flip himself, accomplished it all the old-fashioned way—they *earned* it. After all, when it came to the remarkable talent that was Flip Wilson, "What you saw—is what you got!"

## MEMORABLE MOMENTS

Were you watching when . . .

- Flip and Ed Sullivan could have danced all night, when Flip gave seventy-year-old Ed a lesson in jive dancing and disco moves!
- Flip was merely returning a favor—earlier, "Old Stone Face" congratulated former *Sullivan* regular Flip on landing his own show. He then proceeded to instruct the young upstart on how to be a proper variety-show emcee, Sullivan-style. (Things like making sure hands are arched on hips like a washing machine agitator . . . just the right way to waggle that index finger and stare down the camera . . . and most importantly, how to look mean and angry when addressing the audience!)
- Flip met his match on the dance floor, though, when he tried to instruct Big Bird in the finer points of jive dancing and doing the double-hustle.
- Guest star Aretha Franklin proved an amazing musical tour de force when she paid homage to fellow R&B and jazz legends Della Reese, Sarah Vaughan, Diana Ross, Ella Fitzgerald, and Dionne Warwick, by doing near-flawless imitations of their singing (as well as her own).
- Geraldine was a micro-mini-uniformed naughty nurse to hospital patient Bill Cosby, in a situation where the comic possibilities practically explain themselves.
- None other than Sir Paul McCartney made an ultra-rare guest appearance with his wife Linda and his post-Beatles band Wings, in 1972. The group capped off with a Wings number in a psychedelic, computer-generated electronic background sequence that was state-of-the-art for its time.
- Geraldine finally met her match when guest star Ralph Edwards said, "Tonight, Geraldine Jones, THIS IS YOUR LIFE!" Lucky for Ralph, Geraldine's jealous boyfriend Killer didn't show up that evening—or he'd have gotten an eyeful of mini-skirted Geraldine's flirting, grabbing, and come-ons at poor Ralph!
- Guest star George Carlin and Flip recapped the year 1971 playing newscasters Harry Wayne and Phil Newton—bringing you (of course) "The Wayne–Newton Report!"
- Private eye Danny Danger faced off against his least formidable adversary, Tim Conway's Little Old Man (a crime boss in this one), in a sort-of crossover from the two most popular variety shows of their time.
- Geraldine's analyst (Perry Como) asks her if she's having problems finding a man. "Honey," Geraldine sassed, "the day I have trouble findin' a man, I won't need no

psychiatrist—I'd need a *undertaker*!" Later on in the session, Geraldine balks at Dr. Como's (circa 1970) fee of $35 an hour. "Don't worry," the good doctor said, while escorting Geraldine to lie down on the therapy couch. "We can make arrangements for payment." "Yeah?" Geraldine exclaimed, pointing at the couch. "That's what I'm worried about—the *arrangements*!"

- Reverend Leroy must have really taken in some collection at one of his church services in 1973—the Temptations were his backup choir, singing a stoned-soul version of "Let It Be," while Rev. Leroy and Redd Foxx preached it to the masses!

- Geraldine and Lucille Ball got in a fight with each other over a man—and the man in question was none other than seventy-year-old Ed Sullivan! Ed settled the fracas by pushing the two ladies apart—right by the boobs! Lucy didn't mind, but Geraldine put her hand on her hip and sassed, "What you say, honey?"

  That impertinence was evidently enough for Ed to make up his mind. "Lllllu-uuucccy," he gestured with a sweep of his arms. "Yyyyyyooouu know, you're the only gal . . . for me!" "Oh Eddie," Lucy melted, "when you say things like that, you make me feel like I'm the Toast of the Town!"

- After his show left the airwaves, Flip Wilson explained his success, and that of his most popular alter ego. "The secret of my success with Geraldine is that she's not a put-down of Black women—in fact, she's a celebration of the Black woman! She's smart, loyal, trustful—and sassy. Most drag impersonations *are* a drag. But women can like Geraldine, men can like Geraldine, everyone can like Geraldine." Flip would later recall that, "Geraldine was [everyone's] favorite," including his own—but he added, with a wry grin, "Flip was my hero."

## QUOTABLE QUOTES

- "What you see is what you get!"
- "The Debbil made me do it!"

## BACKSTAGE PASS

Flip was vacationing abroad in the summer of 1971 just before production was about to gear up for the 1971–72 season. His manager and executive producer Monte Kay and producer Bob Henry interrupted his travels to conduct a conference call with him about possible guest stars for the fall 1971 premiere. Only the most desirable, "name" guests were to be considered for a show as important as the first one of the season. So far, they had lined up an A-list slate of Ed Sullivan, Lucille Ball, and the Osmond family.

Flip was thrilled. "That's great!" he exclaimed. "So what's the problem?" Bob Henry stammered, "Well, Flip—nothing—except, well—there aren't any black performers on the show!"

Flip responded, laughing, "Well, what the hell am I?"

# MELLOW GOLD

**The Light Pop Stars—Some a Little Bit Country,
Some a Little Bit Rock-and-Roll—Who Went Variety in the '70s**

## The Tony Orlando & Dawn Rainbow Hour

*Network: CBS; On the air: December 4, 1974–December 28, 1976*

Singer Tony Orlando had moved behind the scenes as a music producer and agent by the end of the 1960s, after enjoying only minor success as a recording artist. However, a friend of his who was producing a groovy little song called "Candida" needed a male vocalist (preferably a Hispanic one, given the song's title and theme) to sing lead on the track. The background vocals were already recorded by a duo of established studio singers named Telma Hopkins and Joyce Vincent Williams, two talented and sexy young black ladies who called their act Dawn. Tony agreed to do the song, more as a favor to an old friend than anything else, thinking it would probably go nowhere fast.

Obviously, Tony misjudged that one a wee bit. "Candida" became a huge hit across the radio dial in the summer of 1970, and the new "group" was soon beseiged with offers for a full album and follow-up recordings. (Tony only actually met Dawn after the song became at hit!) By the time 1973 rolled around, Tony Orlando & Dawn had had one hit after another, with songs like "Has Anybody Seen My Sweet Gypsy Rose," "Knock Three Times," and "Tie a Yellow Ribbon Round the Ole Oak Tree" (the last of which, of course, became the welcome-home anthem for Vietnam veterans, and in early 1981, the hostages released from Iran).

Talk shows, variety shows, and specials all beckoned the threesome, who happily obliged, as Tony, Joyce, and Telma showed their flair for comedy and friendly, vivacious personalities. To CBS chief Fred Silverman, giving the group their own variety show was a no-brainer, especially since by 1974 he was losing his unstoppable *Sonny & Cher* show to divorce. *Tony Orlando & Dawn* debuted in *Sonny & Cher*'s old Wednesday night at 8:00 time slot, leading into William Conrad's huge (in more ways than one) detective drama *Cannon*. Despite heavy fire from NBC's new *Little House on the Prairie,* the show immediately claimed a strong second place and an occasional win in the ratings.

It was easy to see why. The compulsively watchable show was as campy and shticky as a Chuck Barris production, and kicked off with one smiley-face '70s pop anthem after another. The show's disco-era, mirror-walled audience—complete with game-show "chase lights" and brown shag carpeting—only underlined the feel. And the show had regular *Sonny & Cher*–style comedy sketches and musical salutes, as well as the popular recurring characters Lou Effie and Mo'Reen (Joyce and

Tony Orlando and Dawn let the sunshine in on their *Rainbow Hour*.

Telma, of course), a sort of cross between Florida and Willona on *Good Times* and *Laverne and Shirley*.

Above all, the show captured the same sunny, infectious enthusiasm that made Tony Orlando and Dawn such a popular recording act. If you were looking for a feel-good, Vegas-ized variety show, you didn't need to look any further than *Tony Orlando & Dawn*. And it should be noted that the show was the first successful variety show ever hosted by a Hispanic man, let alone one alongside two black ladies.

After two years of solid achievement on Wednesday nights, CBS moved the show to Tuesdays in the fall of 1976, to try to blunt ABC's new sitcoms. Unfortunately, it didn't. (Interestingly, the show was replaced by a variety series hosted by the Jackson Five, which was irregularly scheduled and beset by the same behind-the-scenes dramas and problems that any *Behind the Music* or *True Hollywood Story* fan knows by heart.)

And speaking of scandal and heartbreak, less than a month after *The Tony Orlando & Dawn Rainbow Hour* finished, Tony's world was rocked by the tragic death of one of his best friends, the young comedian and *Chico & the Man* star Freddie Prinze, who committed suicide in January 1977. Tony would spend the next year in a nightmare of drug and alcohol dependency, and another year after that trying to dig his way out before it was too late for him too. Happily, Tony was back in action by the end of 1978, making numerous talk-show and game-show appearances, as he shared his triumph over dependency while rebuilding a new "dawn" in his career as a solo act.

Joyce Vincent Wilson also continued a relatively successful if lower-key career, while Telma Hopkins took off, cast alongside her fellow singing diva and close friend, stage star Nell Carter, in the 1981–87 NBC sitcom *Gimme a Break*. Telma followed that with another sitcom role less than two years later, in the long running 1989–98 ABC "TGIF" comedy hit *Family Matters*.

## The Glen Campbell Goodtime Hour

*Network: CBS; On the air: January 29, 1969–June 13, 1972*

After making a huge splash on the radio in the late '60s with his hits "Galveston" and "By the Time I Get to Phoenix," and successfully hosting *The Summer Brothers Smothers Show*, Glen Campbell was offered his own big-time variety show by CBS in early 1969. And the Glen Campbell show delivered exactly what its title promised—a good time.

As far as the show's format and execution, it was as likeably middle-of-the-road as the music it presented. It lacked the flair, energy, and cutting-edge production techniques of *Laugh-In, Flip Wilson*, and *Sonny & Cher*, but it also lacked the cringe-inducing lameness and cornpone hillbilly antics of its CBS contemporaries *Hee-Haw* and *The Jim Nabors Hour*. *The Glen Campbell Goodtime Hour* was the first country-and-western show that was cool for both regular country fans and young city folk alike. Glen set the tenor of the show himself, and like his personality, the show was funny, warm, and a nice enough way to spend an hour on a Sunday night.

When the show started in early 1969, it was a temporary stopgap on Wednesday nights in the 7:30 leadoff hour. Its success in that early hour prompted rival net NBC to "checkerboard" their early evenings with nearly one variety show per night by fall 1970. When *The Leslie Uggams Show* fell out, *Hee-Haw* came truckin' on into Wednesdays at 7:30, and Campbell was rewarded for his success by being promoted to the golden Sunday night 9:00 hour that *The Smothers Brothers* had had for two years. And while it didn't do quite as well as the Smotherses did in their prime, it nonetheless kept *Bonanza* and ABC's world-premiere movies from completely dominating the evening, with a top twenty finish.

Still, despite Campbell's considerable talent and likability, as the '70s got under way the variety format started its slow fade. Even worse, Campbell was struggling with substance-abuse problems, raising a young family, and a nonstop touring and recording schedule that, combined with the rigors of taping the show, left him with barely enough time left to breathe. After a respectable three-and-a-half year run, the show quietly closed up shop in 1972.

Glen Campbell fortunately overcame the dependency problems that his packed work schedule caused him in the late '80s and early '90s. Glen also enjoyed several more top radio hits, such as 1975's smash "Rhinestone Cowboy," and continued to be a popular guest star on TV specials and at the Grand Ole Opry.

## Donny & Marie

*Network: ABC; On the air: January 23, 1976–May 27, 1979*
The multi-instrumental, singing Osmond family of youngsters received their first big break as regular performers on Andy Williams's 1962–71 variety show on NBC. By the end of that show's run, the youngest brother of the group, deep-eyed, wavy-haired Donny, had become a teenager. And he'd also become the hottest and—to the junior-high set anyway—sexiest teenage idol this side of the *Partridge Family*'s David Cassidy. Barely a week went by without Donny's face on a teen magazine or fan article. Meanwhile, singing sister Marie was finding her fortune as a country and western singer, after her 1972 smash "Paper Roses." Marie soon equalled her slightly older brother in fawning media coverage and cutesy TV gigs.

Fred Silverman was not unaware of these things as he crossed the TV divide, leaving his five years at the helm of CBS's programming department in 1975 to head ABC for three years. Silverman had already seen *Sonny & Cher* become a cultural phenomenon on his watch at CBS, not to mention Carol Burnett in her prime at the pinnacle of CBS's *All in the Family/Mary Tyler Moore* Saturday night lineup.

And after taking a beating with the deserved failure of the outrageous *Saturday Night Live with Howard Cosell,* Silverman was determined to bring on a new variety show with the kitchen-sink verve that had been his trademark at CBS. Silverman contacted veteran entertainers and TV producers Sid and Marty Krofft with his idea for a teenage version of *Sonny & Cher* and *Flip Wilson.*

The freethinking fifth-generation puppeteer duo, who had already brought the wonders of *Pufnstuf, Lidsville, The Bugaloos, Sigmund & the Sea Monsters,* and *Land of the Lost* to the air, moved in to take on their next challenge. And Fred Silverman moved the new show into the stage at Los Angeles independent station KTLA's Golden West Videotape Center in December of 1975, which had previously been occupied by ABC's 1974–75 sitcom *That's My Mama.*

In January of 1976, *Donny & Marie* burst on the scene with an electrified opening montage and a huge, theater-like stage and set. The teenage duo also had the hardest workload in the business, having to appear in nearly every musical number and comedy sketch and reading so many lines that they had to use cue cards and TelePrompTers just to get through.

The crew at the Golden West Videotape Center soon figured out why ABC wanted them to deal with the show instead of staging it at their own Prospect-Talmadge studios. ABC chief Fred Silverman wanted to bring the live excitement of Ice Capades and "Holiday on Ice" to the show, considering that Donny, Marie, and their siblings were proficient ice skaters thanks to their upbringing in Salt Lake City. KTLA's technical crew had to configure an ice-show skating-rink stage, complete with technical banks (and keep it maintained so the ice wouldn't melt under the lights)—and then strike the stage and the ice floor at the end of taping, so that their other clients could rent the stages.

However, it was this battle over studio space that would prove a nail in the show's coffin as time went on. While *Donny & Marie* performed adequately in the ratings, it was never a huge Top 25 hit, on an ABC that was filled to the brim with chart-toppers in the late '70s. But the show did deliver a cascade of stay-at-home families on its Friday-night time slot, and was as big as anyone dreamed it would be with the teenybopper set.

Riding high, the Osmonds announced the surprising decision that they would leave Hollywood in 1978—but remain with the show. The Osmond family was pioneering a concept later used to far greater success by Dolly Parton in the late '80s with her Dollywood, building an Osmond family media complex in Provo, Utah. Donny and his brothers wanted to tape the show there, back home, where they felt they belonged.

ABC and the staff at Golden West Videotape were infuriated by this move, coming after they'd spent money like drunken soldiers building huge multiple sets and the ice rink for the show in Los Angeles. But the larger Osmond family was homesick for Salt Lake City. Especially since Donny and Marie had precious little in the way of support or refuge in decadent, disco-era Hollywood. The two young performers would work twelve- and fourteen-hour days for three or four days a week rehearsing and filming spot segments, and then do the show, only to start up again. The drug and disco atmopshere of the Hollywood scene offered little recourse—except temptations to violate their Mormon commandments and get wasted, while already under tremendous pressure.

It wouldn't have made much difference anyway. In the spring of 1978, CBS debuted a show tailor-made to grab the youngsters that were *Donny & Marie*'s lifeblood: the comic-book action series *The Incredible Hulk.* Not even Donny's singing and smiles or Marie's wholesome sexiness could match the muscles of the Hulk. And by year's end, CBS would own the rest of the night with the new hits *Dukes of Hazzard* and *Dallas.* ABC tried a last-ditch attempt at relieving the impossible workload on Donny (who'd recently married) and Marie by bringing on the whole family (and retitling the show *The Osmond Family Hour*), but it was too late. The ice melted for *Donny & Marie* in the spring of 1979.

Eighteen months after *The Osmond Family Show* faded to black, Marie Osmond was back in the solo spotlight with *Marie* on NBC, for nine months in 1981. Donny pursued a highly successful careeer in the 1980s and '90s in theatre and musicals, including a bravura performance as the lead in the Broadway smash *Joseph and the Amazing Technicolor Dreamcoat.* And in 1998, Donny and Marie reunited for a five-day-a-week daytime talk show, appropriately enough titled *Donny & Marie,* which was a favorite of the Fox network stations for its two-year run. Marie Osmond had to take a leave of absence from the show for a while in 1999, though, when she suffered from depression and some private family issues.

Fortunately, the always-spunky Marie bounced back, while Donny moved on to host a two-year revival of the classic game show *Pyramid* from 2002 to 2004. Fittingly, it was taped right at his old home stage, at KTLA's studios in Los Angeles.

## The Captain & Tennille

*Network: ABC; On the air: September 20, 1976–March 14, 1977*
The most blatant attempt yet to clone CBS's success with *The Sonny & Cher Comedy Hour, The Captain & Tennille* featured the highly popular recording duo of Daryl "The Captain" Dragon (so nicknamed for the anchor-crest captain's hat that was his trademark) and vivacious, sexy singer Toni Tennille. The duo had been a successful lounge and touring act for a while in the late '60s and '70s, and had struck mellow gold in 1975 with their catchy chart-topper "Love Will Keep Us Together."

The show failed to capture the dynamic stage magic that the Captain & Tennille delivered in their sold-out Las Vegas, Palm Beach, Martha's Vineyard, and Hawaiian shows. Not much attention was paid to the show's format—in addition to the song duets (certainly the show's highlight) and the usual guest-star shots, there were lots of long comedy sketches—but without any identifiable recurring or loveable characters, and certainly nothing on the level of Cher's "Vamp" numbers or Flip Wilson's Geraldine bits. One source described the duo as not looking particularly "comfortable" with the weekly effort, and it showed.

After their own show's cancellation, the Captain & Tennille kept up an active presence in what remained of variety TV, on *The Midnight Special* and Johnny Carson in particular. In 1980 they once again hit the top of the charts, with the seductive hit "Do That to Me One More Time." And later that year, Toni Tennille tried to strike out on her own (while remaining married to "the Captain," as she still is) with a daytime talk show, which only lasted a few months.

The Captain & Tennille are still together, and still doing it one more time, as one of the grooviest classic soft rock acts around. (The two made a laugh-out-loud commercial for a phone company a while back—singing an outrageously campy version of "Do That to Me One More Time.")

## Make Your Own Kind of Music (The Carpenters Hour)

*Network: NBC; On the air: July 20, 1971–September 7, 1971*
Not two years after their first smash album, 1969's *Offering*, followed closely by "Close to You" and "We've Only Just Begun," easy-listening royalty Richard and Karen Carpenter were given their own summer replacement series on NBC in 1971. Despite being a high-quality and enjoyable hour with many top-name guests and a fresh approach, the show left the airwaves for good after its summer tryout ended, even though NBC hoped to have the brother-and-sister act back by midseason. In one of those rare cases of stars being (at least temporarily) *too* successful to have their own TV show, the Carpenters were so big in 1971 that they decided they neither wanted nor needed the stress of being tied down to a weekly, twenty-six-episode series.

An ironic postscript to their NBC summer show was the fact that later on in their careers, the Carpenters did make several TV specials—for rival network ABC. Proof that the Carpenters might not have been ready for prime time's compromises back in 1971 came with their last special nine years later, three years before Karen's tragic 1983 death.

It was appropriately called *Music, Music, Music*—an avant-garde program which featured no sketches or comedy routines (really, almost no spoken dialogue at all), flowing quickly from one number or performance video to the next. But the ABC exec in charge of the show felt that the show was a little *too* artistic and out of the ordinary, and he angrily bellowed at Richard Carpenter (as if it were the worst insult he could give to a program), "Whaddaya think this is, kid—a PBS special?"

## The Golddiggers

*Network: NBC/Syndicated first-run; On the air: 1968–1973*
From 1968 to 1970, Dean Martin's busy cast of chorus girls and singers known as The Golddiggers

took over for their boss as Dino took the summers off. The gorgeous gals' first summer series in 1968 boasted a quintessential '60s Vegas lineup of Frank Sinatra Jr., Joey Heatherton, and Paul Lynde saluting the swingin' big band era of the '30s and '40s. For 1969's jaunt Lou Rawls, Paul Lynde, and Tommy Tune saluted the days of old vaudeville, and 1970's tripped-out trip brought things right up to date in mod London, with Charles Nelson Reilly, Tommy Tune, and Marty Feldman.

After the Golddiggers struck ratings gold three summers in a row, producer Greg Garrison green-lit a once-a-week, syndicated variety show for the girls on their own. The twenty-six half hours a season were taped in marathon sessions like a talk or game show, with two or three episodes shot per taping day, during Dean's summer hiatuses in 1971 and 1972. The hectic pace of the tapings (only compounded by the fact that some of the show's segments were shot on location at beaches and amusement parks), and the decline in popularity of the parent *Martin* show closed down the "Gold" mine in '72. But that didn't stop many of the Golddigger girls from graduating to many successful behind-the-scenes careers in film and TV production.

## The Bobby Darin Amusement Company

*Network: NBC; On the air: July 27, 1972–April 27, 1973*
After half a decade of top hits in the late '50s and early '60s, followed by great success in movies and Las Vegas, the supremely talented Bobby Darin finally got his own show on NBC in 1972. By then, the thirty-five-year-old singer had considerably broadened his repertoire to include folk songs (Darin was committed to the peace movement) and the newer hits of the English rock bands at the height of their popularity at the time. The fast-paced and fun show lived up to its name, especially as he surrounded himself with a dream supporting cast of loony laugh-makers like campy comedian Rip Taylor and game-show guru Geoff Edwards.

Bobby was as good in the comedy sketches as he was the with the music moments, too, with characters as wide-ranging and poignant as "Dusty John" (a lost-soul, space-cadet hippie) and "Angie and Carmine" (Bobby and series regular Dick Bakalayan as two young Italian pallies from da Bronx). And most hilariously of all, Bobby's wigged-out answer to Marlon Brando—yes, you got it, "The Godmother."

Tragically, even as the show's artistic and ratings success grew, Bobby Darin's health began to fail. Stricken with rheumatic fever as a child and having several heart ailments throughout his life (including having already undergone open-heart surgery), the pressure of carrying the show just became too much. Less than nine months after the series last telecast, Darin underwent another risky surgery to repair a faulty heart valve, and serious complications arose. On December 20, 1973, just eight months after the premature death of *The Bobby Darin Amusement Company,* the world lost a remarkably talented and kind actor and singer named Bobby Darin, at the age of thirty-seven.

## The Bobby Goldsboro Show

*Syndicated first-run; On the air: September 1972–September 1975*

Bobby Goldsboro, the pop singer who was briefly the bon ami of Vicki Lawrence, cranked up his syndicated variety effort from Golden West Videotape Center, a low-budget, somewhat groan-inducing half hour that was still a big hit with the kids during its pre–*Muppet Show* era. The show's "announcer" was a puppet frog named Calvin Calaveras (hmm, a talking frog puppet—where could they have gotten *that* idea from . . . ) and Bobby had the help of another puppet, a grinning hippie sidekick named Jonathan Rebel, as he proceeded with the program.

## The Bobby Vinton Show

*Syndicated first-run; On the air: September 1975–September 1977*

Bobby Vinton, the Polish-American pop star who became an early-'60s sensation with his tremulous tenor voice on songs like "Roses are Red, My Love" and "Blue Velvet" (when he wasn't playing his clarinet, saxophone, or trumpet) got his crack at variety TV in Toronto in 1975. The show was created and run by the *Sonny & Cher* team of Allan Blye and Chris Bearde, and executive-produced and distributed in the States by syndicated TV sultans Chuck Barris and Sandy Frank.

The show had a large chorus, including one full-sized Polish mama in full ethnic dress who'd dance the jig as Bobby did his thing, and some notable guest stars. But the frizzy-haired Vinton's talent was enough to keep this show watchable for the people who would want to watch it in the first place, as he belted out his 1974 hit "My Melody of Love" at beginning and end. Meanwhile, Chris Bearde and Chuck Barris were teaming up to create another "variety show" of sorts that would bow less than nine months after this one saw the light of day: a little item called *The Gong Show*.

## The Jacksons

*Network: CBS; On the air: June 16, 1976–March 9, 1977*

Before becoming the King of Pop—and way before his mental-health "issues" with children reduced him to a pathetic punch line for late-night talk show hosts—would you believe that Michael Jackson actually starred in a weekly TV variety show? Sure enough, for four weeks in June and July of 1976, followed by eight more in early 1977, Michael and his siblings (minus Jermaine, who was trying his hand at solo work) headlined a CBS variety show. The program replaced *Tony Orlando & Dawn,* and naturally boasted several sizzling musical moments. But other than that, the show seemed to have no purpose—what little comedy and acting skits were there were labored, to put it mildly, and it was slightly hard to watch the teenagers "introducing" other big-name acts old enough to be their parents.

Like the Captain & Tennille show and the far campier *Brady Bunch Hour*, *The Jacksons* stands as an example of the painful transition variety TV was in between the big hits of the past, and the New Wave of the future (*Saturday Night Live, SCTV, Solid Gold*). The networks were desperately seeking performers with enough star appeal and talent to host a weekly revue, and on that score the Jacksons fit the bill. But in the other elements the show came up short, and the notoriously heavy-handed management of the Jacksons' father, Joe Jackson, was also rather evident in the series.

While Michael soon left to pursue his solo career after the show folded, young sister Janet Jackson became a CBS star in her own right when she moved over to play Willona's daughter Penny, on the sitcom *Good Times,* until it went off in 1979. Of course, Janet's huge career in the '80s and '90s as a pop star was nearly equal to that of her brother.

## Sha Na Na

*Syndicated first-run; On the air: September 1977–September 1981*

Grammy producer Pierre Cosette had just come off of the 1975–77 talk show *Sammy and Company,* starring Sammy Davis Jr. and his irrepressible sidekick William B. Williams, when this even more successful effort of his came to fruition. (Joe Flaherty revealed that Sammy's unintentionally cringe-worthy showbiz sleaze-fest was the inspiration for *SCTV*'s "Sammy Maudlin Show.") Cosette had taped a pilot for what would become *Sha Na Na* in 1975, with guest star Rita Moreno, and pitched it to NBC.

NBC said "no," but their owned-and-operated station group eventually said "yes," and agreed to buy the show in first-run syndication for their evening and weekend "access slots." With *Happy Days* on the air and *American Graffiti* still on everyone's minds, Pierre Cosette felt it was only natural for the upbeat "retro" show to take off. Several dozen other stations followed suit, and in the summer of '77, *Sha Na Na* moved into their digs at KTLA's Golden West Videotape Center to begin taping for the fall.

*Sha Na Na* was a very popular musical group dedicated to remembering and reliving the glory days of early rock-and-roll from the '50s and early '60s. In 1969, shortly after being formed by students at Columbia University, the group scored a gig at the counterculture extravaganza Woodstock, where (much to their own surprise and that of the critics) their retro sound got the audience's groove on, and the group became a hit. By 1977, the group had honed their act to perfection, with Jon "Bowzer" Bauman as the leader of the pack; Screamin' Scott Simon, the wild piano man; Donny York, the sunglasses-wearing beatnik; ballad singer Johnny Contardo; reed man Lennie Baker; Denny Greene, the group's black singer; "Captain Outrageous" Tony Santini; and "Dirty Dan" McBride.

The fast-paced half-hour opened and closed with the group doing one popular song of the past, or occasionally one of the here-and-now, followed by bits and sketches with the guest stars of the week. The show also had an impressive cast of regulars—veteran character actors Kenneth Mars and Jane Dulo made regular appearances, as well as goofy comedian Soupy Sales. The show had plenty of lovable shtick, too, from Bowzer flexing his "muscles" with his large mouth open full tilt, to the boys' victory-sign sign-off, "Grease for Peace!"

The show lived long and prospered on the NBC stations from 1977 to 1980, and in ratings and popularity it was behind only *The Muppet Show* and *SCTV* for syndicated half-hour variety shows. A renewal by the CBS owned-and-operated TV stations—where it replaced the equally popular polyester prime-timer *The Gong Show*—saved the show from the axe in the fall of 1980.

But the era of local stations "checkerboarding" the 7:30–8:00 p.m. period with a different game or variety show each night was coming to an end. New five-night-a-week hits like *Entertainment Tonight, PM Magazine, Family Feud, Tic Tac Dough, People's Court,* and a soon-to-spin-into-action nighttime *Wheel of Fortune* were becoming the local stations' new best friends for weeknight prime-access, while *Solid Gold* and *Star Search* would supply Saturdays. Even hits as big as *The Muppet Show* and *Name That Tune* would be wiped out before the end of the 1980–81 season. And so would *Sha Na Na*.

# The Sonny & Cher Comedy Hour

## Vital Stats

**STARRING**
Sonny Bono and Cher

**ON THE AIR**
August 1, 1971–August 29, 1977

**NETWORK**
CBS

**ANNOUNCERS**
Peter Kellen, Ernie Anderson

**MUSIC AND DANCE**
Jimmy Dale (Musical Director);
Tony Mordente (Choreography)

**ORIGINATION**
CBS Television City, Stage 31

"I got you, babe!"

This wasn't the only time *The Sonny & Cher Comedy Hour* got spaced out.

The way they were, 1974.

*T*he *Sonny & Cher Comedy Hour* was to the early 1970s what *Laugh-In* and *The Smothers Brothers* had been to the late '60s, and what *Saturday Night Live* and *SCTV* would be to the end of the decade. In fact, it's hard to imagine how a show could have been a better "bridge" between the two eras than this one. While it stopped and started and stopped again in its later years—under increasingly unpleasant circumstances—the show's 1971–74 heyday remains the definitive variety show of that time. Here's how it all happened.

In the spring of 1971, CBS was looking for new variety programming to fill their summer schedule. After a decade of country sitcoms and old-fashioned heartland variety shows, the network was anxious for a new series that would recapture some of the Smothers Brothers' freewheeling magic and youthful appeal. CBS had finally realized the mistake they'd made in dismissing that show (they would pay nearly a million dollars in damages from a breach-of-contract lawsuit). Now, it was actively trying to rebuild its image as the most up-to-date, cutting-edge network on the air, with Norman Lear sitcoms and new urban detective dramas.

Sonny Bono took no time at all to learn about CBS's new direction through the Hollywood grapevine. He immediately set to work hitting the phones for an appointment to make his pitch—when he found out to his happy surprise that the feeling from the network's end was mutual. New CBS program czar Fred Silverman had recently seen Sonny & Cher's lounge act in Las Vegas, and he was blown away. He knew that if they could bring the same spark and razzmatazz to a weekly TV show, it would most likely be to the new season what *All in the Family* had been to the last— the most talked-about new show on television.

Salvatore "Sonny" Bono was born on February 16, 1935, in Detroit, Michigan. He spent the late 1950s trying to make it in the music business as a performer and/or an agent and/or—whatever that would get him through the door. By the early '60s, Sonny managed to align himself with maverick young record producer Phil "Wall of Sound" Spector. The indefatigable Sonny played percussion on several recording sessions and worked as Phil's right-hand man with the talent. And it was during this time that he met a gorgeous, doe-eyed seventeen-year-old named Cherilyn Sarkasian LaPiere in 1963.

At the time Cher had just dropped out of high school, where she had been a drama major, in order to go full-tilt in pursuing a career as an actress. Cher had left her central California upbringing and her outgoing, artistic young mother to try and make it on her own in Hollywood, supporting herself by singing backup on commercials and recording sessions.

There was instant karma when Sonny met Cher, and it wasn't long before the two moved in together and began performing their own act, calling themselves Caesar and Cleo. By 1965, the two had come out of the closet with their real names, and not long afterward the couple scored their biggest hit—a song that Sonny had written,

which Cher only reluctantly agreed to sing, as she wasn't convinced it would ever go anywhere. The name of the number was "I Got You, Babe."

After the colossal success of "I Got You, Babe," Sonny and Cher were guesting on every major variety show and special of the day, from *Shindig* to *Ed Sullivan*. The two bridged the gap between mod lounge fashions and flower-power hippiedom, with Cher's long, straight black hair and beatnik eye makeup, and Sonny's fur vests and Prince Valiant haircut. More hits were on the way, like "The Beat Goes On," while the duo became even more in demand on early rock TV shows like *American Bandstand* and variety shows like *Laugh-In* and *Carol Burnett*, as well as in the best rock and folk clubs in the country.

However, by the very end of the '60s, while Sonny & Cher remained popular, they no longer found themselves occupying the peak of stardom. Psychedelic, hard-drug rock had taken over the youth scene, along with violent Vietnam war protests. Sonny and Cher tried expanding their horizons with the almost soft-core (for its day) road film *Chastity*, about the sex-periences of a turned-on hippie hitchhiker (Cher). Not coincidentally the two, married by now, also welcomed their first child into the world that year—a daughter named (of course) Chastity Bono.

But despite being a Zappa-like cult classic and period piece, *Chastity* never achieved box office success. Cher and Sonny started booking gigs in Las Vegas and on the lounge circuit, where they brought an entirely new "experience" to the Strip. Along with the King, Elvis Presley, who also came into town around the same time, Sonny & Cher brought their own revolution to the Vegas scene—which was, up until then, notoriously unfriendly to rock music and the youth movement.

By 1971, Sonny and Cher were making a fine income playing Vegas dates and New York nightclubs. But with a new daughter to raise, the freewheeling hippie couple began to start thinking about settling down and ways to get off the road and spend more time with their daughter. When Sonny finally succeded in getting his summer deal from CBS, the timing couldn't have been better.

And it was indeed the right time for both Sonny & Cher, and *Sonny & Cher*. The summer replacement show instantly established itself as a fresh, new, and different kind of variety show, with its funny and unusual "rolling ball" pop-art animated opening. Sonny made sure that the *Sonny & Cher* show would be *the* most innovative, slickest, and fastest-paced variety hour on television. In some ways it went even beyond the *Smothers Brothers* and Lily Tomlin in experiments and avant-garde production techniques.

Nothing was left untried, and everything was a possible target for *Sonny & Cher*. Each show started off with Sonny and Cher running out on a pop-art stage filled with globe-ball light bulbs with their faces painted on them and doing a high-energy duet of a popular rock song. From using state-of-the-art (for the time) special effects and *Electric Company*–like animated segments to the show's venturesome sexuality and libertarian politics, *The Sonny & Cher Comedy Hour* was a TV heat wave that summer of '71. Quickies, cartoons, "two" or even "three" Chers talking and singing to one another (via chroma-key rear-projection), and musical numbers with the biggest acts in rock-and-roll and Motown became the show's trademarks. Even *Laugh-In* began to look almost passé in comparison.

The sense of not being afraid to try the untried and a new, fresh outlook made the show even more appealing to young baby boomer fans who'd grown up with old-school variety TV and thought they had seen it all. As Lorne Michaels would say of *Saturday Night Live* four years later, it looked as though "the grown-ups had gone home" and a bunch of young-adult "kids" had taken over control of the TV studio.

But the show's dead-on Hollywood style and top-flight production values left no doubt that both the people in front of and behind the camera knew exactly what they were doing. By the end of the show's summer run in early September 1971, *Sonny & Cher* had become just what Fred Silverman had dared hope for—second only to Archie Bunker himself as a topic of "buzzworthy" water-cooler conversation and newspaper articles about TV.

After the smashing summer success, it was only a question of when, not if *The Sonny & Cher Comedy Hour* would return to the CBS schedule. On December 27, 1971, *Sonny & Cher* replaced the soon-to-end sitcoms *Arnie* and *My Three Sons* in the 10:00–11:00 Monday night perch. With *Monday Night Football* almost over with for the season, and the Mack-truck strength of lead-ins Lucille Ball and Doris Day (not to mention *Laugh-In*'s leftover viewers), it was the right show in the right place at the right time.

*The Sonny & Cher Comedy Hour* wasted no time whatsoever in establishing itself as the hippest and most "in" show on CBS to watch. The show would start with a high-energy music number, laced with Sonny's sleazy comments about how talented or good in bed or handsome he (thought he) was (and Cher's definitive rolled-eyed put-downs), before capping off for the big finish. Then there'd be sketches with the guest stars and animated bits. And almost always, somewhere in there would be the segment that would become Cher's signature.

"She was a scamp, a camp, and a bit of a tramp! She was a V-A-M-P—VAMP!" Cher would sing, wearing a wide-open red dress, perched on a vaudeville upright piano that Sonny (in turn-of-the-century ruffle shirts, arm bands, and waiter's slacks) would be playing. Then Cher would "salute" the "Vamp of the Week"—a lineup of notable ladies including Betsy Ross, Snow White, Lady Godiva, Cinderella, The Bride of Frankenstein, and endless others. There was also white-trashy, polyester-clad, cigarette-smoking "Laverne," who wore the same kind of old-lady pointy-edged glasses that Lisa Loopner on *Saturday Night Live* and Edith Prickley on *SCTV* would use to make their questionable fashion statements.

You could always count on at least one jaw-dropping, Ed Sullivan–level show-

stopping musical number in the middle of the show. And that's not even counting the guest stars. Considering that the Supremes, Three Dog Night, and others in that echelon dropped by regularly, it goes without saying that the show had the best music in town until *SNL* and *The Midnight Special* came on the scene. Cher would be in her most outrageous Bob Mackie costumes—which showed her navel, her cleavage, and almost everything else on her stunning figure—backed by her handsome and mostly under forty studio musicians, while the go-go and disco lights went flashing at lightning pace.

By the fall of 1972, CBS tried to counteract NBC's brand-new hit *Sanford & Son* and ABC's teenybopper-friendly *Brady Bunch* by placing the equally hot new show against them on Friday nights at 8:00. However, they had the home court advantage, so CBS quickly shifted the show to Carol Burnett's Wednesday night kickoff of 8:00, as Carol went to cap off the best night in television, CBS's peerless Saturday night comedy lineup.

In its new Wednesday-night time period, leading into hits like *Cannon* and *Kojak*, *The Sonny & Cher Comedy Hour* blew the lid off the place. By the time the 1973–74 season started, it had become the single most popular variety show on television. Cher was also making solo recordings (with Sonny's full knowledge and approval, using the house band's musicians) which soared even higher than the show's record-breaking ratings. "Gypsies, Tramps, and Thieves," "Half-Breed," and "Dark Lady" were inescapable Number One hits on radio stations in the early '70s. And the hard-bodied, leather-wearing Cher was behind only Tina Turner, Grace Slick, and the late Janis Joplin when it came to a grrrrrl sportin' a 'tude as a rock star back then.

As 1973 ended and 1974 began, it seemed like Sonny and Cher were at the top of the world. But that was just for the benefit of the Hollywood cameras. In real life, everything was just about to come crashing down. By 1974, Cher was no longer the naive seventeen-year-old Sonny had started dating back in the mid-1960s. She was by far the bigger and more talented star of the two, and she knew it. But according to her, Sonny still talked down to her, insisting on running every aspect of the show and their career his way, or the highway. The same professionalism and caretaking that had seemed so reassuring and protective back when Cher was a vulnerable teenager now made Sonny seem like the quintessential jealous, chauvinistic husband. For the singer who was the very symbol of the liberated woman, it was a crushing irony indeed.

As the show went on, the not-so-happily married couple resolved to remain living together at home and raise Chastity with one another. But in all other respects, later reports of their marriage euphemistically described them as "leading separate lives." And not far into 1974, the dam finally broke.

On February 24, 1974, just days after taping the last episode of the season, the stressed-out duo finally filed for divorce. Both sides would allege that the other had "taken over" and "poisoned" the marriage, the finances, and the show. The split shocked the entire nation, and was as big-time a Hollywood event as the breakups of the biggest movie stars. CBS was frantic to keep their number-one show, the anchor of Wednesday nights and by far the youngest-skewing program that they had. But the two people who made *The Sonny & Cher Comedy Hour* possible had bigger things on their minds. The bitter divorce made it all too clear that it just wouldn't be possible for them to continue working together (at least for the time being). Like someone putting a beloved pet to sleep, the network realized it had no choice anymore. CBS cancelled *The Sonny & Cher Comedy Hour* in the summer of 1974.

However, that didn't mean that Sonny and Cher were finished in television—either one of them.

While even Sonny's most die-hard fans admit that Cher was and is the bigger star of the two, it was actually Sonny that the network heads wanted first crack at. It was widely known in Hollywood circles that he did most of the writing and formatting of the whole Sonny-and-Cher "act" (something that Cher openly acknowledged even after the breakup). ABC got there first, and *The Sonny Comedy Revue* opened in the late summer of 1974, as a replacement for the venerable Efrem Zimbalist crime drama *The FBI*.

The fact that the quintessential '60s hippie was replacing the quintessential Johnson/Nixon era "law and order" program was only the first hint that the new hour was headed for a very rocky road. *The Sonny Comedy Revue* proved to be just what the tenor of its title implied—a plaintive, trying-hard attempt to make it on its own. Sonny put the full force of his personality and energy into the new program, and played it for all it was worth. But it was embarrassing to see nebbishy, shabby Sonny up there introducing other comedy acts who all seemed bigger than he was—even when they weren't. Like Pat Paulsen and Don Knotts, Sonny Bono was in the Rolls-Royce class of being a comedy partner, a second banana, and reacting to other people. But on his own, without someone to bounce back on, *The Sonny Comedy Revue* was the sound of one hand clapping. It was cancelled by Christmas.

Just six weeks after *The Sonny Comedy Revue* met its end, it was Cher's turn to go solo in February of 1975, back on CBS. Cher pulled out all the stops to open her program with A-list guest stars like Flip Wilson, Elton John, and Bette Midler. Needless to say, since then TV still hasn't seen a costume layout like the one that fearsome foursome had! (There was evidently some discord between Cher and Flip Wilson on the set—Cher recalled later in her memoirs that Flip showed up in the beginning, walked out halfway through the taping, and never came back.)

Nonetheless, the *Cher* show's premiere was the biggest party TV had seen in a while, ending with an electrifying three-way concert between Cher, Bette, and Elton, in full costumes on a white art deco set filled with bubbles and balloons. Cher appointed her agent (and by this time her lover), young music mogul-to-be David

Geffen, as her de facto producer, while CBS hired TV's top producer of innovative variety, George Schlatter of *Laugh-In*, to run the show. Between the three of them, there was virtually no guest they couldn't get, no censor they couldn't outfox, and no act that was too outrageous.

The *Cher* show led the league as easily the most ahead-of-its-time variety show of the era until *Saturday Night Live* itself, later that year. (Indeed, one of *SNL*'s founding writers, *National Lampoon* legend Anne Beatts—nicknamed "The Ball Buster" for her take-no-prisoners wit—considered Cher's show one of the few things she truly liked or cared to watch on 1975 television.) No one could be mistaken about the show after seeing its powerhouse opening sequence—a fast-paced montage of Cher in all her various guises, with a computer-generated lightning bolt striking, and a driving disco theme song.

In the women's-movement era of 1975, Cher's show defined freedom. The twenty-nine-year-old singer had liberated herself from a claustrophobic marriage with no apologies, and reveled in her new role of Hollywood's hottest single. Cher enjoyed her post-Sonny status, and flaunted on the air her new lifestyle with rock-and-roll boyfriends like David Geffen and Gregg Allman. And Cher's gowns and dresses were, as always, the sexiest things ever seen on network television.

The show moved full-speed ahead, with all the quickies and rear-projection camera tricks that were the trademarks of *The Sonny & Cher Comedy Hour*, plus show-stopping solo numbers by Cher of everything from show tunes and light classics like "Send in the Clowns" to high-energy Doobie Brothers and Led Zeppelin hits. Perched in a powerhouse "hammock" between *60 Minutes* and *Kojak* on Sunday nights, Cher's show succeeded even beyond what CBS had hoped for, beating both *Walt Disney* and *The Six Million Dollar Man*—at least at first.

Cher (and *Cher*) took some time off after the thirteen-week spring 1975 trial run to recuperate and gear up for the fall. And considering what her personal life was like, she needed it! After dumping David Geffen in the spring of '75 to date Gregg Allman, Cher married Allman (who fathered her son Elijah), and then promptly filed for dissolution within the same month.

Still, Cher looked like a paragon of responsibility and stability compared to what CBS was doing with her show. Instead of solidifying Cher's "ownership" of the Sunday night leadoff hour with best-of-*Cher* show reruns, CBS yanked the show and replaced it with a disastrous summer replacement *Joey and Dad*, starring Joey Heatherton and her father Ray (a prominent kids' show host in his day). Despite the notable talents of Ms. Heatherton, the poorly formatted and ill-conceived hour was a poor showcase for her, and it completely lacked the cutting edge and definitive hipness of Cher's show. By late summer, CBS was back to second or third place in the time slot, and hurried Cher back on the air the first week in September.

Cher's fall 1975 premiere was as fantastic as ever, with the Muppets, the Smothers

Sonny and Cher put Chastity to bed . . . on national television.

A drag-queen's dream team: Bette Midler, Elton John, and Cher.

Cher's too-sexy Snow White seduces Jerry Lewis in 1972.

Brothers, and others brought aboard. There was even more participation from the cheering, sign-holding audience, as the divine diva slid out into the audience section of her stage on an extending platform, surrounded by her studly young studio musicians. Despite the firm competition, the show was still doing well in the ratings—certainly better than any other variety hour CBS could have installed at 8:00 Sunday nights. But it was no longer a cakewalk the way it had been the previous season.

More to the point, Cher was beginning to feel in the starkest possible way how lonely it is at the top, and how tiring the job of carrying CBS's premiere variety showcase was by herself. Just two years earlier, she'd had a somewhat stable married life to a man eleven years her senior, who knew the intricacies of show business inside and out. One year earlier, she'd had a boyfriend who was the most influential young record exec of his time, who could guarantee any music or hip comedy act this side of the Beatles or the Stones as guests for the asking. Now, it was just Cher and George Schlatter, and a network that was placing more demands on her program than ever.

All this would prompt Cher to make, by 1975's end, what was perceived as one of the worst career moves in TV history.

Cher "reunited" with Sonny.

It was a bad decision, the inevitable failure of which was obvious to anyone and everyone—except for the two stars. Sonny had found high-profile work increasingly difficult to get after the cancellation of *The Sonny Comedy Revue*. Even his Las Vegas and Lake Tahoe booking agents were holding back from him. "Who wants to see Sonny without Cher?" And once again, the production teams changed, as George Schlatter, who could forsee all too well how uncomfortable this "marriage" of convenience would be, decided to walk. Nick Vanoff of *Hollywood Palace* fame was brought in to recreate the show—for the third time.

*The Sonny & Cher Show* of February 1976 had enough of a curiosity factor from viewers and enough leftover "oomph" from Cher's solo show to end up fairly high in the standings for what was left of the season. But the show was knocked into next week by the strength of *The Six Million Dollar Man* and *Quincy* the following year. Artistically, the show was exactly what you would expect it to have been. Cher, for her part, actually said she "enjoyed" doing the divorce-era *Sonny & Cher* show most of all—feeling that she was liberated and independent and could do what she wanted, yet with Sonny still there to back her up, surrounded by old friends.

It's likely that she was the only one who felt that way. Sonny and Cher's talent and knack for music and comedy hadn't changed—but the dynamics of their relationship and the show had changed forever. Watching the newly divorced duo deliver insults and one-liners to one another made the show queasy and unsettling, not fun and fancy-free. And instead of laughing *with* Sonny and Cher, by 1977 it was obvious that what little remained of the audience was laughing *at* Sonny and Cher.

By the spring of 1977, production ceased on the show—this time for good—and Sonny and Cher finally went their separate ways. While they reportedly kept in contact with each other as friends (and as Chastity's parents), it would be another full decade before the two of them would be reunited on stage.

Following the demise of the TV show in 1977, Cher immediately moved to Las Vegas and went to work on a weekly live "Cher Show" for the casino-palace stages. The Las Vegas "Cher" revue proved to be a natural and even more outrageous extension of her 1975 series, with elaborate sets, buff-body male dancers, mile-high staircases, and near-nude costumes that were way too hot even for 1970s TV.

From 1978 through '80, Cher's live show packed 'em in with lines around the block. Cher's revue ranked right up there with long-established Strip players like Dean Martin, Frank Sinatra, Kenny Rogers, Dolly Parton, Redd Foxx, and Wayne Newton when it came to bringing in the audiences—and the money! Just as importantly, Cher's act was also by *far* one of the hippest in all of Vegas. Only the likes of Steve Martin, Donna Summer, Tina Turner, and Richard Pryor could claim the same level of in-crowd cachet among the Vegas set. Cher attracted legions of brand-new young fans who had little use for the gambling mecca before, packing the showrooms and discos on the fabled Vegas Strip night after night.

But despite the huge success, colossal paychecks, and love-letter reviews Cher had been getting, Cher made a critical choice in 1980 that changed the direction of her life and career forever. The rock-and-roll superstar decided to give up the security of paid-for penthouse suites and door-to-door limousines and the star stature she enjoyed as a singer to finally pursue her long-delayed dream of a career in the movies as an actress.

While Cher struck out on her own, Sonny Bono could only wish he had such problems. By the early 1980s, Sonny still had semi-frequent work thrown to him from his good friend Aaron Spelling, on such shows as *Love Boat, Charlie's Angels, Fantasy Island, Hart to Hart,* and *Hotel,* plus the usual talk- and game-show appearances and guest shots on holiday specials.

It was obvious, though, that after his 1974 debacle Sonny would probably never again be tapped by the Big Three networks to star in his own prime-time variety show or be approved for the lead in a sitcom. Sonny hardly had the voice to make it as a solo singer, nor did he have the verve or cachet for a kick-ass solo "comedy revue" on stage, like Richard, Steve, Jerry, Lily, or Gilda. As the MTV era took hold, Sonny Bono began to feel like the very definition of the term "has-been."

But Cher's reputation and Hollywood clout only continued to grow. After her 1982 triumph in *Come Back to the Five-and-Dime, Jimmy Dean, Jimmy Dean,* Cher was tapped by director Mike Nichols for a meaty role alongside Meryl Streep and Kurt Russell in his upcoming 1983 movie *Silkwood.* Cher was offered the controversial part of the (fictional) lesbian best friend of allegedly murdered nuclear engineer Karen Silkwood.

Cher received an Oscar nomination for her gritty, courageous performance, erasing all traces of the high-fashion disco glamour that had been her trademark for the past fifteen years. Cher hoped that the motion-picture moguls would take notice—and they did. It would take only one more movie to solidify her new (and deserved) reputation as one of the best actresses in all Hollywood. Cher's next film filled the bill. For her next project in 1984, Cher chose *Mask*—the touching story of an intelligent, good-natured teenager (Eric Stoltz), horribly disfigured by an elephantiasis-like deformity. Cher would play his indomitable trailer-park mother with a foul mouth, a heart of gold, and a will of pure iron. Cher again chose to play a woman who was both tough as nails and vulnerable—a natural continuation of her roles in *Jimmy Dean* and *Silkwood*. Like the actress who played her, Cher's character made no apologies for the way she lived her life. The gorgeous superstar had chosen another role without any trace of glamour or chic and continued to make her working class, salt-of-the-earth characters absolutely believable as real people.

By 1987, Cher was riding so high in her movie career that she was offered a triple-header of to-die-for movie roles. She started the year alongside Dennis Quaid with the meaty role of a prosecutor who risks it all to stop a murderer from going free, in the courtroom thriller *Suspect*. Then she moved on to put a devilish Jack Nicholson in his place, alongside powerhouses Susan Sarandon and Michelle Pfeiffer in *The Witches of Eastwick*.

And to finish, Cher saved the best for last—that of her starring role in *Moonstruck*, alongside Olympia Dukakis and Nicolas Cage. In the spring of 1988, Cher would receive the ultimate proof of her talents as an actress, with the 1987 Oscar for Best Actress.

But what should have been the crowning achievement of Cher's career—her Oscar win—instead turned out to be its downfall. After a lifetime of nonstop touring, performing, and living the rock-and-roll life, and enough heartbreaks and dramas to put her in a league with Liz Taylor and Princess Di, Cher found herself totally exhausted by the end of the '80s. After finishing *Mermaids* in 1990 with a young Winona Ryder, Cher was diagnosed as suffering from chronic fatigue syndrome. And by 1991—little more than three years since her *Moonstruck* Oscar win—Cher was so ill and depressed she could barely get out of bed.

During her absence from the screen, new and younger actresses like Julia Roberts, Meg Ryan, and Sharon Stone took over the box-office gold at the movies. Cher had a tough road to climb to reclaim her crown in big-budget Hollywood films, and she wasn't ready to risk her recovery by committing herself to the stress of a twenty-four-episodes-a-year sitcom on TV. The woman who was the toast of Hollywood just five years earlier now found herself to be precariously close to the position her ex-husband was in a decade earlier. Cher reached her lowest point in 1992–93, when the

Oscar winning super-actress of just five years earlier reduced herself to agreeing to host a series of infomercials.

Realizing the mistake, Cher gave a front-page interview to *TV Guide* in early 1993 in which she spoke as candidly and openly as always—and let the world know that she was preparing to rise yet again. Cher acknowledged that her stint as a cosmetics pitchwoman was "cheesy" and "uncool," but with her usual nonchalantly hip, what's-the-big-deal attitude, Cher also made it clear that she had nothing left to prove to anyone. Fast approaching fifty, she had begun to regain her energy and health, and she was still as sexy, athletic, and fat-free as most women half her age. She had already conquered movies, TV, and music, and Cher made it clear that she was just getting started.

Over on the Sonny side of the street, by the early 1990s, Sonny Bono had embarked upon a new career as a successful restauranteur in Palm Springs, and was elected mayor of the celebrity capital in 1988. Less than six years later, in 1994, pop-culture's most recognizable hippie found himself running for Congress—as a Republican. (Sonny had always been a staunch Republican, although his leather and fur vests and peace-sign belt buckles might not have been the usual image for his party.) What's more, riding on the heels of the "Republican Revolution" that year, Sonny won.

Unfortunately, that victory would prove to be the final triumph for the unstoppable funnyman who'd pulled himself up from the ethnic ghettos of Detroit to worldwide superstardom. Just three years later, shortly after New Year's 1998, the era of Sonny & Cher came to a permanent end. While celebrating the holidays with his third wife Mary in Lake Tahoe, Sonny Bono lost control on the ski slopes, and accidentally ploughed into a tree while going downhill at top speed. It broke his neck on impact. He was just shy of sixty-three years old.

Chastity Bono broke the news to her mother. The indestructible superstar gave the euology, weeping openly, at Congressman Bono's state funeral in Palm Springs. The service was packed to the rafters with the biggest names from both Hollywood and Washington.

Cher was sincere in her grief over "Sonn," and later that year hosted a prime-time CBS special looking back on the magical mystery world of Sonny & Cher. But by 1998, Cher had already triumphed over so many other obstacles that would have sent most entertainers down for the count. It was only second nature for her to climb back on top. Hard-driving pop hits like "Song for the Lonely" and "Believe" propelled her back to the top of the charts. Once again, Cher was pursued by every booking agent in the country for live performances and music videos.

In late 2002, Cher gave a "farewell" tour from live performing, which was standing room only from coast to coast. Still fabulous at fifty-six, Cher announced that she'd "been an evil frickin' diva for forty years," and that the time had come to turn

Yes, fashions *were* that bad in the '70s.

her crown over to a younger generation. But as always, Cher had the last word—one that might just as well apply to her and Sonny's variety show of the 1970s.

Cher said that she wanted Britney, Christina, Mariah, Beyoncé, Lee Ann, and the rest to be able to look back at her career (being the ultimate diva role model) and learn from her example of how she had gone from Grammys to Emmys to Oscars and back again. And with her gorgeous grin spreading across her face, Cher said once they did, she had just one thing left to say to her successors:

"Follow THAT, bitches!"

## FUN FACTS

- Cher was born Cherilyn LaPierre in central California on May 20, 1946. She moved in with Sonny after high school at seventeen and had her first hit single before she turned twenty.
- Despite being the quintessential "flower child" hippie couple, Sonny & Cher vocally disapproved of hard drugs—but not out of moral prudishness, it was just that Cher's "drug" of choice was always health food and physical fitness.
- Cher broke it off with bisexual boyfriend David Geffen in early 1975 when she went to an L.A. disco and made eye contact with a partying Gregg Allman (some say outside the men's room)—and promptly showed David the door that same night!
- Unbelievably, Cher was once almost denied entrance to New York's ultra-exclusive Studio 54. "But I'm CHER!" she cried, flabbergasted that she would be waved aside at the fabled velvet rope line, with the other pathetic "wannabes" clamoring outside the discotheque. (Later on, Studio 54 chief Steve Rubell apologized for the blunder and escorted Cher in himself.)
- Sonny Bono was driven to run for Palm Springs mayor after one too many battles with municipal red tape over his restaurant. Who knew that within barely half a decade, he'd go from chicken cacciatore to Congress?
- When she delivered Sonny's eulogy in 1998, Cher finished her speech with a remembrance from her childhood. In her early days, she said, there used to be a feature in *Reader's Digest* called "The Most Unforgettable Person I Ever Met." "And to me," Cher cried, "that person was Sonny Bono. And no matter where I go or who I meet, that person will always be 'Sonn.'"
- No matter how many shows aired since, or who they starred, the groundbreaking, countercultural, and above all *fun* universe of *The Sonny & Cher Comedy Hour* will forever remain one of the most unforgettable shows in TV history.

## MEMORABLE MOMENTS

Were you watching when . . .

- Sonny and Cher brought baby daughter Chastity on the air for the first time? It was one of the first times the stars of a national show would bring their actual

child on the air, let alone sing and play with her onstage. In the era of women's liberation, Cher also proved that being a new mom didn't mean having to surrender one ounce of sex appeal.

- Snow White wasn't so snow white or Disney-clean after Cher got done with her! The "Vamp" of the week in the show's fall 1972 premiere, Cher's Snow was a cheating hausfrau who was getting it on with all seven dwarves (each played by a bucktoothed Jerry Lewis)—not to mention the milkman!

- Later that same show, shy intellectual Sonny might have been searching for Bobby Fischer, but only came up with Jerry Lewis, when the gentleman's game of chess became a contact sport between the two of them!

- Cher played the most literal "vamp" of all—Vampira—in an ultra-campy spoof that Ed Wood would have no doubt approved of.

- Legendary tough-guy movie and TV star William "Cannon" Conrad sang Christmas carols with Sonny & Cher in the Christmas 1972 program.

- No show this side of *Sesame Street* got more out of cartoon features than *Sonny & Cher*. Joni Mitchell's "Big Yellow Taxi," Three Dog Night's number-one hit "Black and White," and Cher's own hit "Half-Breed" were just a few of the songs visualized in memorable animated segments. Seven years before MTV's birth in 1981, these up-to-the-second spots were among TV's first "music videos."

- Cher sang the Beatles' "Something" to a beastly giant Muppet who kept knocking over things on the elaborate, Roman-columned love set background!

- Physical-fitness goddess Cher and her cast decided to "Shape Up America!" in a bouncy musical salute to health and fitness in her fall 1975 premiere—all wearing bicentennially correct red, white, and blue workout uniforms!

- How about when a gold tuxedo–wearing Dick Smothers played "Chuck Embarrassing" in an out-of-this-world S&M spoof of *Treasure Hunt*, with Cher and Tommy Smothers as a greedy husband-and-wife team?

- Lawrence Welk had to surrender his crown as TV's King of the Bubbles in 1975, when Cher kicked off her show's open in a wild and frothy, balloon-and-bubble bedecked set with Bette Midler and Elton John joining in the fun.

- Cher sang "I'm a W-O-M-A-N" with that other sex goddess of the '60s and '70s, Raquel Welch.

- Carol Burnett came out on the stage at the open of one *Cher* show in a floor-length Cher wig, pretending to be stoned and telling her audience to "Stay Cool" while wearing way-too-tight, cleavage-showing clothes!

- Cher had her boyfriend (and later husband-for-a-month) Gregg Allman as a guest on her show, and sang several rocked-out duets with the Allman Brothers Band.

- Sonny & Cher had an impromptu reunion on the David Letterman show in 1987, and at Letterman and Paul Shaffer's prodding, finally agreed to sing "I Got

You Babe" together. Letterman, the audience, and the band gave a wall-to-wall standing ovation.

- With his usual sense of humor about himself, Sonny poked fun at his image in a great guest shot on *The Golden Girls* in 1988. He was the man of Dorothy's dreams in an episode-long dream sequence where Blanche was reunited with her late husband (who'd died back in 1979). "That's Sonny Bono!" Blanche's husband exclaimed. "He's a major star!" Blanche rolled her eyes and muttered, "Boy, you *have* been gone a long time!"

# definitely Not Ready for prime time!

## TV's Most Outrageous Variety Shows Ever

These camp classics are variety TV's answer to an Ed Wood movie—they're so bad, they're good!

### Turn-On

*Network: ABC; On the air: February 5, 1969*

It is a cruel irony indeed that the worst-received variety show of the 1960s—branded by Alex McNeil in *Total Television* as "television's most notorious flop"—was brought to you by the same people who did the *best* variety show of the '60s, *Rowan & Martin's Laugh-In*. It was also one of the only shows in TV history to be axed after just one telecast. (The only other show to have that dubious accomplishment at the time was CBS's 1961 game show disaster *You're In The Picture*—so bad that host Jackie Gleason apologized for it on air the following week.)

*Turn-On* was ABC's most desperate, tearing-their-hair-out attempt to get a hold on CBS and NBC's variety-show successes in the late '60s. At the time, third-place ABC didn't exactly have a long line of A-list stars queueing up to host their own show on the network. And their only remaining hits in the genre—*The Lawrence Welk Show* and *The Hollywood Palace*—were getting older every day. The network was desperately trying to build credibility with the city dwelling sophisticates who found Dean Martin, *Laugh-In,* and the Smothers Brothers so irresistible, but ABC's "kiddie network" image worked against it. They found a moderate hit with Tom Jones, but they bungled their chance at getting the Smothers Brothers show from CBS. And their attempts to build shows around Englebert Humperdinck, David Steinberg, the Lennon Sisters, and Pearl Bailey would all fail.

*Turn-On* had been developed by George Schlatter and Ed Friendly as a pilot for NBC, but the network saw it for what it was—style over substance, sound and fury signifying little—and rejected it despite *Laugh-In*'s success. CBS also turned it down. The show was even more risqué than the Smothers Brothers was, and CBS didn't relish the thought of fights with the censors.

But when ABC heard about the show, they practically begged Schlatter and Friendly to put it on their airwaves as soon as possible. Having seen *Laugh-In* work a miracle against even *Gunsmoke* and *Lucy,* they pinned almost all their hopes on the new show's success, as if it was already a sure thing.

*Turn-On* wasn't really all *that* bad a show—but twenty years before Seinfeld's premiere, it was perhaps TV's first "show about nothing." The program had no fixed host or central star. Instead, it was a mixture of quickies, comedy sketches, blackouts, and musical moments. The show went from one moment to the next using "inserts" of psychedelic video effects and driving electronic rock music.

*Turn-On* was the 1969 TV equivalent of the "shock and awe" strategy. Not only did the show have up-to-the-second production techniques, it was also determined to break all the rules, even in its first night out. One sketch had the word "SEX" flashed on and off the screen while various actors tried to "avoid" it and made funny faces around it; another featured a vending machine for birth-control pills (shocking to Middle America in 1969). The show also featured just-this-side-of-*Fritz the Cat* "adult cartoons," provided by the Bill Melendez animation studio.

ABC's phone switchboards definitely "turned on" when America saw *Turn-On*. *Lawrence Welk* and *Hollywood Palace* this was not! The soap-loving housewives and snug cozy-mystery fans that had been addicted to the show it "turned off" (the Wednesday editon of *Peyton Place*) must have wondered if somebody had dropped acid into their TV set.

An interesting irony is that the flashy production techniques first used on the adults-only *Turn-On* soon became the blueprint for attention span–challenged children's TV shows like *Sesame Street* and *Electric Company*—not to mention being a primordial incarnation of the music video format, too!

Another bitter irony is that the failure of this supposedly sophisticated, "adult" effort made ABC especially jumpy about seeing to it that their young variety stars were squeaky clean. It also affected their decision to postpone rescuing the Smothers Brothers into summer 1970 (by which time all of ABC's variety shows, even the established ones, were failing), instead of grabbing it while it was fresh off CBS's presses in June of '69. At least the show had an impressive cast: Tim Conway, Teresa Graves, Bonnie Boland, Hamilton Camp, Chuck McCann, Mel Stuart, Debbie Macomber, and Carol Wayne were among the regulars for the one telecast that it lasted before ABC "turned off" *Turn-On*.

## The Beautiful Phyllis Diller Show

*Network: NBC; On the air: September 15, 1968–December 22, 1968*
Fresh from her 1966 sitcom *The Pruitts of Southampton,* wiggy comedienne Phyllis Diller launched her hour-long variety program following *Bonanza* with kooky comedy veterans Norm Crosby and Rip Taylor on hand for support. The show wasn't all that terrible, and it boasted work by a then lit-tle-known writer named Lorne Michaels, as well as a top-flight production team including longtime Emmy and Oscar producer Bob Finkel. However, the program's humorous title and its almost instant death opposite *Mission: Impossible* earned it a place amongst TV's biggest "groaners" in the variety-show field.

## What's It All About, World?

*Network: ABC; On the air: February 6, 1969–May 1, 1969*

In many ways even more embarrassing than *Turn-On,* this variety hour, hosted by Dean Jones, was an attempted satire of the Hollywood TV and movie industry and of the dizzying spin-basket of changes that the late 1960s brought. However, the show ended up (according to iconoclastic author Harlan Ellison) as a "horror of right-wing imbecility."

Dick Clair and Jenna McMahon (the comedy team who became Carol Burnett's head writers and created *Mama's Family* and *Facts of Life*), young black sitcom actor Scoey Mitchell, and young-man's-Pat-Paulsen comedian Dennis Allen (later to join *Laugh-In*) were among the more notable regulars while it lasted. After six weeks on the air, the show reverted from its superficial resemblances to *Laugh-In* and Dean Martin (the "conversations," the quickies, etc.), and tried to become a straight star-appeal variety hour, imaginatively retitling itself *The Dean Jones Variety Hour.* By the end of April, ABC had said that their world was all about Nielsens and Arbitrons, and retitled the show *cancelled.*

## Saturday Night Live with Howard Cosell

*Network: ABC; On the air: September 20, 1975–January 17, 1976*

No, this wasn't the "real" *Saturday Night Live,* which also premiered in the fall of 1975, over on NBC. This abomination was perhaps the first major network variety show to be made with an executive producer who had no background in comedy, talk, game, or music shows whatsoever—and worse, a host who displayed not even the slightest talent for music, comedy, or dance.

ABC had been out of the variety-show business for four years by the time this series was conceived in 1975. For all intents and purposes, ABC had abandoned the format with their variety-show genocide of 1971, with Pearl Bailey, Tom Jones, Johnny Cash, and Lawrence Welk summarily excised from the schedule in one fell swoop. After that, ABC's only desultory attempts at the form were a last-minute *Comedy Hour* with Rich Little that barely lasted six weeks, and a big-budget catastrophe with Julie Andrews a year later.

It is hard to conceive of a more inept way to bring the format back than this show, which selected—of all people—*Monday Night Football* anchor Howard Cosell as its standard bearer. The show's genesis was a 1974 special conceived by legendary ABC Sports chieftain Roone Arledge, called *Frank Sinatra: The Main Event,* a live, satellite broadcast concert with Frank Sinatra from the ring at Madison Square Garden, with the absolute peak of the Hollywood A-list—Redford, Streisand, Newman, and others—invited to front-row, on-camera seats. Howard Cosell was tabbed to emcee the "Event"—dressed in an outrageous purple tuxedo with chiffon ruffles—introducing Sinatra at the top of the show boxing-ring announcer–style, from the center stage at the Gardens.

Following the astonishingly high ratings for the concert, ABC wondered if perhaps it could recapture some of that magic week after week, with an endlessly running series of lesser "events." The network wanted Cosell to host the show, partly because he was one of the few "names" ABC had in its stable in 1975, and also in light of the Sinatra affair's success (which could hardly be attributed to Cosell, but still . . .).

The network purposely did not want an established comedian or rock singer to host the program, on the theory that they would upstage the acts that would be invited on the show. The network had decided that they wanted an *Ed Sullivan Show/Hollywood Palace* style "video vaudeville" updated for the new generation, with a host there to introduce the acts and provide continuity.

Even in light of that, ABC would have been far better off choosing an established talk- or game-show host, or a nationally known radio personality like Don Imus, "the Real" Don Steele, or Robert W. Morgan to host the series. Howard Cosell was undoubtedly one of the greatest sports journalists of our time. But, love him or hate him, having him host a fun, freewheeling variety hour in the hip, disco-trendy world of 1975 was a casting catastrophe on a par with asking Mike Wallace to take over the Martha Stewart show or Barbara Walters to host *The Price Is Right*.

Cosell's strangled-prose way of speaking and awkward stage manners were painfully obvious even beyond camp value—he made Ed Sullivan and Lawrence Welk "seem positively graceful by comparison," wrote *TV Guide* journalist Doug Hill. With almost Olympian arrogance, Cosell suggested backstage that the show reunite the Beatles at once, on the air—just like that! As if John, Paul, George, and Ringo were just waiting around for Cosell to snap his fingers!

After getting a desperately needed reality check, a vengeful Cosell and Arledge then ludicrously tried to hype the show's opening act, the bubble-gum rock group the Bay City Rollers, as being the "Next Beatles." (Yeah, right.) Meanwhile, the show's budget reached a stratosphere even higher than the egos of host and producer, as Arledge tried to modernize the program's look by having on-location satellite pickups of different acts from all over the globe.

Things grew even more frantic at ABC when they learned how the show they still thought (without the slightest justification) would be their biggest fall hit had fared, as the November 1975 "sweeps" started rolling in. After the initial shock value and curiosity wore off, ABC's so-called *Saturday Night Live* was pummeled so badly by *The Jeffersons* that it was movin' on down to the very bottom of the ratings.

Also, another infinitely superior *Saturday Night Live* had started over on NBC and was *really* revolutionizing the variety-show format in a way that the Cosell crew couldn't even dream of doing. On January 17, 1976, ABC's *Saturday Night Live* was dead on arrival.

The only good thing about the show was that it provided the first big break into TV of a young comedian/actor named Bill Murray, who would end up on the "real" *Saturday Night Live* just one year later and help make it the classic it was. NBC's *SNL* also paid humorous homage to the Cosell show in the naming of their repertory company. Cosell's show had haughtily christened its cast of regulars "The Prime Time Players"—to which Lorne Michaels responded by calling *his* cast, "The Not Ready for Prime Time Players."

## The Brady Bunch Hour

*Network: ABC; On the air: January 23, 1977–May 25, 1977*

Ranking in the Top Five of *TV Guide*'s "Worst Shows of All Time" list, this show is perhaps the best (worst?) example of Hollywood's unslakable compulsion to rip off, spin off, sequelize, go for the safe bet, and bleed any proven moneymaking formula until it runs bone dry.

Television's most indestructible family had already been featured in a sitcom and a cartoon, and had just been "reunited" in a 1976 special that had scored high ratings for newly first-place ABC by the time this show started. Meanwhile, what was supposed to have been ABC's signature variety effort for the season, *The Captain & Tennille,* was going nowhere against *Little House on the Prairie* and *Rhoda.* But the eager, let's-put-on-a-show shtick of *Donny & Marie* was doing big numbers and generating huge talk-show appearances and fan-mag covers for its youthful stars.

While the original *Brady* series was deservedly beloved by the children of divorcing "Me Generation" parents for its portrayal of happy home life, this show would have betrayed the entire merit of the original program if it weren't so silly to begin with. A successful architect and a fashionable housewife all of a sudden chucking it all to become entertainers? And hadn't this ground already been a wee bit covered by the Bradys' longtime Friday-night neighbors, the rock-singing Partridge Family?

*The Brady Bunch Hour* was more than unbearable—it was unbelievable, even for the most die-hard Brady fans. The show's crassness was so unrelenting, you wouldn't have been surprised to see Bill Murray's "Nick the Lounge Singer" or *SCTV*'s "Johnny LaRue" drop by for a cameo appearance. Intentionally or not, every variety-show cliché was there—hard closeups of Greg or Marcia-Marcia-Marcia mugging for the camera, so-called "witty" patter in between cringy musical numbers, and costumes that were outrageous even for the late '70s (suburban soccer-mom Carol wearing plungy rhinestone-studded evening gowns; Mike in a shocking-orange Cat-in-the-Hat suit complete with ruffle shirt, top hat, and cane . . . you get the idea).

The most interesting thing about the show was that the one person most would have thought would've been the most reluctant to do it was actually its biggest booster. Robert Reed's fights with *Brady* creator/producer Sherwood Schwartz over the original show's direction were near legendary. (He had taken the Mike Brady part under duress, as an actor under contract to Paramount/Desilu.) Stage-trained *Defenders* and *Mannix* veteran Reed wanted the show's plots to be

You think *this* is bad? You should see it in color!

more believable and to move closer to a family-oriented version of the MTM sitcoms, with humor based on the interplay of the characters. Schwartz disagreed and, probably prudently, insisted on aiming the sitcom's mentality squarely at the junior-high set.

However, when it came time to do the variety hour, Reed approached the show with an enthusiasm and workload that surpassed and amazed everyone, including his colleague, variety-and-Vegas veteran Florence Henderson. "Robert wanted to prove that he could sing and dance, as well as act," Florence would later recall in interviews.

Reed and Henderson continued relatively successful careers, with Reed's life tragically ending in May 1992 from cancer and AIDS. During the next decade, there would be other *Brady* specials and limited series (*The Brady Brides, The Bradys*), and even a hit movie in 1995 starring Gary Cole and Shelley Long as the patron saints of suburbia themselves.

Happily, in all the other versions, as well as the inviolable cable reruns of the original show, the Bradys were back where they belonged, solving the problems of everyday life with a smile, a laugh, and a batch of Alice's homebaked cookies. But while *The Brady Bunch Hour* may be gone, to the people who witnessed it firsthand, it will probably never be forgotten!

## Pink Lady

*Network: NBC; On the air: March 1, 1980–April 11, 1980*

Considered by many critics to be perhaps the worst TV show of all time, the almost indescribably campy *Pink Lady* well earned its place alongside such atomic bombs as *Turn-On, You're in the Picture, Supertrain,* and *My Mother the Car.* While the show arguably broke down some barriers in putting two Japanese women in starring roles, the program did for Asian Americans pretty much what *Amos & Andy* did for blacks.

The premise of the show was simple: handsome young comedian Jeff Altman, caught between the dynamic duo of Mei Nemoto and Kei Masuda—Japan's number-one soft-rock act of the time, Pink Lady. The fact that Mei and Kei barely spoke English bothered NBC chief Fred Silverman not at all, as the twentysomething beauties were well endowed in more than just their singing voices!

(Interestingly, as the show was being developed in the fall of 1979, NBC's detective hit *Rockford Files* had a hilarious subplot in one of its episodes about the misadventures of a sexy Japanese country singer who couldn't speak English. Proving that NBC wasn't oblivious to the dig, *Pink Lady* briefly replaced the soon-to-end *Rockford Files* on Fridays, when Jimbo raced over to Thursday nights at 10:00 for his final remaining episodes in NBC prime that spring.)

The fact that other infinitely superior shows of the time (like *Hawaii Five-0* and *Magnum, P.I.* and the miniseries *Shogun*) were finally giving Asian actors relatively important roles to play made *Pink Lady* "rook" even more insulting. And the show was so jaw-droppingly sexist it made Dean Martin's show look like it had been written by Gloria Steinem and Gloria Allred. Even *Pink Lady*'s opening sequence was an eye-rolling travesty, as a computer-generated pink origami bird flew across a space skyline and exploded into the title *Pink Lady—and Jeff.*

A hilariously bad example of the show's humor was a "Sam Spade" style detective sketch. Jeff, doing a horrible Bogey-by-way-of-Clark Gable impersonation (complete with trenchcoat) tells Pink Lady that "nothing they could offer him" would prevent him from putting them under arrest. "Noww evenn diss?" leers Kei, putting Jeff's hand right over her nipple. When Jeff demurs, an insulted Mei and Kei growl, "How-a you rike a knucow sanwich?" shaking their fists at him. *Pink Lady* achieved the near-impossible accomplishment of making its competition *(The Dukes of Hazzard)* look like *Masterpiece Theatre* in comparison.

The network tried boosting the show's popularity by signing A-list movie and TV guest stars like Larry Hagman, Suzanne Somers, and others. But performing in the midst of this, the big-name guests seemed about as comfortable as they would be in an operating room. Even by late '70s standards, *Pink Lady* ginsu-knifed good taste into a fricasee. NBC karate-chopped the show after just six weeks.

# Who Turned Out the Lights?

New beginnings,
and the end
of an era.

AFTER THE GREAT prime-time variety shows of the 1960s and '70s started running their courses, TV executives were of two minds when it came to the genre. Half of them were ready to let the variety formats die of attrition—to use a phrase of TV and film historian Hal Erikson, some execs felt the formats were just "too tired-blooded . . . too 1950s." Those execs were ready to let variety shows, like their game- and talk-show cousins, become the province of prime-access nighttime syndication, and concentrate the networks' programming on sexy sitcoms, hard-hitting filmed dramas, and movies.

The network decision-makers that wanted to keep variety shows alive were becoming almost frantic in their attempts to try to find the Next Big Thing. *Laugh-In*, the Smotherses, and Sonny & Cher were so innovative, Carol Burnett, Dean Martin, and Flip Wilson were so brilliant . . . now, how can we follow that?

Unfortunately, they couldn't—as the previous spot illustrates. At least, not in network prime time. But a whole new world of adventure was about to bloom outside of the watchful eyes of eight to eleven o'clock, in the realm of late-night TV. There they could get away with far more venturesome content and hipper, not-for-everyone comedians and performers.

## THE MIDNIGHT SPECIAL

On February 2, 1973, *The Midnight Special* rolled into the KNBC Studios "railway station," and occupied a parking lot there for eight years. Starring legendary rock DJ Wolfman Jack, *The Midnight Special* became must-see TV for almost every young rock, R&B, and jazz fan coming home from the clubs or discos with their dates . . . or trying to forget a dateless Friday night alone.

The show's genesis was an August 1972 "Get Out the Vote" special, hosted by John Denver and Mama Cass Elliott that celebrated the recent rollback of the voting age from twenty-one to eighteen, in response to Vietnam veterans who resented being old enough to be drafted but too young to vote. Twenty years before MTV would try to "rock the vote," this special attempted to do exactly that. And knowing that NBC would never put an all rock-and-roll, hard-edged, countercultural show in prime time, producer Burt Sugarman asked for a slot at 1:00 a.m. on a Friday night, right after Johnny Carson signed off. Despite the network's doubts that a late-late night show would work, the 1972 special broke the needle on the ratings chart, and had some of the purest youth demographics in TV history.

Within six months of its premiere, *The Midnight Special* had scored Ray Charles, Aretha Franklin, Joan Baez, Jerry Lee Lewis, Waylon Jennings, Billy Preston, the Doobie Brothers, the Pointer Sisters, Steely Dan, and the Bee Gees, plus comedians like George Carlin, Joan Rivers, and Steve Martin. Mick Jagger and David Bowie were also on the way, and the first show kicked off with the one other person most identified with the series besides Wolfman Jack, the Australian singer and actress (and feminist icon) Helen Reddy.

Rock bands who would have laughed at an invite from Mike, Merv, Dinah, or Carol lined up for the new show, while the biggest managers in Hollywood never failed to return a phone call from young talent booker Susan Richards. The show's boogie-nights "look" was blatantly patterned after the trendiest Hollywood and Manhattan nightclubs like the Whiskey-a-Go-Go, the Troubadour, and of course, Studio 54. Soon scads of young folk from L.A., Orange County, and San Diego turned the show's Tuesday-night tapings into a regular rock-and-roll "be-in," coming in for the show's start in the early evening and staying until they closed out the studio late at night.

By the mid-1970s, *The Midnight Special* was firmly established as a Friday-night ritual in singles' apartments, college dorms, bars, and high school party houses across the United States and Canada. The show quickly inspired imitators like *Don Kirshner's Rock Concert* and Dick Clark's *In Concert* segment of ABC's *Wide World of Entertainment*. ABBA, Herb Alpert, the Beach Boys, the Bee Gees, Blood Sweat & Tears, Chicago, Cher, Eric Clapton, Joe Cocker, Alice Cooper, Aretha Franklin, Elton John, KC and the Sunshine Band, BB King, Bob Marley & the Wailers, Little Richard, Olivia Newton-John, Lou Reed, David Bowie, the Rolling Stones, and Rod Stewart and the Faces were just a small sampling of the acts who rocked the *Midnight Special* stage.

## SATURDAY NIGHT LIVE

After *The Midnight Special* proved that late-night programming could be far more than just Johnny Carson or Merv Griffin and the late movie, NBC was eager to capitalize and build on the new trend. In late 1974, innovative NBC prexy Herb Schlosser ordered the development of a weekly sketch-comedy variety show, one that would be aimed at the same youth-demographic *Midnight Special* audience that was singlehandedly keeping NBC in the hip variety business. Schlosser also wanted to air the show "live, from New York," as much of NBC's Rockefeller Center studios were sitting idle as game, talk, and variety shows moved to Hollywood. Most importantly, the new show had to be a place to develop new young talent and build for the future. Entrenched NBC execs (and Carson confidants) Dave Tebet and Fred DeCordova turned the comedy world upside down looking for "the next white Gentile comedian" who would be fit to slip into Johnny's shoes once he called it quits.

Feeling that NBC had already pushed the boundaries as far as they could go in prime time—and in light of the relaxed standards and relative freedom from letter-writers and pressure groups that a late-night slot afforded—Schlosser opened a Saturday night time slot at 11:30 for the new program. And when NBC hired a young producer/writer named Lorne Michaels to run the new show, they got all that they had hoped for—and a helluva lot more.

*Saturday Night Live* premiered on NBC on October 11, 1975, in what was previously the deadest of the dead time slots in television. From the first segment of the show (a sketch with John Belushi and the ghoulish writer-comedian Michael "Mr. Mike" O'Donoghue, called "The Wolverines"), "you knew you weren't watching George Gobel or Garry Moore, or whatever comedy *had* been," as Mr. Mike himself gloated. (The opening skit portrayed a Russian immigrant being taught look-and-say reading by his foreign language teacher, who died of a heart attack during the lesson—only for the immigrant to grab his chest and keel over, rotely imitating the teacher. Then Chevy Chase came out and introduced a new catchphrase to the American lexicon—"Live from New York—it's *Saturday Night!*")

It wasn't just that *Saturday Night Live* was funny; as one famous book on the series noted, it was the *way* the show was funny. The Baby Boomers who'd come of age with the counterculture and their younger brothers and sisters coming to adulthood in the disco era realized that this was a show that was made by and for *them*. Not the widdle kids, not Granny and Grandpa—a show *just* for them. Michael O'Donoghue wasn't kidding when he said that *Saturday Night Live* would be defined as much by what it wasn't as by what it was. *SNL*'s humor reflected an entire attitude, a knowing code that spoke more directly to its target audience than any show in TV history.

It was an almost too perfect irony that the last series to tape in NBC's flagship Studio 8H before *SNL* was the long-running comedy game show *What's My Line*, which had just wrapped a few months earlier, not long before host Larry Blyden's death that June. *What's My Line*'s style of comedy—campy slapstick gags and quickie interviews crossed with old-Hollywood and Broadway sophistication—embodied everything that *SNL* was reacting against. Indeed, many times a proposed sketch would be summarily rejected during meetings with the epithet, "That's just too Carol Burnett!"

The sets were deliberately grungy and run-down, with bad lighting and K-Mart videotape resolution, conveying an underground comedy or jazz club's view of the streets of New York. Even the *Smothers Brothers Comedy Hour* looked squeaky clean compared to this. The entire atmosphere and attitude was straight out of a Velvet Underground record or a grungy Warhol art movie. With the possible exceptions of the *Cher* show's edgier moments and *The Midnight Special*, *Saturday Night Live* was the antithesis of every other variety show then on television.

More books and articles have probably been written about the many lives of *Saturday Night Live* than about any other variety show in history, even including Gleason, Sid Caesar, and Carson. Suffice it to say that in its landmark first five years on television (which almost every fan agrees were the series' peak), virtually every performer who starred on the show—Dan Aykroyd, John Belushi, Chevy Chase, Jane Curtin, Garrett Morris, Bill Murray, Laraine Newman, Gilda Radner—skyrocketed to stardom. In later years, the program would launch the careers of Eddie Murphy,

Mike Myers, Dana Carvey, Dennis Miller, Adam Sandler, and Will Ferrell, to name a few.

The show also gave birth to more catchphrases and cultural references than even *Laugh-In* at its height—from "But Nooooooooooooooo!" to "Jane, you ignorant slut" to "Never mind!" to "Goodnight, and have a pleasant tomorrow." And the characters—the Coneheads, Barbara Wawa, Emily Litella, Roseanne Roseannadanna, the Nerds, the equally nerdy Swinging Czech Brothers, Father Guido Sarducci, and the candygram-delivering Land Shark became *the* pop-culture for the teens and twentysomethings of the late '70s. And the show even eclipsed *The Midnight Special* as the hot destination for the top rock bands until MTV came on the scene.

## THE MUPPET SHOW

Even as the adults-only antics of *SNL* and *Midnight Special* raged around it, another very different family-variety show was about to launch in 1976.

Jim Henson had learned to be careful what he wished for. After spending the '60s making regular appearances on talk and variety shows and doing creative commercials for various sponsors with his crew of Muppet creations, he eagerly signed on to co-create *Sesame Street* with Joan Ganz Cooney in 1969. Henson would be proud of his work on that landmark PBS children's show from beginning to end, and he personally voiced characters like Ernie (of Bert and Ernie fame) and brought his signature Muppets—Rowlf the Dog and Kermit the Frog—aboard the show.

By the mid-1970s, though, Henson wanted to show that the Muppets were capable of more than just teaching kindergarteners their ABCs. He was eager to use the characters he'd developed and some new ones too, to make some gentle social satire and "adult" (in the sense of somewhat sophisticated, as opposed to explicit) comedy.

As such, he was happy when NBC signed him to create some offbeat Muppet characters for *Saturday Night Live*. But Henson was, as *SNL* historians Doug Hill and Jeff Weingrad noted, "far more sympathetic with the sunnier side of the '60s counterculture" than the "hard-edged, negative, and decadent" self-conscious hipness that was *SNL*'s stock in trade. Henson walked off the show before the 1975–76 season finished, and Lorne Michaels held the door for him.

But Henson's brief tenure on *Saturday Night Live* had been a successful failure—it caught the eye of British media mogul Sir Lew Grade and his ITC film and television emprire. Henson's work on adults-only *SNL* and the hip and sexy *Cher* show convinced him that grown-ups might watch a show starring the Muppets, as well as just families with small children. Grade agreed to bankroll a weekly half-hour "Muppet show," which he could get on the air in British prime time with no questions asked.

In the States, Grade would take the show into the world of first-run syndication, aiming it at the early evening prime-access slots that had already proven so lucrative for *Lawrence Welk*, *Hee-Haw*, and a slew of nighttime game shows. By the spring of

1976, the CBS owned-and-operated stations had signed on—with more than a hundred other U.S. stations following suit. And one of Canada's TV networks had purchased the program for their prime-time schedule as well.

*The Muppet Show* was a success beyond Henson or Grade's wildest dreams. It was not only an island of family entertainment in the era of disco, drugs, and decadence; it was something that adults could *also* watch without cringing or gagging from sticky-sweetness. Some of Hollywood's biggest movie stars lined up to be on the show. In fact, *The Muppet Show* arguably had more big-name guest stars than any TV show in history, perhaps even including Ed Sullivan and Johnny Carson. Everyone from Peter Sellers to James Coburn to Carol Burnett, from Gilda Radner to Dizzy Gillespie to Elton John, from the cast of *Star Wars* to Beverly Sills to Sylvester Stallone, would join Kermit and Miss Piggy during the show's five-year run.

But the heart and soul of *The Muppet Show* was, of course, the Muppets themselves. A new crew of puppets were tailored for the show, so many that it would be impossible to enumerate all of them in detail. The following are a few of the most popular characters.

- Fozzie the Bear—a hyper-enthusiastic, shaggy, not-so-old vaudeville pro, whose repertoire of over-the-road jokes were a cross between Uncle Miltie and the Unknown Comic.
- Gonzo the Great, a purple weirdo with a question-mark-shaped nose who would do anything to get a great performance despite his contempt for the audience—or to charm his way into the heart of his longtime love, Camilla the Chicken.
- Smiling stage manager Scooter, with his electric-green jacket and wide-eye eyeglasses.
- The Swedish Chef, a mustachioed miscreant who chortled his way through throwing together (literally—his kitchen often looked like a white tornado of flour and sugar) one gourmet delicacy after another.
- Dr. Teeth and the Electric Mayhem Band, featuring spaced-out hippie Janice, wild-eyed John Belushi wannabe Animal (on the drums, of course), and a blaring horn section that would have made Doc and Maynard proud.
- For contrast there was Sam the American Eagle, whose somber baritone and gray-colored body took up where President Nixon had left off.
- Statler and Waldorf—the two cranky old theater-critic curmudgeons who sat in the balcony, cheering and jeering each show.
- And of course, the lady we cannot forget (lest we receive a karate-chop to the neck), the World's Greatest Star—Miss Piggy. One book accurately noted that she was conceived as a satire on the "overnight superstar" phenomenon then striking such notables as Farrah Fawcett, Suzanne Somers, Jamie Lee Curtis, and Bo Derek. No doubt the full-figured Piggy would have no qualms about putting

herself in that kind of rarefied company with regards to her looks and sex appeal. Not to be outdone by her rivals, she made a sexy bikini photo poster, workout videos, and frequent cover shots on *TV Guide, People,* and fashion and women's magazines. Miss Piggy had enough mood swings to qualify for a month's worth of Midol and practiced more kung-fu moves than any actress this side of a Pam Grier "blaxploitation" movie. She even launched a write-in candidacy for the 1979 Best Actress Oscar for her work in *The Muppet Movie,* to show Meryl, Sally, and Bette who the real Queen of Hollywood was! In real life, the man who voiced her was Jim Henson's longtime best friend, the respected film director Frank Oz.

Like the show, *The Muppet Movie* attracted the top of the star list, with Bob Hope, John Denver, Telly Savalas, Cloris Leachman, Charles Durning, Milton Berle, and Orson Welles, as well as legendary ventriloquist (and father of Candice) Edgar Bergen, who made his last-ever appearance in the film. Bergen died in September 1978, just after completing his role, at the age of seventy-five. Henson paid his idol the ultimate compliment by dedicating the movie to his memory when it was released the following summer.

After five years of production, with well over a hundred episodes "in the can," *The Muppet Show* decided to go out while it was still at the height of its popularity, after a more than respectable run. *Sesame Street* would still provide homes for the Muppets, and the reruns, movie offers, nonstop merchandising, and cable TV specials brought in enough to keep Miss Piggy in diamonds and Gucci forever.

*The Muppet Show* came to a permanent and poignant end just nine years later, when Jim Henson died in May 1990 at the age of fifty-three. It was all too appropriate that Henson made his own "rainbow connection" the very same day as his fellow variety all-star Sammy Davis Jr. But while Jim Henson is gone, Kermit the Frog, Bert and Ernie, Miss Piggy, Big Bird and all the rest are still alive and well, and far more than just cloth and fur for their fans. Probably no other single entertainer had more of an influence or immediate impact on Generation X and Y's first television memories than Jim Henson, and that's some kind of legacy.

## SCTV

Meanwhile, back where their parents' TV shows were concerned, the third trilon to the axis of after-hours variety entertainment also started in 1976. Strictly speaking, this show was a Canadian series that was syndicated in the United States. But it ran on so many NBC outlets (including all their top-market stations in L.A., New York, San Francisco, Chicago, and so on) that it was essentially an NBC show. And in fact it actually became one when it left syndication for a network berth in the spring of 1981.

Second City was the premiere acting and comedy troupe of the 1960s and '70s, with alumni including Mike Nichols, Elaine May, Valerie Harper, and David Steinberg, as well as a slew of future regulars on *Saturday Night Live*. The major branch of Second City was set up in Chicago in the late 1950s (then the "second city" to New York, as L.A. was just beginning its suburban postwar growth spurt.) But the Toronto arm of the troupe would eclipse its parent by the mid-'70s, with a membership including John Candy, Gilda Radner, Eugene Levy, Dan Aykroyd, and Valri Bromfield, among others.

The repertory company performed in numerous stage plays, comedy revues, stand-up nights, and so on. Mainstream fame eluded them, though; their comic sensibilities weren't exactly the stuff of big-budget Hollywood movies and TV shows. But the talent that the company possessed along with their ability to perform sketches and characters to the same perfection as the Carol Burnett and *Laugh-In* crews simply begged for national media exposure.

Second City toppers Bernard Sahlins and Andrew Alexander came up with a masterstroke. If Second City was going to launch itself in a television show, why not make the show a satire of television itself—especially in light of the fact that the biggest movie in fall 1976 (besides maybe *Rocky* and *Taxi Driver*) was Paddy Chayevsky's immortal satire *Network*. They would have a near-limitless supply of material to draw upon, and of course, the most popular segments and characters could return time and time again. For a show being made by and for Baby Boomers—the first generation to grow up with television and take it for granted, it would be the perfect format.

In August 1976, everyone's favorite classic of Canucks run amok was finally born, as the *SCTV* network signed on the air on Canadian television. With a cast of comedy black belts like John Candy, Joe Flaherty, Harold Ramis, Andrea Martin, Catherine O'Hara, Dave Thomas, and (later on) Martin Short and Rick Moranis, the show had the most impressive talent roster of any program, perhaps even including *SNL*, of its time.

Within a year, Sahlins managed to get his ultimate wish for U.S. success when the Rhodes Communications arm of Filmways picked up the new show for syndicated distribution. Scores of NBC affilliates bought *SCTV* and most of them scheduled the half-hour show right behind *Saturday Night Live* after *SNL*'s 1:00 a.m. sign-off, giving it the perfect lead-in.

In the alternate universe of *Second City TV* (most people called it *SCTV* anyway), *SCTV* was the "call letters" of Channel 109 in Melonville, owned by a particularly crude and egomaniacal owner rumored to have ties to the mob named Guy Caballero (Joe Flaherty). Guy was the kind of guy who used a wheelchair even though he could walk (and even tap-dance) just to make a cheap ploy for sympathy and respect. (Of course, his favorite show was *Ironside*.) He invariably made his fashion statement in white *Saturday Night Fever* disco suits and garish hats.

Guy's first lieutenant in command of the station was the haplessly handsome Moe Green (played by Harold Ramis) who was kidnapped and presumably "cancelled" in 1978 by the "Lutonian Liberation Front." (When a shocked Guy was asked to take funds away from his Rolls-Royce payments and vacation homes just this one time—to pay the unimaginably high $2,000 ransom—he more or less told them to go ahead and off the little twerp.) Guy got just what he wanted in Moe's successor, the fabulously sleazy Edith Prickley, expertly played by Andrea Martin.

Like a $1.98 version of Joan Collins on *Dynasty*, Edith was the perfect mistress for a station as off the wall as Melonville's finest. With her Cruella De Vil leopard outfits, horn-rimmed glasses, and Tammy Faye makeup, Edith took guilt-free pleasure in luring men she'd just met into her bedroom, destroying actors' careers, and crudely promoting shows of the lowest class while cancelling others just for fun.

There were hints that she and Guy were partners on and off duty, but the eye-popping imagery of such a thing was probably best left only to the imagination. The station-syndication veteran also brought new meaning to the phrase "access slot" when she voyaged into the cable-TV world of adult cinema, with the scorching hot epic, "Prickley Heat." (If the movie ever made home video, it would probably be more at home in the "horror" section.)

The regular "shows" on *SCTV*'s schedule were things like *The Sammy Maudlin Show*, which Joe Flaherty revealed was patterned directly after the unintentional mid-'70s sleazefest *Sammy & Company*, starring Sammy Davis Jr. and his fawning second banana William B. Williams. Sammy's favorite guest was stand-up comedian and lounge singer Bobby Bittman (Eugene Levy), who looked and acted like the long-lost son of Chuck Barris—with his king-size "Jewish Afro," open silk shirts, ring-studded fingers, and gold disco chains crossing his hairy chest. The chain-smoking Bobby's frequent companion was spaced-out Vegas bimbo Lola Heatherton (Catherine O'Hara), or her Close Personal Friend, Lorna Minnelli (also Catherine).

There were also kiddie classics like "Officer Friendly" (who wasn't), and "Kaptain Kombat," who schooled his preteen viewers on the finer points of guerrilla warfare, assisted by his friend Gunny Rabbit. In one of the show's funniest sketches, "Battle of the PBS Stars," Julia Child (John Candy in a dress) faced off against Mister Rogers, with little "King Friday" rooting for him on the sidelines!

Joe and Eugene also made a memorable team as *SCTV*'s anchormen, the right-on Floyd Robertson, and the even more-on Earl Camembert. Earl mispronounced even his own last name, and his less-than-tasteful suits looked like they came from a jumble sale at *Let's Make a Deal*.

Then there were various game shows, hosted by emcees like Alex Trebell and Twink Winkindale, followed by the soap opera *Days of the Week*, which sounded like an *Electric Company* sketch and didn't look much better. In prime time, there were offerings like *The Fracases*, a spoof on the Norman Lear era of screaming, Very Special Episode social-relevance sitcoms (particularly *One Day at a Time*) and innumerable parodies of dramas like *Ironside*, *Dallas*, and *Kojak*, not to mention Joe's mean, temper-tantrumming, jut-jawed version of *Quincy*.

## THE BEGINNING OF THE END

By the end of the 1970s, though, even these three flagships were about to hit an iceberg. In 1978, Fred Silverman completed the three-network hat trick by moving first from running CBS and then from ABC to take over NBC, which had been mired badly in third place for three years. He zeroed in on *Saturday Night Live* with a vengeance as soon as he got there, thinking that the late-night showcase might be a font of new talent for his ailing prime-time schedule. One of Silverman's first moves was to offer Gilda Radner a multi-million-dollar deal for a prime-time variety hour to compete with his own signature ABC creation, *Charlie's Angels*.

Furious at the unwanted intrusion on his turf, Lorne assiduously advised Gilda not to take the deal, and even promised to pay for a one-woman Broadway show that he would film for the movies at his own expense, if she told Silverman "no." That was just the first battle in what would become an all-out war.

Lorne made Fred Silverman himself a "character" on the show, with John Belushi playing the NBC chief as the crudest of the crude studio execs. One takeoff on *Charlie's Angels* had the Angels (Gilda, Jane Curtin, and guest host Kate Jackson) assigned to perform such missions impossible as assassinating Johnny Carson and seducing NBC's best talent away for picture deals. In it, "Silverman" revealed he was still working for CBS and ABC, and was out to covertly destroy NBC from within, so that the other two networks could sop up what was left. When Kate Jackson said she felt guilty about what she was doing, that maybe TV could be a place of high quality and artistic freedom, "Silverman" slapped her, shouting, "Don't you ever say that about prime time again!"

In 1979, John Belushi left *SNL*, and he took his best friend Dan Aykroyd with him. The two were not only the hottest comedians in television; they had a platinum record of their famous Blues Brothers act in the stores, and they had played sold-out concert tours. And after John's box-office shattering success in 1978's slob comedy *Animal House*, Universal Studios couldn't wait to get John and Dan to do a *Blues Brothers* feature.

Chevy Chase had left the show long beforehand, after a breakout first season, to take advantage of solo specials from NBC and write-your-ticket Hollywood movie deals (most notably with Goldie Hawn in *Foul Play*, *Caddyshack* with Bill Murray, the *National Lampoon* movies, and his signature role as quirky reporter *Fletch*).

In 1980, any hope of keeping what remained of the original cast and crew was shattered by a blistering "editorial" that head writer Al Franken delivered on the final "Weekend Update" parody newscast of the season. Called "Limo for the Lame-O," it was a devastating attack on Fred Silverman that went far beyond John Belushi's satirization of the boss. At one point, Franken brought up a chart of the Top Ten TV shows of 1979–80, noting that "you see some *A*s, *B*s, *C*s, and *S*s [for ABC and CBS shows]—but not one *N*. And you know why? Because Silverman is a lame-o!" After Franken ruefully noted that Silverman had a paid-for penthouse and door-to-door limo service, when as talented a writer as himself had to make do on his own, he called out the chief as "indecisive and weak!"

Fred Silverman was so furious he practically threw something at his TV set. After five years, Lorne was leaving day-to-day involvement in *SNL* to take advantage of a development deal at Paramount Studios, and he insisted that Al Franken (and his comedy partner Tom Davis) become the next producers of *Saturday Night Live*. But Silverman told his lieutenant—a young exec named Brandon Tartikoff—that he would fire Tartikoff on the spot if he even *considered* giving the job to Franken.

However, due to the show's top-rated success and dream demographics, NBC refused to cancel the show outright. Instead, associate producer Jean Doumanian was promoted to produce the show—really, to recreate it—with an entirely new cast and crew.

In fairness to Jean Doumanian, who would go on to produce numerous films and projects with her friend Woody Allen, her unerring eye for talent unearthed such comic geniuses as Gilbert Gottfried, Eddie Murphy, and Joe Piscopo, and she discovered young character actors like Denny Dillon and Charles Rocket. But Jean's treatment of the new show's writing staff was an absolute disgrace as she became more overwhelmed by the impossible job. And matters weren't helped any when NBC execs started punishing her for all of Lorne's excesses.

She fired the show's new head writer, the novelist and *New York Times* magazine columnist Peter Tauber, before the first show of the season even aired, after Tauber insisted she back off the apprentice writers and demanded to protect them from her criticism and interference. She then hired former *Smothers Brothers* scribe Mason Williams, but by then Jean had become so swamped that Williams was shocked at what he described as her "incompetence." He ditched the show before Christmas.

No doubt Tauber was equally shocked while he was there. Not only was he threatened during his work routine; when it came to the show's youngest and least experienced writers, Jean made Judge Judy look like Mother Teresa. She sent them one vicious, suggestion-less memo after another, including such lines as "This has just *got* to be funnier! I don't get it—What's the point?" and an all-time low of "You see this thing? And I hope you *hate* it—because *you* wrote it!"

After his dismissal, Tauber told the press in detail what was going on. And by the start of 1981, every tabloid and TV entertainment-magazine was zeroing in on the "new" and not-so-improved *SNL* with a vengeance. NBC's most prestigious and profitable late-night series besides Johnny Carson himself was now being referred to as "Saturday Night Dead On Arrival" and "Saturday Night Vile."

The end finally came in February 1981, during a spoof of *Dallas*'s famous "Who Shot

JR?" masterpiece—when a tipsy Charles Rocket, playing J.R., told guest host (and *Dallas* costar) Charlene Tilton, live on the air, that he wanted to know just "who the *fuck* did it!" Fred Silverman demanded that Jean Doumanian be fired at once. And by the first week in March, her time on the show was history.

Cancelling the show was still out of the question at this point, but now *Saturday Night Live* wasn't just in critical condition—as the cardiologists say, it was in "V-fib." The program needed a producer strong enough, connected enough, and with enough of a platform to wrestle the show back on track and chart a new direction with a firm hand. But the established comedy screenwriters from the film industry and the sitcom veterans with a track record could see that the *SNL* ship was sinking fast.

Brandon Tartikoff lobbied hard for the one man he thought could turn *Saturday Night Live* around before it was too late. Dick Ebersol, who was legendary ABC sports topper Roone Arledge's right-hand man during the early 1970s and had helped Lorne Michaels get the original *Saturday Night Live* off the ground back in 1975, had been producing *The Midnight Special* alongside Stan Harris for the past five years.

*The Midnight Special* itself was "on the bubble" for renewal after over eight years on the air. The same rock acts, record labels, and managers that had been begging the show for exposure only a few years ago were now paying attention to the development of a new cable network called MTV, which was only a few months away from launch. Already *The Midnight Special* was reduced to producing filler segments of interviews with sitcom and movie stars, as live performances (and even videos) with new rock bands and hip stand-up comedians became fewer and further between.

When Brandon Tartikoff started romancing Dick Ebersol to take over *SNL*, that finally flipped the coin for the other show. *The Midnight Special* went into permanent midnight on May 1, 1981. The series appropriately closed with a final re-airing of the original "Get Out the Vote" special that had started it all.

But another NBC executive, fearing that *Saturday Night Live* might not be able to survive with or without Dick Ebersol, had already made an aggressive move to option the syndicated show that had been *Saturday Night*'s de facto follow-up for the past four years. *SCTV* had had a rocky road in its parent Canada the past year, bouncing from one Canadian network to another, and changing studio locations in the process, which resulted in a protracted hiatus of new episodes being produced the past year. By the end of 1980, though, it was ramped up and running with new episodes—and as soon as NBC exec Irv Segelstein had heard the news, he cleared *SCTV* as an official NBC show.

With NBC giving *SNL* one last chance to prove itself, the new *SCTV* moved into the *Midnight Special*'s old Friday night railway station starting in May of 1981. The new show would be ninety minutes long instead of the syndicated show's thirty, which resulted in much more money and production values—but also awkward music video segments to fill the gaps, and longer, more elaborate sketches taking the place of the *Laugh-In*–like quickness of the earlier episodes' skits.

However, like *Laugh-In* and *Saturday Night Live*, the SCTV talent pool had become so high-profile during the past few years that it also became the go-to place to find new talent. John Candy, Martin Short, and Rick Moranis in particular had film offers coming every which way, while Joe Flaherty, Dave Thomas, and Andrea Martin would become guest-starring sitcom royalty in the later '80s and '90s. Harold Ramis left the show way back when Moe Green had died in 1978 to become a top comedy screenwriter and director, with hits like *Animal House, Ghostbusters,* and *Caddyshack* just for starters. And Catherine O'Hara and Eugene Levy would amass a fine body of comical character work on the stage and screen.

All of that, plus the crushing pressure of writing and performing ninety minutes' worth of elaborate sketches, spoofs, and video segments pointed in only one direction. With its fans still wanting more, SCTV signed off the air for good in June of 1983.

By 1984, *Saturday Night Live* had finally started to turn itself around under the leadership of Dick Ebersol. The show was a ratings success once again, and departing cast member Eddie Murphy achieved true A-list stardom in films like *48 Hrs* and *Beverly Hills Cop,* along with his HBO comedy concerts.

And while no one would confuse the show with *Lawrence Welk* or *Carol Burnett,* Dick Ebersol had managed to steer the groundbreaking program away from the cutting-edge, in-group hipness that had typified the 1975–80 era. He ruled out all but the broadest political satire, and selected mainstream TV faces and up-and-coming young movie stars as guest hosts—rather than the hard-living journalists, "name" movie stars, and hip stand-up comics that the earlier show had insisted on.

But after four years, Dick Ebersol had had enough. He had other fish to fry in the TV world, plus a new marriage to actress Susan Saint James (then starring alongside *SNL* vet Jane Curtin in the CBS sitcom *Kate & Allie*). Meanwhile, Lorne Michaels hadn't had the success that he had hoped for in the motion-picture world, with only a few modest comedy hits to his credit. His production company, Broadway Video, still owned much of the show, and he found that he missed the power seat and adrenaline rush that the live countdown to Saturday night gave him each week. In September 1985, the prodigal Lorne returned.

He's still there as of this writing. *SNL* continued its tradition of changing its cast and characters more often than some people change underwear, as each new mini-generation of comedians comes and inevitably goes on to other, if not always bigger and better things. But Lorne Michaels' leadership has remained the show's enduring constant. And it is an ironic combination of those two things that helped the ever-youthful *Saturday Night Live* stay alive for more than thirty years—to become the oldest remaining variety show on network television.

# POSTMODERN CLASSICS

**The Hippest of the Hip and the Hottest of the Hot**

## That Was the Week That Was

*Network: NBC; On the air: January 10, 1964–May 4, 1965*

Based on a British TV series that satirized current events, *TW3* (as it came to be abbreviated) was brought to you by Ed Friendly, who would later modify the show's format into what became *Rowan & Martin's Laugh-In.* The show was successful in the ratings, and became the must-see TV for critics, columnists, and intellectuals. *TW3* went several steps beyond even the Smothers Brothers in its to-the-point political satire—Catholics, Jews, Democrats, and Republicans all got the *TW3* treatment by name—and as such, in the polarized world of Johnson-vs-Goldwater 1964 and '65, the show was quickly escorted off the air.

In addition to stellar writing and execution, *TW3* had perhaps the most talented cast of regulars ever to appear on a variety revue, certainly in a league with *Saturday Night Live* and *SCTV* (both of which openly acknowledged *TW3* for inspiring their own shows). Alan Alda, David Frost, Phyllis Newman, Henry Morgan, Skitch Henderson, Caterina Valente, Nancy Ames, and Buck Henry were all regular stars of the show—which, even forty years later, is gone but definitely not forgotten!

## Shindig

*Network: ABC; On the air: September 16, 1964–January 8, 1966*

## Hullabaloo

*Network: NBC; On the air: January 12, 1965–August 29, 1966*

TV's first honest-to-goodness prime-time rock-and-roll show, *Shindig* (and its NBC imitation *Hullabaloo*), opened the door for countless short-lived music shows in the '60s, and the most successful music show of the '70s, *The Midnight Special.* Unlike Ed Sullivan, Bing Crosby, or even Dick Clark, *Shindig* was actually hosted by someone in his twenties who could effortlessly fit in with the all-youth motif of the program. Jimmy O'Neill, a California disk jockey, was tapped to emcee *Shindig,* which featured the Righteous Brothers, Bobby Sherman, and Glen Campbell as regulars, and was partially responsible for launching their stellar careers. The show also booked its share of star power, including the Rolling Stones, the Byrds, the Everly Brothers, and the Who, whose appearance on *Shindig* was their first on American television. Even the Beatles dropped by once, in October of 1964.

Unfortunately, as rock went counterculture and racial crises made the booking of R&B and Motown artists a delicate matter, *Shindig* got the axe at ABC, as the network searched for the Next Big Thing that would be their next fad or trend to ride. (They got it, at least temporarily: *Shindig* was replaced by the huge hit *Batman,* which also had its wings clipped in the spring of 1968 despite its popularity because trend-happy ABC figured it had run its course.) Within another eight months, *Hullabaloo* was gone too.

## The Jonathan Winters Show

*Network: CBS; On the air: December 27, 1967–May 22, 1969/Syndicated first-run 1972–74*
Jonathan Winters, the irrepressible comedy genius whose diverse characters were like someone with multiple-personality syndrome who'd mastered it, came to CBS late in 1967 to replace the risible *Dundee and the Culhane.* Winters' endless supply of characters put him in Flip Wilson territory when it came to being a one-man repertory company. He could play everyone and everything from Binky the effete preppie to Maudie Frickett, the by-golly-gumption Midwestern granny who was the inspiration for her likely cousin, Johnny Carson's Aunt Blabby.

The *Jonathan Winters Show* was also far ahead of its time in being one of the first truly unique, improvisational variety shows since the earliest days of the medium. With a dream supporting cast including Alice Ghostley, Paul Lynde, Cliff "Charley Weaver" Arquette, and future *Falcon Crest* diva Abby Dalton, the show prospered at 10:00 Wednesday nights and was still doing well when it flip-flopped with new detective hit *Hawaii Five-0* in December 1968, moving to Thursdays at 8:00. (In the 1969 film *Midnight Cowboy,* a giant billboard of Winters can be glimpsed in the scene where Ratso and Joe Buck walk on an elevated platform near an abandoned brick building.)

CBS decided to cancel the ultra-politically incorrect *Gomer Pyle* in 1969—but they still wanted to retain Jim Nabors in a weekly variety series. The 8:00 Thursday slot, bolstered by the kid-com *Family Affair,* was the ideal spot for it. To make room for that show, the same year that CBS axed the Smothers Brothers it also bid adieu to the *Wacky World of Jonathan Winters* (which is what he called his 1972–74 syndicated follow-up, produced by Dean Martin topper Greg Garrison).

After that, Winters joined his costars as a regular on the original *Hollywood Squares,* and he was one of Mike Douglas's favorite guests on his long-running talk show. In 1981, he became Mearth, the middle-aged "son" of Pam Dawber and Robin Williams, who hatched from a giant egg Mork had "given birth to" on *Mork & Mindy*'s last season. (Winters was and is Robin Williams's comedy idol, and he personally picked Winters for the part.) The years since have only confirmed Jonathan Winters's presence in comedy as one of the most innovative funnymen since Kovacs and Berle, and one of the biggest influences on the Baby-Boom comedians who would take over TV in the '70s and '80s.

## Monty Python's Flying Circus

*Produced 1969–1974 for the BBC*

*Monty Python's Flying Circus* was in some ways the biggest comedy watershed to hit the screen since *Laugh-In* and *All in the Family* on either side of the "Pond." "Monty Python" was not a person, but rather the offbeat name for the equally offbeat troupe of young comic actors from Britain who starred in the series.

The show starred a team of talent all-stars like Eric Idle, John Cleese, Michael Palin, Terry Jones, Terry Gilliam, and Graham Chapman. One of the unique things about the show (and what made it must-see TV for young counterculture-vultures) was that every single cast member was a mod young white man. That didn't stop them from tackling their opposites, though—it was rare indeed for a *Python* episode to go by without featuring one or more of the guys in outrageous drag and wigs and push-up bras, or in stuffy powdered wigs as old British duffers. Rather than offensive, the unabashed silliness of the show, combined with its scalpel-sharp satire, just made this part of the series even funnier and somehow more appropriate.

*Monty Python's Flying Circus* was a spoof on "civilized" (especially British) society. And it skewered the British government with the same elan that *The Smothers Brothers* and *Laugh-In* showed to stuffy U.S. institutions, satirizing the social-democratic bureacracy with things like "The Ministry of Silly Walks," when they weren't playing games like "Confuse the Cat." It was also top-heavy on vaguely grotesque (and almost surely heavily influenced by drugs) psychedelic animated segments designed by *Python* regular Terry Gilliam, with things like people's heads popping open only to reveal mold, gangrene, and grass within, or tripped-out outer space segments. (Interestingly, Gilliam was the troupe's sole American performer.)

The show would go from filmed, movie-like pieces to shot-on-videotape sketches and skits and back again without warning, and made *Laugh-In* seem positively orderly by comparison. The closest the program ever came to providing a "bridge" between one psychedelic or offbeat segment and another was what soon became the show's signature phrase. "And now for something completely different!"

As Alex McNeil noted in *Total Television,* in the five years the series was in regular production only forty-five episodes were made. The reason most people in the United States and Canada think of it as having been a weekly series was that late in the show's run it was brought to stateside public television as a regular weekly offering. Almost all of the series' principals became major stars—especially Eric Idle and John Cleese, the latter of whom starred in the classic "Brit-com" *Fawlty Towers.* (Sadly, Graham Chapman died of cancer in 1989.) All of the *Python* regulars had relatively successful movie careers, including the spin-off films *Monty Python and the Holy Grail, Monty Python's The Meaning of Life, The Life of Brian,* and—of course—*And Now for Something Completely Different.*

And now for something . . . well, you know.

## The Benny Hill Show

*Produced 1969–1989 for Thames TV/Britain*

Britain's bawdiest comic was already relatively well known in the States and Canada in the late '60s and '70s, due to the notoriety of his U.K. series of variety specials and their ultra-explicit sexual jokes and nudity. But the show didn't make it across the pond as a regular feature until January of 1979, when Taffner Associates brought edited half-hour portions of the shows to syndication. (Taffner would also later distribute reruns of the sexy 1977–84 ABC sictom *Three's Company*, itself based on the British comedy *Man About the House*.)

The syndicated series nabbed high-profile 7:30 p.m. access slots on local independent stations in New York, Los Angeles, and Boston, and equally high-ticket 11:00 p.m. and midnight slots in dozens of other cities. It was no accident that Taffner chose to bring the show to syndication,

"I say! Is that a salute, or are you just happy to see me?"

where as long as it met the most basic FCC standards of decency and a local station manager could be convinced to buy it, it would be OK. That sure beat dealing with the inevitable armies of Broadcast Standards censors on one of the networks. The show blended footage from 1960s and '70s specials with newly produced ones hot off the presses.

The show's beloved supporting cast became celebrities on both sides of the Pond: full-sized old buffer Bob Todd—perhaps the real-life inspiration for *The Muppet Show*'s "Statler and Waldorf," who could play stuffy British stock characters and boozing beer hounds with equal skill; lovable dirty old man "Little" Jackie Wright, with his Buddy Holly glasses and his bald pate that Benny couldn't resist lightly slap-slap-slap-slap-slapping in his funny fast films; dignified announcer-chap Henry McGee, with his tall, commanding, aristocratic mien and delivery; and of course, the scintillating group of scantily clad "birds," humorously known as "Hill's Angels." Hill's Angels did *Laugh-In*–style quickies and go-go breaks, big production numbers, and performed in "naughty bits" with Benny like his workout videos (he lifts one cheerleader girl up and down on his face), or the innumerable spoofs of shows like *Charlie's Angels* and porno movies and slasher films.

Of course, Benny himself (and the rest of the guys) had no problem dressing up as women in drag—like his mumbling old Miss Ellie in the *Dallas* sketches, or his Elizabeth Taylor or Queen Elizabeth impersonations. Benny was also a Gleason-like one man company of his own characters—lecherous newscaster Humphrey Bumphrey, the none-too-bright daredevil Captain Fred Scuttle, Professor Marvel, and all the rest.

*The Benny Hill Show* truly was the Benny Hill show: Hill saw to almost every aspect of production, and wrote the vast bulk of the skits, sketches, and even the lyrics to the songs himself. His shows never lost their popularity either in the U.K. or in North America, but in 1989, the management at Thames Television had decided that the sixty-five year old comedian had finally run his course. Benny was furious at the abrupt dismissal after making "millions of pounds" for the company, and he set to work planning specials for rival networks and an American tour.

Sadly, though, it never came to pass. Benny Hill died of a heart attack at age sixty-eight in the spring of 1992. His obituary was front-page news worldwide, proving that he was in many people's minds, *the* preeminent British comedian from the 1940s onward. Unfortunately, after Benny's death his shows faded from public view, but they still turn up every now and then—and are thus all the more savored as the guilty-pleasure "naughty bits" that they are!

## Solid Gold

*Syndicated first-run: 1980–1988*
They say that success is the best revenge, and so it is fitting that after stars like Pearl Bailey and Leslie Uggams faced the very worst in discrimination and one unjustified cancellation after another,

the last big variety hour of the '70s was hosted by two black ladies. And when you remember that those ladies were R&B legend Dionne Warwick and Fifth Dimension queen Marilyn McCoo—well, to paraphrase their fellow diva Carly Simon, "nobody could have done it better."

More importantly, while network execs embarrassed themselves in the latter half of the '70s trying to find a variety-show format that would be new and hip and exciting, it was this non-network, access-syndicated series that finally lived up to the ideal. *This* was the one that ABC, CBS, or NBC should have put on all along!

Longtime television executive Al Masini and his colleague and friend Bill Andrews created this show as the first regular weekly offering of Masini's "Operation Prime Time" series of syndicated specials and movie events in the late '70s. OPT had been a smashing success with TV movies and miniseries like *The Bastard* and *The Gossip Columnist,* and Masini wanted his next project to be a two-hour, top-name rock-and-roll TV special. Titled *Solid Gold '79,* the show counted down the hottest hits of 1979, and was hosted by top entertainers Glen Campbell and Dionne Warwick. The smashing success of the show prompted Masini to convert the format into a full-bore weekly series to begin in the fall.

At the same time, Bill Andrews had just finished overseeing the final episodes of *The $1.98 Beauty Contest* and the launch of the equally campy *Face the Music* for syndication superstar Sandy Frank. After leaving Frank's employ in March 1980, around the same time *Solid Gold '79* aired, Andrews was in just the right place to be Masini's right-hand man on the project. The show moved into the old *Donny & Marie* studio at KTLA's Golden West Videotape Complex (where variety and game-show legends *Sha Na Na* and *Name That Tune* were finishing their final seasons). In September 1980, *Solid Gold* glittered its way into weekend prime-access on scores of TV stations from coast to coast.

The white-hot show became the biggest reason for young people to stay at home on Saturday nights since *The Mary Tyler Moore Show* had gone off the air. And *Solid Gold* moved at the fastest pace since *Laugh-In* itself. It was a full hour's worth of top ten countdowns and up-to-the-minute performances, backed up by Dionne or Marilyn's star power—and of course, the Solid Gold Dancers.

*Solid Gold* found a way to beat back the music-video challenge and bring the old "dance show" format of things like *American Bandstand* and *Soul* Train into the '80s. The show had a professional troupe of high-energy, buff-bodied male and female dancers, with teeth and personalities almost as perfect as their zero-fat, Nautilized bodies. Aside from maybe "Hill's Angels," the Solid Gold Dancers became the hottest and sexiest variety show troupe that the tube had ever seen. And they kept the viewers riveted to their seats as they turned the weekly Top Ten Countdown into borderline S&M "performance art" with their sizzling dance routines.

*Solid Gold's* impact was felt immediately. No longer were hillbilly relics like *Hee-Haw* or old reliables like *Lawrence Welk* and *Match Game PM* the most desirable shows in weekend syndication. With Dionne or Marilyn there; an assortment of "guest hosts" like Andy Gibb, Rick Dees, and others; plus music videos hot off the presses and the Solid Gold Dancers, having a few big-name stars perform live was only frosting on the cake. But no sooner was the show on the air than one huge name after another in rock, jazz, or R&B would try to get a booking on the show. The fact that the show didn't really "need" big stars, with all the other things it had going for it, only made the show more alluring to even the most egotistical and prima-donna of stars.

And despite being, along with *Dance Fever* and *The Gong Show,* the quintessential disco-era show, *Solid Gold* more than flourished as the 1980s got fully under way. The show had built-in chic, glitz and glamour, and it utilized every computer, videotape, and editing trick in the book. And the Solid Gold Dancers performed one decadent dance routine after another, with artsy, almost-shocking segments that could almost have come right out of *Velvet Goldmine*. Who can forget those sl-l-l-iiiiding disco poles and mirrors and zooming photography set to the beat of the music, or their on-the-spot music videos with the guest stars?

A sad epitaph for the show came as *Solid Gold's* final episodes aired. Longtime cohost Andy Gibb died after years of struggle with substance abuse in the spring of 1988. By that time *Solid Gold* had become a victim of its own success—it had already rewritten the rules for TV variety and opened the bank accounts and financial floodgates for big-budget hours in weekend syndication, like the *Star Trek* spin-offs and the soon-to-come *Hercules* and *Xena*. The show had also been bumping-and-grinding for a more than respectable eight-year run, and it was time to give all those calf muscles and Elvis-pelvises a break!

*Solid Gold* certainly left its glitter-stained mark on things, though. It stands as one of TV's last-ever successful variety shows, and was among the last remnants of late '70s disco culture to survive and thrive on television. And after twenty years of some of the most innovative, risky, and beloved shows in television history, it is appropriately with this fabulous, funny classic that the "golden" age of TV variety finally came to a close.

# CONCLUSION

And so ends our tripped-out trip back in time to celebrate TV's biggest and best variety shows of the psychedelic '60s and the sexy '70s. When *Solid* Gold gave it up for good in '88, any remnant of the "boogie nights" era in TV was gone forever.

As a matter of fact, variety TV itself was near terminally ill by then. Within two years, Tracey Ullman would end her weekly Fox variety show (although its spin-off, *The Simpsons*, launched in 1989, became one of TV's longest-running series ever). Less than six years after *Solid Gold*'s disco ball exploded, the era of the prime-time variety show ended completely when Jim Carrey became a movie star and the Wayans Brothers left for their own WB sitcom, as Fox's *In Living Color* ran dry in the spring of 1994.

But even despite those body blows, variety TV isn't completely dead. *Saturday Night Live* continues in late night, of course, and in 1995 Fox launched the late-night sketch comedy *Mad TV,* which has also proven a long-lasting success. Cable TV offers specials with stand-up comedians and occasional musicians, and PBS regularly brings live jazz and progressive rock shows into America's living rooms. And there are reality shows with a variety aspect—most notably the number-one-rated show of recent years, Fox's *American Idol*.

And if anything is to be gained by this book beyond entertainment and a few happy reminiscences, it is to memorialize the phoenix-like powers of rebirth and renewal that the variety format exemplified during America's most turbulent era. Perhaps a new generation of "really big shews" is just around the corner, redesigned and ready to take on the twenty-first century, with another crew of soon-to-be-stars who'll make us think, make us cry, and make us laugh—and above all, make us glad we had this time together.

# Index

## A

Acuff, Roy, 56, 59
Ailes, Roger, 141
Akins, Claude, xviii
Alda, Alan, 130, 220
Aldridge, Sheila, 41
Alexander, Andrew, 214
Ali, Muhammad, 161
Allen, Dennis, 129, 138, 200
Allen, Fred, 8
Allen, Gracie, 8
Allen, Robert, 43
Allen, Steve, xiv–xv, 8, 11, 16, 107
Allen, Woody, xiii, xix, 217
Allman, Gregg, 188, 195–96
Allred, Gloria, 205
Alpert, Herb, 209
Altman, Jeff, 204
Altman, Robert, 146
Ames, Nancy, 130, 220
Anderson, Ernie, 105, 113, 125, 181
Anderson, Lynn, 35, 44, 46
Anderson, Paul Thomas, 125, 146
Anderson, Ron, 47
Andrews, Bill, 226
Andrews, Julie, 22, 76–77, 108, 200
Arledge, Roone, 200, 218
Armstrong, Louis, xiv, 4, 11, 18, 33
Arthur, Bea, 74, 110, 123
Astaire, Fred, 7
Aubrey, James T. Jr., 88
Aykroyd, Dan, 210, 214, 216
Aylesworth, John, 57

## B

Bacharach, Burt, 36
Baez, Joan, 92–93, 95, 208

Bailey, Pearl, 11, 77, 149–50, 152, 198, 200, 225
Bakalayan, Dick, 177
Bakely, Bonny Lee, 70
Baker, Lennie, 180
Balden, Elaine, 41
Balden, Jim, 41
Ball, Lucille, xiii, 13, 74, 132, 163, 169, 185
Ballard, Bob, 27
Barber, Ava, 41, 46
Barker, Bob, xiii
Barone, Anita, 115
Barrett, Rona, 133
Barris, Chuck, 56–57, 98, 147, 170, 178, 215
Bay City Rollers, The, 201
Beatles, The, ix, 5, 12–13, 15–16, 18–19, 21, 35–36, 99–100, 131, 133, 144, 190, 196, 201, 220
Beatts, Anne, 188
Beatty, Ned, 113
Bee Gees, The, 208–9
Belafonte, Harry, 7, 11, 92, 95, 157, 162
Belland, Bruce, 125
Belushi, John, 210, 212, 216
Bendix, William, xiii
Benny, Jack, xiii, 5–6, 8, 12, 37, 50
Benton, Barbi, 59
Bergen, Candice, 146, 213
Bergen, Edgar, 213
Berle, Milton, x, xii–xiii, xix, 6, 8, 11, 15, 28, 158, 212, 213
Berlin, Irving, 7, 37
Bernard, Ian, 129
Berry, Ken, 109, 113
Beyoncé, 195
Biviano, Lin, 46

Black, Shirley Temple, 143
Blake, Robert, 70
Blanc, Mel, xiii
Blyden, Larry, 210
Blye, Allan, 76, 86, 152, 178
Bogonia, Ruby, 142
Boland, Bonnie, 125, 199
Bono, Chastity, 184, 189, 193
Bono, Sonny, 181–87, 191, 193, 195–97
Boone, Daniel, 160
Boone, Pat, xi
Borge, Victor, 7
Bowie, David, 208–9
Bowzer, 179–80
Boyd, Malcolm, 90
Boylan, Barbara, 32
Brady Bunch, The, 179, 202, 204
Brando, Marlon, 177
Brewer, Teresa, 7
Brill, Charlie, 21
Brillstein, Bernie, 57
Bromfield, Valri, 214
Brooks, Albert, 15, 20
Brooks, Foster, 78
Brooks, Mel, xii, xix, 112, 117
Brown, Chelsea, 129, 135, 147
Brown, James, 12, 19
Brown, Johnny, 129, 138, 149
Brown, Les, 52–53, 61, 125, 157
Bruce, Lenny, 131
Buckley, William F., 144
Bugaloos, The, 174
Burgess, Bobby, 32, 35, 47
Burnett, Carol, ix, xii, xv, 8, 16, 41, 55, 76–77, 84, 86, 95, 105–23, 125–26, 147, 173, 184, 186, 196, 200, 208, 210, 212, 214, 219
Burns, George, xix, 5, 8–9, 12

Burns, Ken, 33
Burr, Raymond, 97
Burton, Richard, 22
Bush, Barbara, 44
Buzzi, Ruth, 124, 129, 133, 135–36, 139, 147
Byner, John, xi, 8
Byrds, The, 220

## C

Caesar, Sid, xii, xix, 10–11, 15, 210
Cage, Nicolas, 192
Callas, Maria, 22
Camp, Hamilton, 199
Campbell, Glen, 36, 56, 81, 90–91, 99, 125, 149, 172–73, 220, 226
Candy, John, 214–15, 219
Captain and Tenille, The, 175–76
Carlin, George, 5, 12, 15, 168, 208
Carne, Judy, 25, 129, 132–33, 135, 143–44, 147
Carney, Art, xiii, xvii, xix
Carpenter, Karen, 123, 176
Carpenter, Richard, 176
Carrey, Jim, 229
Carroll, Diahann, 148, 157, 162
Carruthers, Bill, 52, 54
Carson, Johnny, 16, 44, 72, 93, 159, 162, 176, 208–10, 212, 216–17, 221
Carter, Lynda, 117
Carter, Nell, 172
Carvey, Dana, 211
Cash, Johnny, 25, 52–54, 56–58, 93, 99, 102, 130, 200
Cash, June Carter, 54
Cassidy, David, 75, 173
Castle, Jo Ann, 32–33, 37, 39, 43–44, 46, 124
Castro, Fidel, 11
Cates, George, 27, 41
Cavett, Dick, 15, 93
Chambers, Ernie, xvii, 86
Chapman, Graham, 222
Charles, Ray, 117, 123, 208
Charmoli, Tony, xii
Charo, 106
Chase, Chevy, 144, 210, 216
Chayevsky, Paddy, 214

Cher, ix, xviii, 51, 65, 76, 94, 101, 106, 109, 138, 143, 147, 163, 166, 170, 172–76, 178, 181–97, 208–11
Child, Julia, 133
Clair, Dick, 200
Clapton, Eric, 209
Clark, Dick, 55, 209, 220
Clark, Petula, 162
Clark, Roy, 58–59
Clayton-Thomas, David, 97
Cleese, John, 222
Cline, Patsy, 52
Clinton, Hillary, 60
Clooney, Rosemary, 7, 71
Coburn, James, 212
Coca, Imogene, xii
Cocker, Joe, 209
Cole, Gary, 204
Cole, Nat King, xiv, 33, 148, 150, 157, 160
Coleman, Dabney, 146
Collins, Dorothy, xii
Collins, Joan, 215
Collins, Judy, xvii, 54
Como, Perry, xiv, xix, 35, 123, 149, 156, 168
Conrad, William, 170, 196
Contardo, Johnny, 180
Conti, Tom, 75
Conway, Tim, 105, 107, 109, 112–13, 117–18, 121, 124–27, 143, 168, 199
Cooney, Joan Ganz, 211
Cooper, Alice, 209
Cosby, Bill, 13, 77–78, 148, 157, 161, 168
Cosell, Howard, 174, 200–1
Cosette, Pierre, 143, 179
Crocetti, Dino, 62–63
Cronyn, Hume, 77
Crosby, Bing, xiv, 6, 24, 38, 48–49, 123, 156, 220
Crosby, Norm, 199
Crowe, Cameron, 146
Cruise, Tom, 126
Cuesta, Henry, 40
Curtin, Jane, 210, 216, 219
Curtis, Jamie Lee, 147, 212

## D

Dale, Dick, 43, 46
Dale, Jimmy, 181
Dalton, Abby, 221
Dandridge, Dorothy, 157
Dann, Michael, 85, 88–89, 91, 94, 125
Darin, Bobby, 16, 167, 177–178
Davis, Sammy Jr., xv, 11, 16, 18, 25, 33, 63, 69–70, 123, 133, 143, 157, 179, 213
Davis, Tom, 217
Dawber, Pam, 221
Dawson, Richard, 70, 76, 129, 138, 146
Day, Dennis, xiii
Day, Doris, 78, 109, 185
Dayan, Moshe, 143
Dean, Jimmy, 191–92
DeCordova, Fred, 209
Dees, Rick, 227
DeGeneres, Ellen, 146
DeLaria, Lea, 146
Delo, Ken, 36, 46, 49
DeLuise, Dom, 61, 67, 73
Denver, John, 47, 208, 213
Derek, Bo, 212
Deutsch, Patti, 129, 138
DeVol, Frank, 43
Diana, Princess, 192
Dickinson, Angie, 63
Diller, Phyllis, 20, 56, 199
Dillon, Denny, 217
Disney, Walt, 7, 21, 48, 50, 78, 109, 160, 188
Donahue, Phil, 122
Doobie Brothers, The, 208
Dorsey, Tommy, 30
Douglas, Michael, 69
Douglas, Mike, 44, 141–42, 221
Doumanian, Jean, 217–18
Drier, Moosie, 129
DuBrow, Rick, 38
Dukakis, Olympia, 192
Dulles, John Foster, 107
Dulo, Jane, 180
Dumont, Margaret, 24
Duncan, Arthur, 33, 39, 47
Durante, Jimmy, xv, 74, 100
Durning, Charles, 213
Dylan, Bob, 19, 54

## E

Ebersol, Dick, 218–19
Echeverria, Rudy, 47
Eden, Barbara, 143
Edwards, Blake, 77
Edwards, Dave, 43
Edwards, Geoff, 177
Edwards, Ralph, 24, 125, 168
Ehrhardt, Ernie, 43
Einstein, Bob, 76, 81, 97, 152
Ellington, Duke, ix, 13, 30
Elliott, Mama Cass, xvii, 123, 208
Ellison, Harlan, 200
Emery, Ralph, 46, 55, 57
English, Ralna, 29, 36, 44, 46
Erikson, Hal, 208
Eubanks, Bob, 99
Everly Brothers, The, 220

## F

Fabray, Nanette, xiii
Falan, Tanya, 35, 48
Falana, Lola, 78
Farrell, Gail, 36, 41, 47
Fawcett, Farrah, 212
Fay, Maegan, 115
Fedderson, Don, 31, 38, 40, 43
Feeney, Joe, 29, 31, 46, 50
Feldman, Marty, 177
Feliciano, Jose, 23
Ferrell, Will, 211
Field, Sally, 113, 121, 143
Fields, Totie, 20
Fields, W. C., 133
Fischer, Bobby, 196
Fisher, Gail, 148, 162
Fitzgerald, Ella, ix, xiv, 11, 16, 18, 22, 123, 156, 168
Flagg, Fannie, 76
Flaherty, Joe, 179, 214–15, 219
Floren, Myron, 27, 29–30, 34, 47, 49
Flynn, Joe, 124
Flynn, Salli, 36, 41
Fonda, Jane, 146
Fontaine, Frank, xiii, 8
Ford, Tennessee Ernie, xv, 47, 52
Fosse, Bob, xii
Fountain, Pete, 33

Foxx, Redd, 152, 157, 169, 191
Frank, Sandy, 56, 178, 226
Franken, Al, 216–17
Franklin, Aretha, 12, 22, 163–64, 168, 208–9
Freberg, Stan, 35
French, Leigh, 81, 89, 91, 97
Friendly, Ed, 130, 140, 147, 198, 220
Fritz, Ken, 102
Frost, David, 130, 220
Frye, David, 89

## G

Gable, Clark, 21, 110
Garagiola, Joe, xv
Garland, Judy, 9, 22, 130–31
Garner, Peggy Ann, 17
Garrison, Greg, 65–66, 69, 177, 221
Geffen, David, 188, 195
Gennaro, Peter, 13
Gentry, Bobbie, 54
Ghostley, Alice, 77, 221
Gibb, Andy, 227
Gibbs, Terry, 99
Gibran, Kahlil, 165
Gibson, Henry, 129, 135–36, 138, 140, 146
Gifford, Kathie Lee, 58, 60
Gillespie, Dizzy, 212
Gilliam, Byron, 129
Gilliam, Terry, 222
Gleason, Jackie, xiii, xvi–xviii, 8, 125, 198
Glover, Savion, 47
Gobel, George, xv, 210
Godfrey, Arthur, xi–xii, xix, 11
Golddiggers, The, 61, 64–66, 69, 72–73, 176–77
Goldsboro, Bobby, 178
Goodman, Benny, xiv, 7–8, 30
Gore, Lesley, 35
Gorme, Eydie, 13, 109, 123
Gorshin, Frank, 8
Gottfried, Gilbert, 217
Grade, Sir Lew, 77, 211
Graham, Billy, 49
Graves, Teresa, 129, 135, 138, 146, 199
Green, Jules, 10

Greene, Denny, 180
Grier, Pam, 213
Griffin, Merv, 55, 93, 97, 209
Griffith, Andy, xvi, 78–79, 109
Griffiths, Sandi, 36, 41
Guest, Judith, 75
Guthrie, Arlo, 54
Guthrie, Woody, 36
Guy, Bobby, 124

## H

Hackett, Buddy, 70
Hagman, Larry, 205
Hall, Monty, 70
Hall, Tom T., 55
Hamilton, Carrie, 115
Hamilton, Joe, 108, 113, 115, 118
Hanks, Tom, xix
Harlan, John, 155
Harper, Valerie, 214
Harrington, Pat, xv
Harris, Charlotte, 32, 41
Harris, David, 93, 95
Harris, Emmylou, 80
Harris, Stan, 102, 218
Hart, Clay, 36
Havens, Bob, 48
Hawn, Goldie, 72, 129, 136, 138–39, 144, 216
Heatherton, Joey, 177, 188
Hefner, Hugh, 59
Hemion, Dwight, xii
Henderson, Florence, 204
Henderson, Skitch, 131, 220
Hendrix, Jimi, 7
Henry, Bob, 160, 169
Henry, Buck, 220
Henson, Jim, 12, 70, 211, 213
Herfurt, Skeets, 43
Hill, Benny, 65, 224–25
Hill, Doug, 84, 201, 211
Hines, Gregory, 33, 47
Hitchcock, Alfred, 107
Holly, Buddy, 12, 36, 225
Hooper, Larry, 46
Hope, Bob, 4, 6–7, 13, 24, 98, 132, 142, 163, 213
Hopkins, Telma, 170, 172

Hopper, Hedda, 6
Horne, Lena, 11
Hovis, Guy, 29, 36, 46
Hudson, Kate, 144
Hudson, Rock, 36, 118
Humperdinck, Englebert, 77, 93, 99, 102–3, 198
Humphrey, Hubert, 89, 141
Humphreys, Paul, 41, 48
Hunt, Helen, 117
Huston, John, 113

**I**

Idle, Eric, 222
Ilson, Saul, xvii, 86
Imus, Don, 201
Ivins, Molly, 60

**J**

Jack, Wolfman, 208–9
Jackson, Janet, 179
Jackson, Joe, 179
Jackson, Kate, 216
Jackson, Mahalia, xiv
Jackson, Michael, 178
Jackson Five, The, 11, 25, 172
Jacobi, Lou, 61
Jagger, Mick, 19, 208
James, Dennis, xix
Janssen, David, 63, 73
Jencks, Richard, 94
Jennings, Waylon, 208
Jensen, Sandi, 36
John, Elton, xvii, 187, 189, 196, 209, 212
Johnson, Arte, 129, 135–36, 138, 140, 144, 146
Johnson, Freddie, 158, 162
Johnson, Lyndon, 88–89, 91
Jones, Allan, 23
Jones, Dean, 200
Jones, Grandpa, 59
Jones, Jack, 23
Jones, Quincy, 78
Jones, Terry, 222
Jones, Tom, 77, 93, 99–100, 198, 200
Joplin, Janis, 7, 19, 102, 186
Jordan, Will, xi, 8

**K**

Kahn, Madeline, 112
Kaufman, Andy, 49, 76
Kay, Monte, 160, 162, 169
Kaye, Danny, xvi, xix, 84, 86
Kean, Jane, xvii
Keaton, Michael, 74–75
Kellen, Peter, 181
Kelly, Emmett, xiii
Kelly, Gene, ix, 21, 74
Kelly, George T., 30
Kennedy, Bobby, 89
Kennedy, John F., 130
Kennedy, Sarah, 129, 138
Keyes, Paul, 141
Kiley, Richard, 22
Kiley, Tim, 12, 86, 160, 162
Kilgore, Jim, 53
Kind, Richard, 115
King, Alan, 13, 16, 20, 25
King, BB, 209
King, Billie Jean, xx
King, Cissy, 35, 39, 41, 47
Kirby, Durward, xv
Kirshner, Don, 209
Kiser, Terry, 115
Kissinger, Henry, 118
Klein, Johnny, 41
Knight, Gladys, 13, 22, 166
Knotts, Don, xv, 78–79, 126, 160, 187
Korman, Harvey, 46, 105, 107, 109, 112, 117–18, 124, 127
Kovacs, Ernie, xii
Krause, Peter, 115
Krofft, Marty, 12, 56, 174
Kurtz, Swoosie, 74

**L**

Lafferty, Perry, 85, 91
Landon, Michael, 147
Landsberg, Klaus, 31
Lane, Kenny, 61, 65
Lange, Hope, 76
Lange, Jim, 98
Lanson, Snooky, xii
LaRosa, Julius, xi
LaRue, Johnny, 202
Laughton, Charles, 17
Lawford, Peter, 63

Lawrence, Carol, 5, 16, 219
Lawrence, Steve, 13, 109, 121, 123
Lawrence, Vicki, 101, 105, 107, 109, 113, 117–18, 124, 178
Leachman, Cloris, 112, 213
Lear, Norman, xviii, 86, 126, 130, 183, 215
Lee, Peggy, ix, 7, 13, 123
Lennon Sisters, 29, 32, 35, 38, 43–44, 48, 93, 100–1, 103, 198
Lennon, Dan, 101
Lennon, John, 51
Lennon, William, 101
Leonard, John, 157
Letterman, David, 16, 74, 196
Levinson, Barry, 125–26
Levy, Eugene, xiv, 214–15, 219
Lewis, Jerry Lee, 208
Lewis, Jerry, xiii, 7, 24, 62–63, 84, 189, 196
Liberace, 31
Lido, Bob, 29, 31, 47
Linn, Roberta, 31
Little, Rich, xix, 8, 77, 200
Livingstone, Mary, xiii
Lloyd, Jeremy, 129
Lollobrigida, Gina, 63, 72
Lon, Alice, 31–32
Long, Shelley, 204
Longet, Claudine, xix
Lott, Trent, 46
Lovitz, John, 147
Ludden, Allen, 108
Lutz, Sam, 31, 38
Lynde, Paul, 177
Lynde, Paul, 48, 221
Lynn, Loretta, 52, 56, 123

**M**

MacDonald, John D., 141
MacGraw, Ali, 133
MacKenzie, Gisele, xii
Mackie, Bob, 186
MacLaine, Shirley, 63
Macomber, Debbie, 199
MacRae, Sheila, xvii
Madden, Dave, 129, 146
Malden, Karl, 69
Maloof, Richard, 37, 47
Mancini, Henry, xvi

Mandrell Sisters, 55–57, 80, 126
Mandrell, Barbara, 55–57, 80, 126
Mandrell, Irlene, 56
Mandrell, Louise, 56
Manzarek, Ray, 16
Marie, Rose, 124
Marley, Bob, 209
Mars, Ken, 113, 121, 180
Marshall, Peter, 46, 142
Martin, Andrea, 214–15, 219
Martin, Ann, 44, 124
Martin, Dean, ix, xiv, xvii, 7, 12, 24, 61–73, 79, 84, 98–99, 107, 131, 133, 147, 149, 159–60, 165, 176, 191, 198, 200, 204, 208, 221
Martin, Dick, 70, 84, 129–33, 140
Martin, Jeanne, 62, 66
Martin, Steve, 36, 81, 86, 96–97, 191, 208
Marvin, Lee, 113
Masini, Al, 226
Mason, Jackie, 13, 16, 21
Masuda, Kei, 204
Mathis, Johnny, 167
May, Elaine, 95, 214
Mayo, Whitman, 152
McAnn, Terry, 123
McCall, Mitzi, 21
McCann, Chuck, 199
McCartney, Linda, 13
McCartney, Paul, 13, 163, 168
McCoo, Marilyn, 126, 226
McDonald, Betty, 62
McGee, Henry, 225
McGuire Sisters, xi
McMahon, Ed, 72
McMahon, Jenna, 200
McNeil, Alex, 198, 222
McQueen, Steve, 133, 135
Meadows, Audrey, xiii, xvii, 71
Meadows, Jayne, xv
Medford, Kay, 61
Medley, Bill, 97
Melendez, Bill, 199
Mercer, Marian, 61
Merman, Ethel, ix, 16
Metrano, Art, 125
Metzger, Mary Lou, 36, 41, 47
Michaels, Lorne, 21, 146, 185, 199, 202, 209, 211, 218–19

Midler, Bette, 187, 189, 196
Miller, Dennis, 211
Miller, Mitch, 148
Mitchell, Joni, 196
Mitchell, Scoey, 200
Moffitt, John, 12–13
Monkees, The, 84
Montgomery, George, xix
Monty Python's Flying Circus, 222–23
Moore, Garry, xv, 107–8, 210
Moore, Mary Tyler, 15, 38, 65, 74–76, 109, 138, 173, 226
Moore, Rudy Ray, 157
Moranis, Rick, 214, 219
Mordente, Tony, 181
Moreno, Rita, 179
Morgan, Henry, 220
Morgan, Robert W., 201
Morris, Garrett, 210
Morrison, Jim, 19–20, 95
Morrow, Karen, 55
Murphy, Eddie, 210, 217, 219
Murray, Bill, 201–2, 210, 216
Myers, Mike, 211

**N**

Nabors, Jim, 54–55, 94, 109, 118, 160, 172, 221
Narz, Jack, x
Navratilova, Martina, xx
Nelson, Craig Richard, 113
Nelson, Craig T., 113
Nemoto, Mei, 204
Netherton, Tom, 40, 47
Nevins, Natalie, 35, 37, 41, 46
Newhart, Bob, 15, 70, 78, 109–10, 140
Newman, Laraine, 210
Newman, Phyllis, 130, 220
Newton, Wayne, 168, 191
Newton-John, Olivia, xix, 209
Nichols, Mike, 191, 214
Nichols, Nichelle, 148, 162
Nicholson, Jack, 192
Nielsen, Leslie, 117
Niverson, Elaine, 41
Nixon, Richard, 88, 133, 141–42
Novak, Kim, xv
Nye, Louis, xv

**O**

O'Connell, Helen, xii
O'Connor, Des, 25
O'Donoghue, Michael, 210
O'Hara, Catherine, 214–15, 219
O'Keefe, Goldie, 89
Olivier, Sir Laurence, 122
Olson, Johnny, xiii, xvii
O'Neill, Jimmy, 220
Orlando, Tony, 170–72, 178
Osmond, Donny, 173–75
Osmond, Marie, 56, 173–75
Osmond Family, xvi, xviii, 169, 173–75
Otwell, David, 41
Owens, Buck, 58
Owens, Gary, xx, 129, 132, 134–37, 142, 147
Oz, Frank, 213

**P**

Paar, Jack, xv, 107
Page, LaWanda, 152–53
Page, Patti, 7
Paley, William S., 6, 88, 94
Palin, Michael, 222
Parker, Chuck, 124
Parsons, Louella, 6
Parton, Dolly, 79, 146, 174, 191
Partridge Family, The, 100, 146, 173, 202
Paul, Ralph, 3
Paulsen, Pat, 81, 87, 89, 97, 187
Pearl, Minnie, 56, 59
Pennington, Janice, 129, 135
Peppiatt, Frank, 57
Perry, Roger, 142
Pfeiffer, Michelle, 192
Phillips, Michelle, 11, 16
Piscopo, Joe, 217
Piven, Jeremy, 115
Pleshette, Suzanne, 109
Pointer Sisters, 123, 208
Poitier, Sidney, 148, 157
Poston, Tom, xv
Power, Shirley Black, 143
Power, Tyrone, 143
Powers, Austin, 133
Precht, Betty, 17
Precht, Bob, 11, 19

Presley, Elvis, 10, 17, 184
Preston, Billy, 208
Price, Kenny, 60
Price, Vincent, xv
Prinze, Freddie, 172
Prohaska, Janos, xvii
Pryor, Richard, 7, 11–12, 15, 125, 150–52, 157, 191

## Q

Quaid, Dennis, 192

## R

Radner, Gilda, 124, 210, 212, 214, 216
Ralston, Bob, 48
Ramis, Harold, 214–15, 219
Randolph, Joyce, xiii
Rashad, Phylicia, 78
Rawls, Lou, 177
Rayburn, Gene, xv
Reagan, Ronald, 88, 143
Reddy, Helen, 209
Reed, Lou, 209
Reed, Robert, 202
Reese, Della, 152–53, 168
Reilly, Charles Nelson, 61, 73, 177
Reiner, Carl, xii, xix, 86
Reiner, Rob, 81, 97
Renner, Fern, 30
Reynolds, Burt, xviii, xx, 16, 55, 132
Richard, Little, 209
Rickles, Don, 70
Righteous Brothers, The, 220
Riley, Jeannine, 59
Rivers, Joan, 4–5, 12–13, 16, 20, 46, 56, 208
Roberts, Jimmy, 31, 48
Roberts, Julia, 192
Rocket, Charles, 217–18
Rodgers, Pamela, 129
Rogers, Kenny, 191
Rogers, Sally, 124
Roman, Lulu, 59–60
Ronstadt, Linda, 80
Rooney, Mickey, 25
Roosevelt, Franklin, x
Rosenhaus, Matthew, 40, 43, 50
Ross, Betsy, 185
Ross, Diana, 11, 25, 168

Rowan, Dan, 129–31, 140–44
Rowe, Misty, 60
Rubell, Steve, 195
Rule, Elton, 149
Russell, Kurt, 144, 191
Russell, Nipsey, 61, 73, 157
Ryan, Meg, 192
Ryder, Winona, 192

## S

Sabich, Spider, xix
Sahl, Mort, 84, 125
Sahlins, Bernard, 214
Saint James, Susan, 36, 219
Sales, Soupy, xviii, 21, 180
Samples, Junior, 59
Sandler, Adam, 211
Santini, Tony, 180
Sarandon, Susan, 192
Sartain, Gailard, 60
Savalas, Telly, 213
Schlatter, George, 130–31, 137–38, 140–41, 147, 188, 190, 198
Schlosser, Herb, 209
Schneider, Jack, 94
Schwartz, Sherwood, 202
Scorsese, Martin, 50
Seeger, Pete, 82, 85, 96
Segelstein, Irv, 218
Sellers, Peter, 63, 73, 212
Severinsen, Doc, 43
Sha Na Na, 55, 97, 147, 179–80, 226
Shaffer, Paul, 196
Sharma, Barbara, 129, 138, 140
Shawn, Dick, 74
Sherman, Bobby, 220
Shimoff, Karel, 22
Shore, Dinah, xiv, xvi, xix, 70, 109–10
Short, Martin, 124, 214, 219
Shuster, Frank, 21
Shuster, Rosie, 21
Sills, Beverly, 22, 212
Silverman, Fred, 55, 125, 170, 173–74, 183, 185, 204, 216–18
Simon, Carly, 226
Simon, Neil, xii, xix
Simon, Paul, 54
Simon, Scott, 179
Sinatra, Frank Jr., 177

Sinatra, Frank, xiv, 8, 63, 70, 72, 130, 144, 177, 191, 200
Sinatra, Nancy, 36
Skelton, Red, xiii, xviii, 6, 8, 84, 86, 125, 160
Slick, Grace, 96, 186
Sloan, Dr. Mark, 76
Smith, Kate, 37
Smothers Brothers, ix, xv, xvii–xviii, 54, 63, 76, 80–97, 101–2, 107, 125, 133, 142, 148, 150, 160, 162, 172–73, 183–84, 198–99, 210, 217, 220–222
Smothers, Dick, 81–97, 142, 196
Smothers, Tommy, 81–97, 142, 196
Solt, Andrew, 16, 25
Somers, Suzanne, 205, 212
Somerville, Dave, 125
Sommer, Elke, 73
Spelling, Aaron, 191
Springfield, Dusty, 22
Stafford, Jo, 7
Stallone, Sylvester, 119, 212
Stanton, Frank, 88–89
Steele, Don, 201
Steely Dan, 208
Steinberg, David, 81, 90, 96, 99, 101, 198, 214
Steinem, Gloria, 205
Stevenson, McLean, 125
Stewart, Martha, 137, 201
Stewart, Rod, 209
Stoltz, Eric, 192
Stone, Sharon, 137, 192
Stones, Rolling, 12, 19, 24, 209, 220
Strasberg, Lee, xix
Streep, Meryl, 191
Streisand, Barbra, 9, 12–13, 22
Struthers, Sally, 125–26
Stuart, Mel, 199
Sues, Alan, 129, 133, 140, 147
Sugarman, Burt, 102, 208
Sullivan, Ed, ix, xi, xv–xvi, 3–23, 28, 33, 35, 38, 53, 62–63, 79, 83–86, 90, 95, 107, 115, 125, 131, 133, 141, 148, 159–60, 168–69, 184, 201, 212, 220
Sullivan, Kathie, 41, 47, 49
Sullivan, Roger, 46
Summer, Donna, 191
Susann, Jacqueline, 88
Sutherland, Joan, 22

**T**

Tandy, Jessica, 77
Tankersley, William, 86, 89
Tann, Georgia, 76
Tartikoff, Brandon, 217–18
Tauber, Peter, 217
Taylor, Elizabeth, 192, 225
Taylor, Rip, 56, 177, 199
Tebet, Dave, 209
Temptations, The, 12, 169
Tennille, Toni, 175–76
Thomas, Dave, 214, 219
Thomas, Marlo, 65
Three Dog Night, 186, 196
Tillis, Mel, 56
Tillstom, Burr, 131
Tilton, Charlene, 218
Tinker, Grant, 74–75
Todd, Bob, 225
Tolsky, Susan, 78
Tomlin, Lily, xix, 94, 102, 129, 137–39,
    146, 164, 184
Topo Gigio, 13
Travolta, John, xix
Triola, Michele, 113
Tune, Tommy, 177
Turner, Jim, 41
Turner, Ted, 60
Turner, Tina, 18, 186, 191
Twitty, Conway, 56
Tyler, Willie, 129, 138

**U**

Uggams, Leslie, 125, 138, 148–49, 173,
    225
Ullman, Tracey, 57, 80, 229

**V**

Valente, Caterina, 130, 220
Van Dyke, Dick, xiii, 74–77, 112, 117,
    124

Van Horne, Harriet, 17
Van Patten, Dick, 112
Van Patten, Joyce, 75
Vanderbilt, Gloria, 137
Vaughan, Sarah, 123, 168
Vereen, Ben, 33
Vines, Lee, 3
Vinton, Bobby, 178

**W**

Waggoner, Lyle, 105, 107, 109, 117
Wagner, Jane, 146
Wallace, George, 89
Wallace, Mike, 201
Walters, Barbara, 201
Warnes, Jennifer, 81, 97
Warren, Bob, 27
Warren, Jennifer, 97
Warwick, Dionne, 13, 64, 126, 168, 226
Wayans Brothers, The, 229
Wayans, Keenan Ivory, 166
Wayne, Carol, 199
Wayne, Harry, 168
Wayne, John, 90, 132
Wayne, Johnny, 21
Weaver, Charley, 59, 221
Weingrad, Jeff, 84, 211
Weinstein, Sylvia, 5
Welch, Raquel, 24, 196
Welk, Christina Schwann, 28
Welk, Fern, 31, 44, 48
Welk, Larry III, 48
Welk, Larry Jr., 30, 32, 48
Welk, Lawrence, ix, xiii–xiv, xvi, 10, 12,
    16, 24, 27–51, 55, 60, 63, 79, 84, 95,
    98, 100–1, 103, 107, 110, 116, 131,
    133, 149, 196, 198–201, 211, 219,
    227
Welk, Ludwig, 28
Welk, Shirley, 48
Welles, Orson, 63, 213
Wences, Señor, 7, 13, 16

Werner, Mort, 132
West, Dottie, 52
White, Betty, 31, 108–9, 116
White, Slappy, 152, 157
Williams, Andy, xvi–xvii, xix, 84, 149,
    160, 173
Williams, Hank, 52
Williams, Joyce Vincent, 170
Williams, Mason, 36, 84–85, 96, 217
Williams, Robin, 221
Williams, William B., 179
Willis, Andra, 35, 47
Wilson, Don, xiii
Wilson, Flip, ix, 11–13, 15, 66, 69, 79,
    86, 138, 148–49, 155–69, 172, 174,
    176, 187, 208, 221
Wilson, Joyce Vincent, 172
Winchell, Walter, 6, 17
Winters, Jonathan, 158, 221
Wonder, Stevie, 35
Wood, Robert, 15, 88, 91, 93–94, 125
Worley, Jo Anne, 124, 129, 135, 138,
    142, 146
Wright, Jackie, 225
Wynette, Tammy, 52, 56

**Y**

York, Donny, 180
Young, Donna Jean, 129, 138
Youngman, Henny, 12, 21

**Z**

Zell, Johnny, 48
Zeppelin, Led, 188
Zepperling, Fred, 48
Zimbalist, Efrem, 187
Zimmer, Norma, 32, 48

# About the Author

Telly R. Davidson has been a regular contributor to Los Angeles's *Entertainment Day* magazine, where he wrote the popular "TV Talk" column. He also contributes his own column regularly to *FilmStew Magazine*. His television work includes being a research consultant on the top-rated NBC specials *Most Outrageous Game Show Moments* (1, 2, 3, 4, 5, and 6) and many other creative projects. He lives in Santa Fe Springs, California.